General Studies

IMO Level 1 & 2, CBSE, ICSE, GCSE, State Boards

Chandan Sengupta

Creative Learning Series

Handbook of General Studies

Chandan Sengupta

This book is prepared for meeting evergrowing demand of students for additional contents to accelerate their regular practices. . This book is designed to provide additional practice problems based on the National Curriculum duly prescribed by the boards concerned. After practicing these worksheets and assignments the fellow students of that particular curriculum will become competent enough in dealing specified tasks of particular types. They also accumulate the minimum requirements a student should have before taking part in Olympiads. It will also accelerate off the school mathematical practices alongside the observations of parents and other peer members. It will also give an adequate support to different tutorials meant for ensuring individual progress.

Revised Publication   : March 2025

Revised Edition   : March 2026

Hard Copies: 10,000

Published by: Chandan Sengupta, Arabinda Nagar, Bankura – 722101 W.B. India

This book is prepared for fellow aspirants of IMO, Olympiads, Talent Search Examinations and School Studies.

Contents

CONTENTS

CONTENTS

Let Us Prepare

Q 1. Snehal is permitted 1000 calories a day on her diet. She consumed 379 calories at lunch and 242 at breakfast. How many calories may she consume at dinner?

Q 2. Prepare suitable mathematical statement to represent each of the following grids.

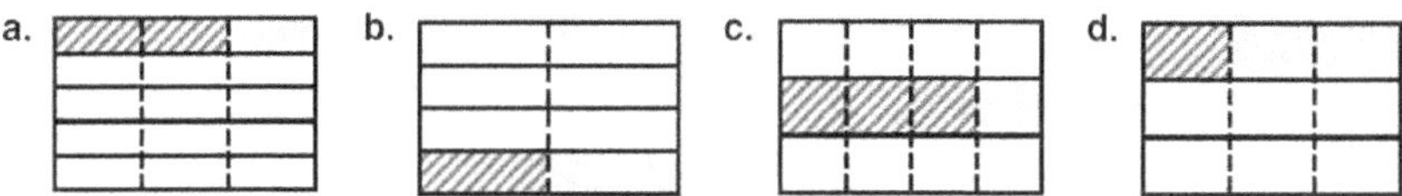

Q 3. One third of a swimming pool is roped off for nonswimmers. Three fourths of this space is used for swimming lessons. What fractional part of the pool is used for swimming lessons?

Q 4. Five sixteenths of the books on the shelf are nonfiction. Three fourths of these books cover topics related to science. One eighth of science books cover Physics. What part of the books on the shelf are Physics books?

Q 5. Half of 250 students attend track and field meet. One fifth of rest of students are included in Basket Ball team. How many students are there in that team?

Q 6. How many equal pieces of wood that weigh between 15 and 16 g can be made from a 110 g block if the whole block is used?

Q 7. There are ….. days in two leap years.

Q 8. The reciprocal of a whole number has ………… a numerator of 1.

[Option: always/ sometimes/ never]

Q 9. If we write all natural numbers from 1 to 200 then what fraction of all numbers starting from 1 to 200 are multiples of 20?

Q 10. Arrange values of a, b, c, d, e and f in ascending order.

1. $\frac{2}{3} \div \frac{5}{6} = \frac{2}{3} \times \frac{6}{5} = a$

2. $\frac{4}{5} \div \frac{4}{7} = \frac{4}{5} \times \frac{7}{4} = d$

3. $\frac{3}{8} \div \frac{15}{16} = \frac{3}{8} \times \frac{?}{?} = b$

4. $\frac{3}{7} \div \frac{6}{7} = \frac{3}{7} \times \frac{?}{?} = e$

5. $\frac{4}{25} \div \frac{2}{3} = \frac{?}{?} \times \frac{?}{?} = c$

6. $\frac{9}{10} \div \frac{3}{5} = \frac{?}{?} \times \frac{?}{?} = f$

Q 11. Simplify: $\frac{1}{2} \times \frac{2}{3} \times \frac{3}{4} \times \dots \left(1 - \frac{1}{1000}\right) \times 2009 \div 1{,}000 = \dots\dots$

Q 13. In March, 812 people came to the Nature Cure Center; in April, 1105; in May, 1229; in June, 270 more people than people came in previous month; and in July, 110 less than the attendance of June. In August, 126 fewer people came to the center than came in July. How many people came in August?

Q 14. What least number should be subtracted from four digit greatest number to obtain a common multiple of 4 and 8?

Q 15. Two thirds of the visitors of Community Centre on Monday were children. Three fourths of the children came on a school trip. The rest, 21 children, came with their families. How many people visited the Community Center on Monday?

Q 16. While working 6 hours a day Nikhil can finish his project works in 8 days. He started working at the rate of four hours a day. Find out the number of additional days for which he has to work.

Q 17. Arrange the following in ascending order.

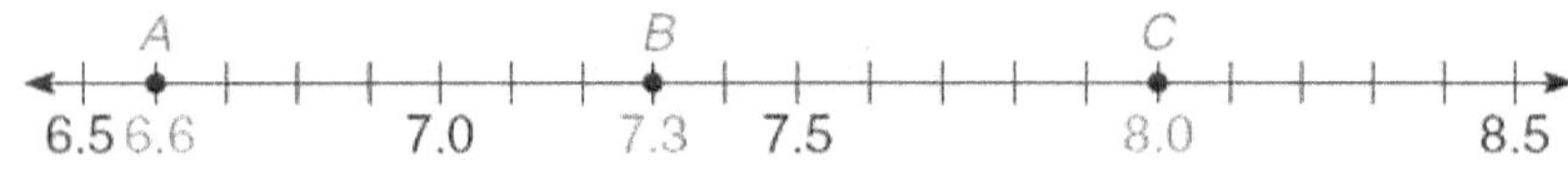

Q 18. What least number should be added to sum of six digit smallest number and five digit greatest number to obtain a common multiple of 3 and 9?

Q 19. Smallest five digit number which can be divided by 9 leaving a remainder 7 is equal to ………………

Basic Operations

Q 1. The juice in a machine costs Rs 20 a bottle. The machine will accept only exact change, it cannot give change, and it will not accept pennies of Rs 1, 2 or half of one hundred. Coins of Rs 5 , Rs 10 and Rs 20 can be used. How many different combinations of coins can Stella use to buy a bottle of juice?

Q 2. There are 936 boys and 1044 girls in the track meet. The coach wants an equal number of boys or girls on each team. What is the greatest number of boys or girls the coach can have on a team? How many teams in all will he have?

Q 3. There were 1,212 students taking part at last week's track and field meet. A little less than half were girls. Write a fraction that might represent the part of the team that was girls.

Q 4. Jan has three times as many baseball cards as Jeric. Jan has 87 baseball cards. How many baseball cards does Jeric have?

Q 5. What least number should be subtracted from sum of six digit smallest number and five digit greatest number to obtain a multiple of 9?

Q 6. John has 459 feet of rope and Jeanine has 603 feet. What is the longest possible length they can cut from each rope so that all the pieces are equal in length?

Q 7. By using suitable addition sentence find out values of A, B and C and arrange them in ascending order.

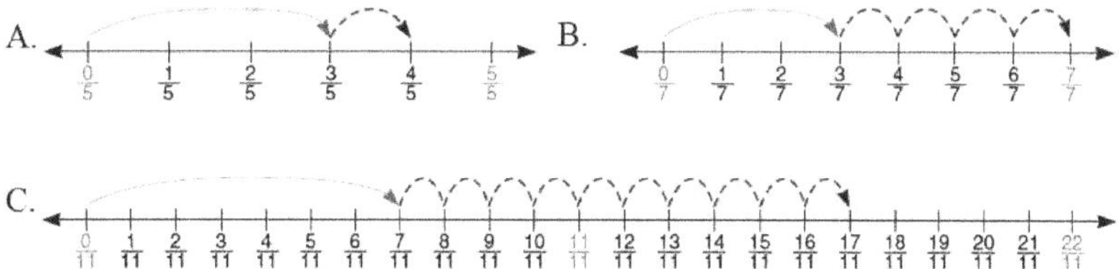

Q 8. Arrange p, q, r and s in ascending order.

a. $\left(\frac{2}{9} + \frac{1}{9}\right) + \frac{4}{9} = \frac{2}{9} + \left(\frac{1}{9} + p\right)$

c. $\frac{3}{10} + \left(\frac{2}{10} + \frac{1}{10}\right) = \left(\frac{3}{10} + q\right) + \frac{1}{10}$

b. $\left(\frac{3}{4} + r\right) + \frac{5}{6} = \frac{3}{4} + \left(\frac{2}{3} + \frac{5}{6}\right)$

d. $s + \left(\frac{1}{2} + \frac{1}{6}\right) = \left(\frac{2}{5} + \frac{1}{2}\right) + \frac{1}{6}$

Q 9. Write subtraction sentence for each of the following and arrange them in ascending order.

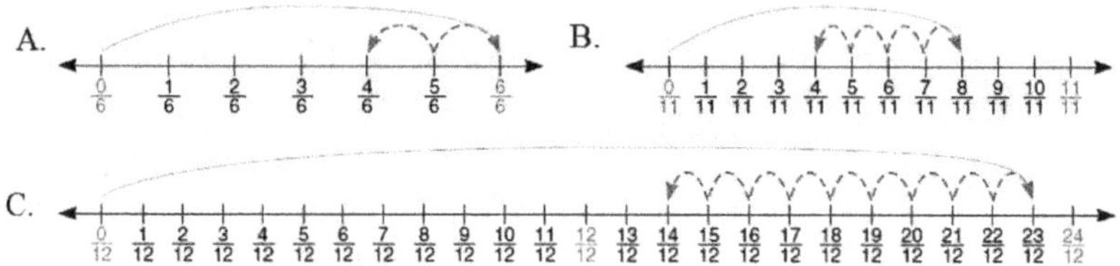

Q 10. Pat, Jett, and Vic went to the library during their break. Jett stayed in the library for quarter of an hour less than Pat. Vic stayed in the library for half of an hour more than Jett. If Vic stayed in the library for 2 ¾ hours, then how much time did each one stay in the library?

Q 11. How many five digit natural numbers are there in all?

Q 12. Use following sticks to construct different figures as per options duly delivered by instructors.

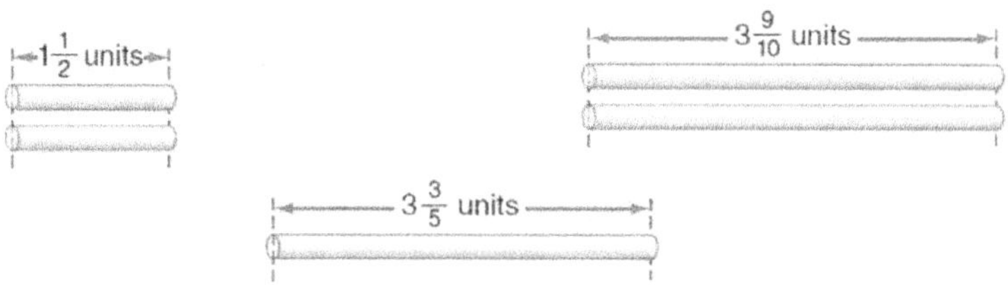

Option A: Largest possible triangle.

Option B: A rectangle.

Option C: Difference of outer boundary between largest triangle and the rectangle will be equal to ……. units.

H. O. T. S.

Q 1. Rumanika sorts 302 letters into the first bin, 413 letters into the second bin, and 524 letters into the third. If the pattern continues, how many letters will she put into the seventh and tenth bins?

Q 2. Zip codes help postal workers sort mail. How many 5-digit zip codes begin with the digits 100_ _?

Q 3. Last year Stella read 24 books. This year she read twice that number. Next year she plans to cover up 32 more books her targeted reading of this year. How many books did Stella read in the all the three consecutive years?

Q 4. Nimmi has cards which is 18 more than ninth multiple of smallest three digit number. She gives an equal number to each of 19 classmates. At most, how many cards does Nimmi give to each classmate?

Q 5. Timothi writes a number pattern in which the first number in the pattern is divisible by 2, the second number is divisible by 3, the third number is divisible by 9, and then the pattern repeats itself. Which of these numbers, 260, 280, 320, and 360 could be the 12th number in Timothi's pattern?

Q 6. In her coin book, Rina wants to arrange 18 French coins, 24 Spanish coins and 36 Indian coins in equal rows on the page. What is the greatest number of coins that she can arrange in each row? How many rows will she have in this way?

Q 7. Three out of 39 visitors to the Book Fair are stamp collectors. What fractional part of the visitors are not stamp collectors?

Q 8. Smallest number of a natural number is 18 and sixth number is 54. If the number increases equally at every step then find out the value of sum of sixth and seventh number of that number series.

Q 9. One seventh of seven million fifty six thousand sixty three = ……

Q 10. One hundred Seven out of 428 stamps in Tina'a collection are from Asia. What fractional part of her collection is not from Asia?

Q 11. Seven twelfths of the flowers in the box are red. Write an equivalent fraction to show what parts of the flowers in the box are not red.

Q 12. Smallest number which can divide 213,321,221 leaving remainder 2 is equal to ………. Another divisor of single digit which divides this number leaving remainder 2 is equal to ……………..

Q 13. What fraction of the following grid is not shaded?

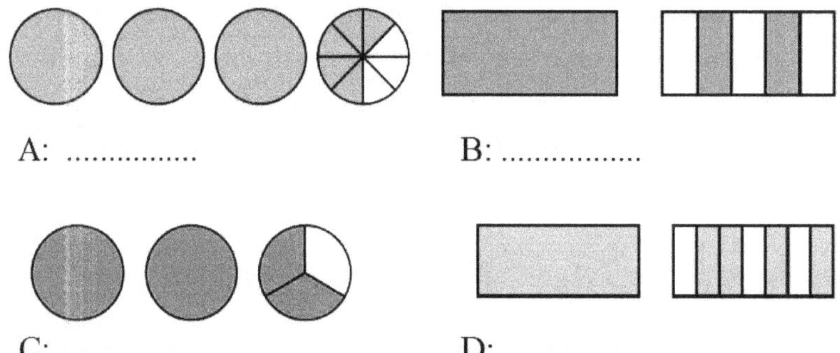

Q 14. Represent the following by using simple fractions.

A: ……………

B: ……………

C: ……………

D: ……………

Q 15. What fraction of all the natural starting from 1 to 250 are multiples of 5?

Q 16. One sixth of one seventh of a natural number is equal to 10,20,301. Find out the number. Also find out sixth multiple of that number.

Exam Race

Q 1. A .... having .... end point(s) can be extended endlessly in one direction.

Q 2. Stella has a CD case that holds 136 CDs. She divides the case into four equal sections for education, cartoons, traditional, and dance music. How many CDs can each section hold?

Q 3. Observe the following bar graph.

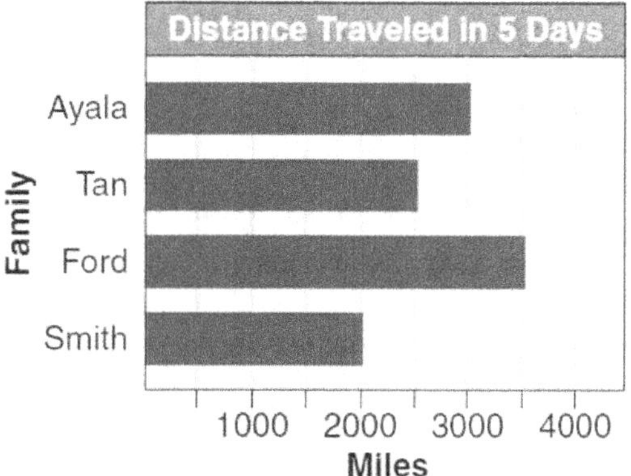

A: How many miles each family travelled each day?

B: Which family travelled maximum distance?

C: Average distance travelled by Ayla, Tan and Smith = ...

Q 4. Each bucket of capacity 20 L are filled with water. Water of all such buckets was finally collected in a container. Four fifth of that container is finally filled up. Half of the empty part of that container can be filled up by using two full bucket of water. What is the capacity of the water container?

Q 5. Two bells toll at an interval of 4 seconds and five seconds respectively. After what time interval these bells toll together?

Q 6. The Art Guild has 1438 flyers to give out. If 8 members of the Guild share the job equally, how many flyers will each give out? How many extra flyers will be needed to ensure equal distribution of the same amongst members?

Q 7. The art club creates holiday cards for the A specialised retirement home. There are 8 members of the club, each of whom creates 25 cards. The 15 residents of the retirement home each take the same number of cards. What is the minimum number of remaining cards?

Q 8. Julia stores 3535 cans of juice on 7 shelves in a stockroom. Each shelf has the same number of cans of juice stored on it. How many cans of juice are stored on each shelf?

Q 9. There are 1250 greeting cards in packs. Each pack holds 16 cards. How many thousands of cards will be there in all?

Q 10. There are 589 people going on a field trip. Nineteen buses are hired for the trip. If the same number of people rides in each bus, how many people ride in each bus?

Q 11. While hunting, a cheetah can cover 1310 ft of ground in as few as 60 strides. About how many feet does it travel in 15 strides?

Q 12. There are 738 children enrolled in Silicon Valley International Public School. If there are 18 classrooms in the school, what is the average number of students in each classroom?

Q 13. A number between 2700 and 2800 when divided by 25 has a quotient that contains three odd digits and has no remainder. Find fifth multiple of that number.

Q 14. There are 43,560 apples to be shipped to stores. If 72 apples are packed in each of the small box and 100 apples are to be shipped in 31 big boxes. One additional large box is used for packing apples what left after packing all the boxes duly assigned for transportation. How many boxes of apples are to be shipped?

Q 15. One fifth of one seventh of 35,70,105 = ……………..

1. Model Papers

Exercise 1

Q 1. Complete the following number pattern.

334^2 $= 111,556$

3334^2 $= 11,115,556$

33334^2 $= 1,111,155,556$

333334^2 $= 111,111,555,556$

33333334^2 $= \dots\dots\dots\dots\dots\dots\dots$

33333333334^2 $= \dots\dots\dots\dots\dots\dots\dots$

Q 2. A set of natural numbers is given below.

2 3 5 7 11 13 17 19 23 29 31 37 41 43 47 53 59 61

67 71 73 79 83 89 97 101 103 107 109 113 127 131 137 139

149 151 157 163 167 173 179 181 191 193 197 199 211 223 227

229 233 239 241 251 257 263 269 271 277 281 283 293 307 311

313 317 331 337 347 349 353 359 367 373 379 383 389 397 401

409 419 421 431 433 439 443 449 457 461 463 467 479 487 491

499

What can be concluded about all these natural numbers?

Q 3. What least number should be subtracted from five digit greatest number to obtain a number divisible by 8?

Q 4. Sum of five consecutive natural numbers is equal to 55,0515. Find out greatest number of this number series.

Q 5. Sonalika wanted to divide three and half cakes amongst her 14 fellow friends. Find out fraction share of each of her friends.

Q 6. Monika saved $138 to buy a bicycle of cost $270. She worked at the Stellar Circus each week and received $30 the first week. For each additional week, She received $2 more than the preceding week. How many weeks did she work to have enough money to pay for the bicycle?

Q 7. How many sheets of paper each with 10 base ten cubes pictured would be needed for 10 thousand? 100 thousand? 1 million? 30 million? 100 million? 2 billion?

Q 8. What least number should be subtracted from four digit greatest number to obtain a common multiple of 2 and 4?

Q 9. Complete the following:

P = 30 tens + 300 hundreds + 290 + 121,121

Q = 40 tens + 12 hundreds – 121,121 – 300

(P + Q) – (20 tens + 300 tens + 110) = ………………

Q 10. Compare place value of underlined digits:

A. 365,12<u>3</u>,145,000   B. 839,200,<u>4</u>30,000

Q 11. Arrange the following in ascending order.

P = three million, five hundred forty thousand, thirty-seven;

Q = forty million, one hundred thousand, two hundred five;

R = two hundred twenty million, five thousand, eight;

S = three billion, six hundred six million, seventy-seven thousand, four hundred three;

Q 12. What least number should be subtracted from sum of five digit smallest number and four digit greatest number to obtain a common multiple of 3 and 9?

2. Olympiads

All numbers formed and displayed in standard form by using digits 0, 1, 2, 3, 4, 5, 6, 7, 8 and 9 are called decimal numbers.

Q 1. How many triangles are there in each of the following?

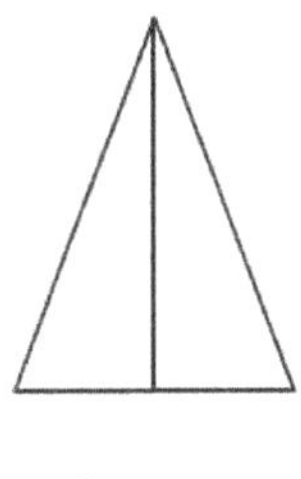 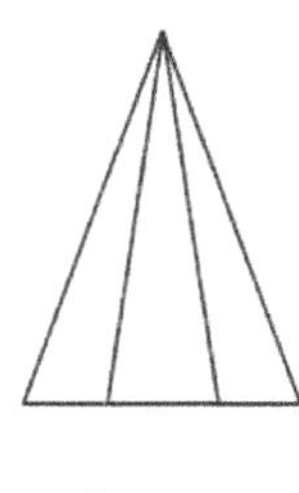 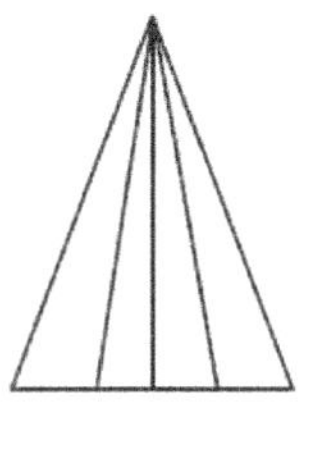 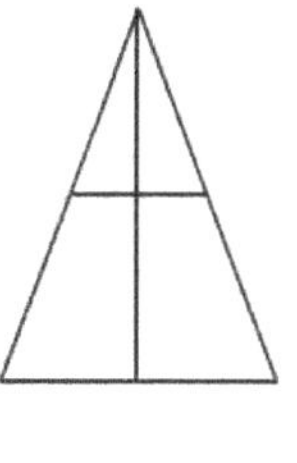

P   Q   R   S

Q 2. Use the given chart to represent natural numbers in Roman Numerals.

I	II	III	IV	V	VI	VII	VIII	IX	X
1	2	3	4	5	6	7	8	9	10
V	X	XV	XX	XXV	XXX	XXXV	XL	XLV	L
5	10	15	20	25	30	35	40	45	50
X	XX	XXX	XL	L	LX	LXX	LXXX	XC	C
10	20	30	40	50	60	70	80	90	100
C	CC	CCC	CD	D	DC	DCC	DCCC	CM	M
100	200	300	400	500	600	700	800	900	1000

A: 3,009 + 2,021 + 132   B: 1000 + 500 + 30 + 9

C: 3,000 + 2 X 300 + 40 X 40 + 121

Q 3. What will be digit at ones place of R in the following?

125 X 12,43,243 X 8 = R

Q 4. There are ……….. end points in a line segment.

Q 5. Calculate outer boundary and area of the following.

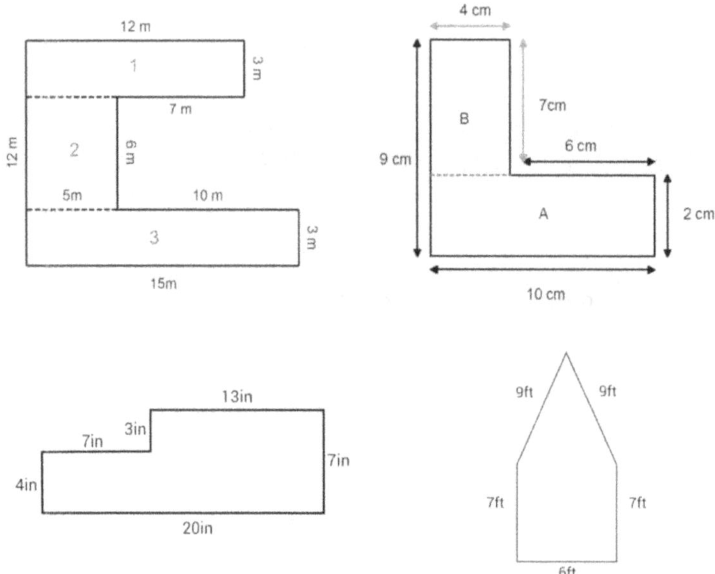

Q 6. Calculate total surface area of the following.

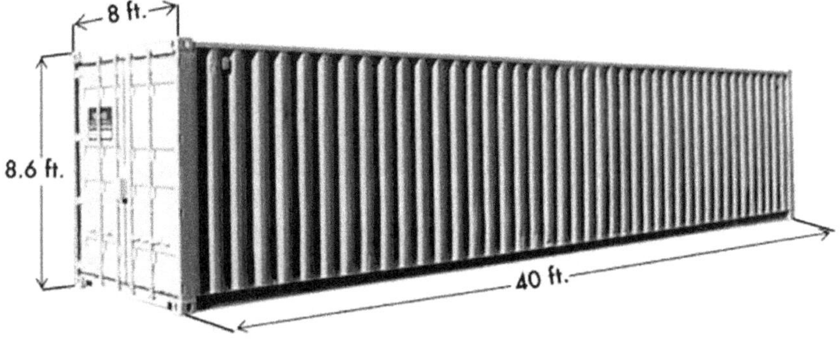

Q 7. Sum of six consecutive number exceeds sixth multiple of six digit smallest number by 21. Find out the greatest number of this number series.

Q 8. Half of a quarter of a given number is equal to 11,11,011. Find out the number.

***.

3. A Test Paper

Q 1. How many seven digit numbers are there in all?

Q 2. Is it possible to draw a triangle having sides 3 cm, 5 cm and 9 cm?

Q 3. Which of the following graph indicates motion of object having uniform speed?

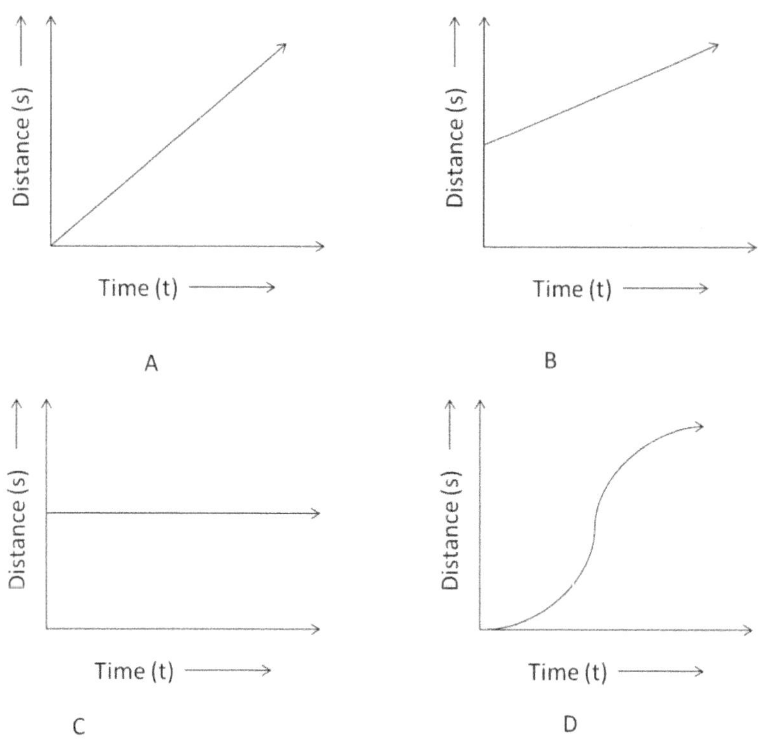

4. $1 + 3 + 5 = 3 \times 3 = 9$; then $1 + 3 + 5 + 7 + 9 + 11 = $ …………

5. How many times does minute hand complete revolving around a dial in a couple of days?

6. Complete the following:

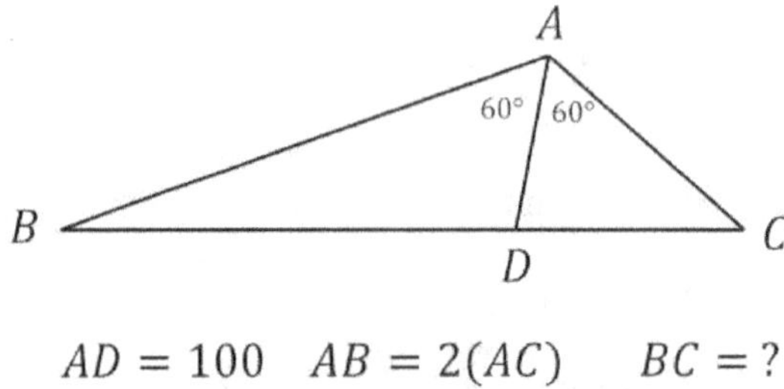

$$AD = 100 \quad AB = 2(AC) \quad BC = ?$$

7. What will be digit at ones place of P in the following?

101,90,239 X 21,23,309 X 21,32,909 X 90,90,909 = P

8. $\frac{11}{12}$ X $\frac{12}{13}$ X $\frac{13}{14}$ X .... $\left(1 - \frac{1}{1000}\right)$ X $\left(1 - \frac{1}{11}\right)$ = ...

9. Observe the following and complete the given pattern:

$$1306 = 1^1 + 3^2 + 0^3 + 6^4; \qquad 1676 = 1^1 + 6^2 + 7^3 + 6^4$$

$$2427 = 2^p + 4^q + 2^r + 7^s \qquad 3435 = 3^3 + 4^4 + 3^3 + 5^5$$

Find out values of p, q, r and s.

10. How many six digit numbers are there in all?

11. Half of a natural number exceeds six digit smallest number by 2,008. Find out the number.

12. What least number should be subtracted from five digit greatest number to make it divisible by 8?

13. If 8 X 125 = 1,000 and 25 X 40 = 1,000 then find out the following:

A: 125 X 3249 X 40 X 8 X 25 ÷ 10,000 = ...

B : 40 X 125 X 25 X 8 ÷ 100,000 = ...

14. Sum of five consecutive natural numbers is equal to 50,5021. Find out the greatest number of this natural number series.

***.

4. Forms and Patterns

1. The number 175 can be expressed as the sum of the increasing powers of its digits: $175 = 1^1 + 7^2 + 5^3$. Some other examples: $135 = 1^1 + 3^2 + 5^3$, $518 = 5^1 + 1^2 + 8^3$, and $598 = 5^1 + 9^2 + 8^3$.

2. $1634 = 1^4 + 6^4 + 3^4 + 4^4$.

Similarly $\qquad 9474 = $ ....

and $\qquad 8208 = $ ....

3. $497 \times 2 = 994$, and $497 + 2 = 499$, then $499 + 2 + 497 \times 2 = $ ....

4. $365 = 10^2 + 11^2 + 12^2 = 13^2 + 14^n$. value of n = ...

5. Given that $31 = 1 + 5 + 5^2 = 1 + 2 + 2^2 + 2^3 + 2^p$. Here p = ...

6. $\qquad 333 \times 777 \qquad = 258{,}741,$

$\qquad 333 \times 444 \qquad = 147{,}852,$

$\qquad 666 \times 777 \qquad = 517{,}842.$

For all these three products same digits are used at different order.

7. $666 = 2^3 + 3^2 + 5^2 + 7^d + 11^2 + 13^2 + 17^2$. Here d = ...

8. Number 9 and 11 are tied in different ways:

$\frac{1}{9} = 0.111111111111111111111...\,,$

and $\frac{1}{11} = 0.090909090909090909090909....$ We know that the product of 9 and 11 is 99 unit fraction: $\frac{1}{99} = 0.01010101010101....$

9. $\frac{1}{27} = 0.037037037037037037...$ and

$\frac{1}{37} = 0.027027027027027027...,$ we work out : $999 = 27 \times 37$.

10. $1111 = 56^2 + 65^2$; $\qquad\qquad 111{,}111 = 55^6 - 44^5$

11. Consider the following divisibility rule: "If the sum of the digits of a number is divisible by 3 (or 9), then the original number is divisible by 3 (or 9)."

For making following numbers divisible by 3 (or 9) we can work out smallest possible value of n in the following.

A: 32,435.n54   B: 2n4, 324,021   C: n21,321,324

D: Is the number 745,785 divisible by 3 or 9?

12. Fact files of the number 29, 49 and 79:

For 29: $(2 + 9) + (2 \times 9) = 11 + 18 = 29$;

For 49: $(4 + 9) + (4 \times 9) = 13 + 36 = 49$

For 79: $(7 + 9) + (7 \times 9) = 16 + 63 = 79$

13. Number 9:

Number 9 = 3 consecutive factorials, such as $9 = 1! + 2! + 3!$

$9^2 = 81$ and $8 + 1 = 9$.

14. Observe the number series and find out the value of p.

A: $987654321 \times 9 = 8888888889$

B: $987654321 \times p = 17777777778$

C: $987654321 \times 27 = 26666666667$

D: $987654321 \times 36 = 35555555556$

E: $987654321 \times 45 = 44444444445$

15. Sum of seven consecutive natural numbers is equal to 77,56,091. In the seven number series the smallest number will be equal to ....

***.

5. Lines and Angles

Q 1. Observe the following figure in which Ray diagram is used to indicate range of vision experienced by a fish.

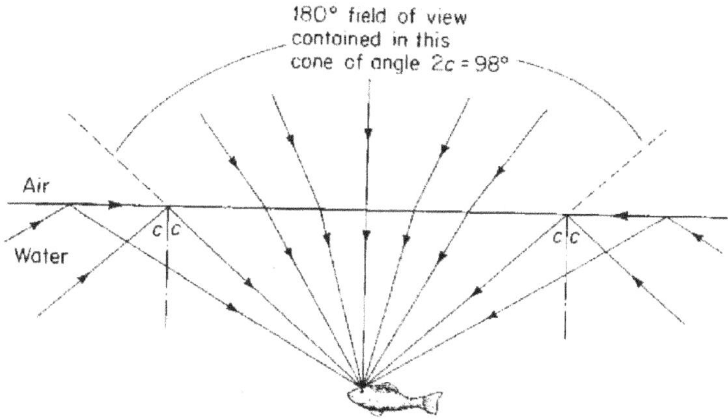

What realm of spherical region of surface water will be covered by visual realm of this diagram?

Q 2. Observe the following diagram and strike out the odd one statement.

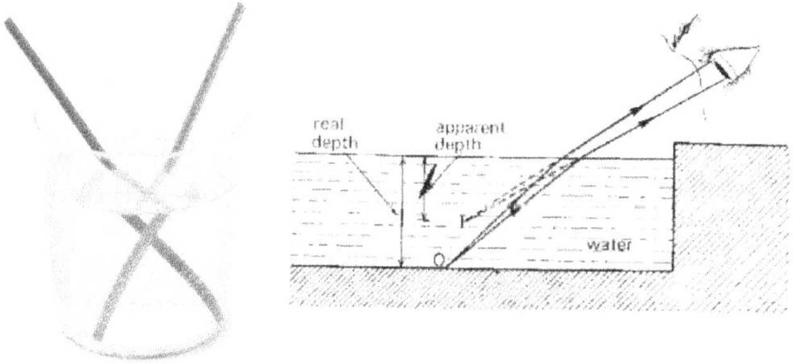

A: light ray bends at the junction of material medium due to difference in optical density of the medium through which rays are propagating.

B. We can recognise the bending of light with our un-aided eye.

C. Light rays passing through transparent medium loses intensity due to presence of impurities in the medium of propagation.

D. Rays of different wavelength propagates differently and often get scattered while passing through different medium of propagation.

E. Apparent depth of a container holding water appears less than the real depth because of bending of light at the junction of the material medium.

Q 3. How many additional bricks are needed to complete the following?

Q 4. How many non-overlapping triangles can be accommodated in a pentagon?

Q 5. Is there any polygon having five vertices and two diagonals?

Q 6. Three interior angles of a triangle are in the ratio of 2: 3: 4. Find out magnitude of the greatest angle of that triangle.

Q 7. How many lines can be drawn by using two out of three non-collinear points?

Q 8. A pair of .... angles can share the common vertex and a common arm.

Q 9. Sum of a given angle and its complementary angle is equal to ......

Q 10. Hour hand of a clock makes .... complete angle while moving throughout a couple of days.

Q 11. A .... has no definite length and no definite endpoints. It can be extended endlessly in either directions.

6. Additional Worksheets

All numbers formed and displayed in standard form by using digits 0, 1, 2, 3, 4, 5, 6, 7, 8 and 9 are called decimal numbers.

Exercise 1

Q 1. Write values of each of the following as displayed in the given number line.

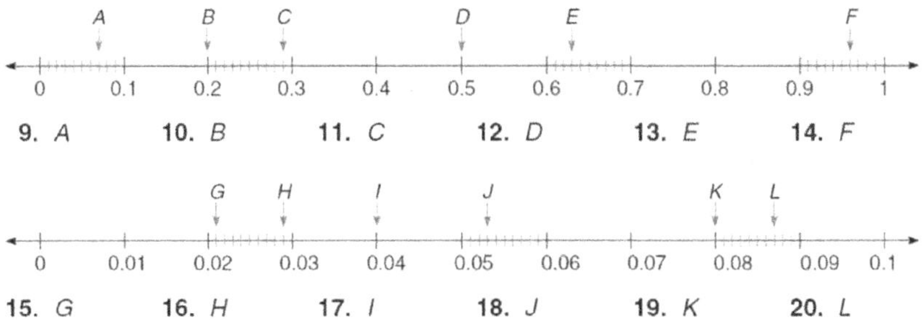

9. A   **10.** B   **11.** C   **12.** D   **13.** E   **14.** F

15. G   **16.** H   **17.** I   **18.** J   **19.** K   **20.** L

Q 2. Compare the following.

$$0.583 + 2.745 \ \ldots\ldots\ldots\ 0.1 + 0.02 + 3.003 + 0.101 - 0.201$$

Q 3. The leading team's score in the Decimal Olympics was 40.816 points. The final team's three players scored 14.21, 12.924, and 13.689 points respectively. Did they have enough points to take the lead?

Q 4. A miniature coal car is 0.39 m tall and a miniature refrigerator car is about 0.5 m tall. Another cupboard is 0.59 m less tall than collective tallness of coal car and refrigerator. Which car is tallest?

Q 5. Nikhil observed that a passenger train takes 36 seconds to cross him when he was standing on a 1.4 km long platform. The train was moving at an average speed of 36 km/h. Find out length of that train.

Exercise 2

Q 1. The average distance from Earth to the planet Saturn is about 773,119,750 miles. Write the word name of this number.

Q 2. 32,530,008 = (3 X A) (2 X B) (5 X C) (3 X D) (8 X E);

Here A + B – D X E = …………

Q 3. Arrange the following in ascending order.

A = One hundred forty-five and two thousandths

B = Sixty-one and three hundred eighteen thousandths

C = One hundred thirty-eight and five hundred forty-one thousandths

Q 4. Ramon puts 104 books in a box. Seventy – eight of the books are textbooks. How many books are not textbooks?

Q 5. Five rivers form a river system and have lengths of 513 miles, 125.32 miles, 209.093 miles, 247 miles and 397.07 miles respectively. Altogether, how long are these rivers?

Q 6. Bobby has 4030 international coins. One hundred twenty-three coins are from China, 1499 from India and 301 from Nepal. How many coins are not from Asia?

Q 7. Sum of seven consecutive natural numbers is equal to 70,77,028. Find out the greatest number of this natural number series.

Q 8. Complete the following:

A. 45,162 + 215.001+ 3614.7 + 3 X 10,000 + 4 X 1000

B. 746,500 + 28,781 + 978,432 + 739,853 + 3,001

C. 204,106 +403 7000 +10,691 + 43 X 1,000 + 1,001

Arrange these three values in ascending order.

Q 9. Half of a quarter of 88,08,016 = ……………………..

Exercise 3

Q 1. Every cubic millimeter of blood contains about 7500 white blood cells. A count less than 1500 above this number is still considered healthy. Is a white cell count of 8750 considered healthy?

Q 2. Light travels at an average speed of 3 lakh km/s. Light from a luminous celestial body reaches the Earth in 8.5 minutes. Calculate distance of that object from the Earth.

Q 3. Earth's total surface area is about 199,560 thousand square miles. Approximately 139,692 thousand square miles are covered with water. About how much of Earth's surface is covered by land? Work out your answer in the nearest million.

Q 4. Observe the following example and represent given numerals in standard form:

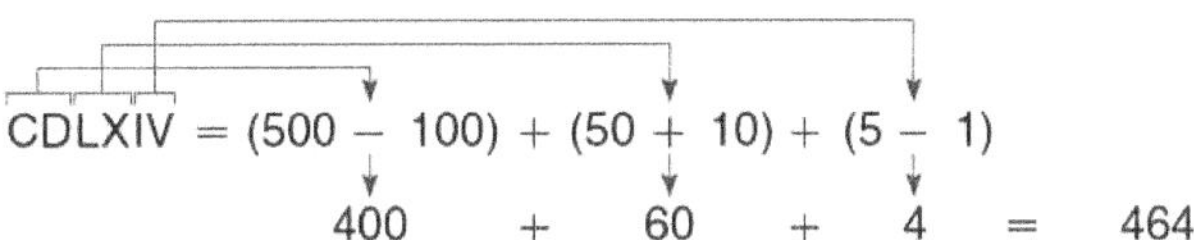

1. CCLXIII = 100 + __ + 50 + __ + __ + __ + __ = __
2. CMXCIV = (1000 − __) + (__ − 10) + (__ − __) = __

3. XXXIV	4. MVII	5. LV	6. DXXI
7. CCLXX	8. DCCXC	9. XCIX	10. MDIII
11. XLVII	12. MCCLVI	13. CXLV	14. MDCCXCI
15. MMCLI	16. MMDCCCIII	17. MDCCLXXXV	18. MDCCCXLV

Q 5. Rumani can finish her project activities in 3 days while working 4 hours a day. Somani can finish similar project activity in4 days while working at the rate of three hours a day. Both of them started working together on their project activities at the rate of two hours a day. In how many days do they finish their project works jointly?

Q 6. One third of one sixth of 18,36,072 = ...

Exercise 4

Q 1. Each of the students of a class donated Rs 50 for an outing. Three teachers contributed Rs 400 each to make the collection Rs 3,200 in all. How many students are there in that class?

Q 2. Tina has a cat, a bird, and a package of birdseed. She wants to get all three home safely, but her bicycle basket will hold only one at a time. The cat will eat the bird if the two are left alone together. The bird will eat the birdseed if they are left alone. How many trips , and in which definite order, does Grace need to make to get everything home safely?

Q 3. Population of a Tibal's village is between 800 and 1000. The sum of the digits in its population is 21, and the digits in the ones and the hundreds places are the same. What might be the population of the village?

Q 4. Between 1800 and 2000, the population of a country increased by 276,113,906. The population was almost 280 million in 1990. If the population increases by the same amount in the next 200 years, will the population in 2200 be more than 1 billion?

Q 5. Find out sum of greatest and smallest number after arranging the following in ascending order.

6,135,936;   6,315,396;   6,531,639;   6,153,693

Q 6. The area of State A is 97,073 square miles and the area of State B is 8,706 square miles more than State A. What is the total area of the two states?

Q 7. In May, 13,637 people attended the circus, which was 8,478 people less than the attendance in June. In July, the attendance was 3,342 more than that of June's. How many people attended the circus in May to July?

Q 8. What least number should be subtracted from six digit greatest number to obtain a number divisible by 8 leaving remainder 3?

Q 9. One fifth of one sixth of 30,60,090 = ...

Exercise 5

Q 1. Stay and Hay discovered that they had visited the same museums in City of Tomb during the summer. Ray visited 2 museums during each of his 3 days there. If Sue visited 3 museums a day, how many days was her trip?

Q 2. A conference hall in a community center has 50 rows of seats with 19 seats in each row. How many people in all can the hall seat?

Q 3. The vendor deputed his men in a theatre and sold 130 sandwiches at each of 8 shows each day for 25 days. One bag of parcel contains 100 sandwiches. How many bags sandwiches in all did the vendor sell?

Q 4. There are 60 reams of paper. Each ream contains 500 sheets. How many sheets are there in all?

Q 5. A point on Earth's equator travels 900 km every hour. What distance will this point travel in a couple of months? [Consider one month equal to 30 days.]

Q 6. Mars orbits the Sun at the rate of 15 miles per second. Calculate the distance travelled by that planet in a day.

Q 7. A wall mount clock takes 4 seconds for striking 4 bells at 4 a.m. Calculate total time to be taken by that clock to strike 10 bells at 10 p.m.

Q 8. A fruit distributor received 656 cartons of plums during the week. The average number of plums per carton is 125. At the end of the week, 79,950 plums had been sold to community market. Were all the plums received sold at the end of the week?

Q 9. Dennis picks an average of 1512 bushel baskets of apples during a promising season. If each basket holds 125 apples, how many thousands of apples does Dennis pick during the season?

Q 10. Sum of five consecutive natural number is equal to 15,45,015. Find sum of smallest and greatest natural number of this number series.

Achievers

Q 1. Half of Water tank A, Quarter of another water tank B and one fifth of water tank C are filled up by a cistern in 20 minutes, 15 minutes and 12 minutes respectively. Calculate total time to be taken by that cistern to fill up all the three water tanks completely.

Q 2. $\left(\dfrac{1}{10} + \dfrac{11}{100} + \dfrac{101}{1000} + \dfrac{1001}{10,000}\right) X\ 0.001\ + 11.1001 =$ ....

Q 3. Rumanika prepared a project activity sheet in 3 days while working at the rate of 4 hours a day. Calculate total number of days to be taken by her to finish ten such works if she prefer working 5 hours a day.

Q 4. Three angles of a triangle are in the ratio of 1: 2: 3. Find out magnitude of the greatest angle of that triangle.

Q 5. Malobika can finish jogging 1 km 200 m in 1 m 40 seconds. Rumani can jog at an average speed of 8 m/s. Who jogs faster and by how much?

Q 6. Observe the following diagram and select the statement which requires modification.

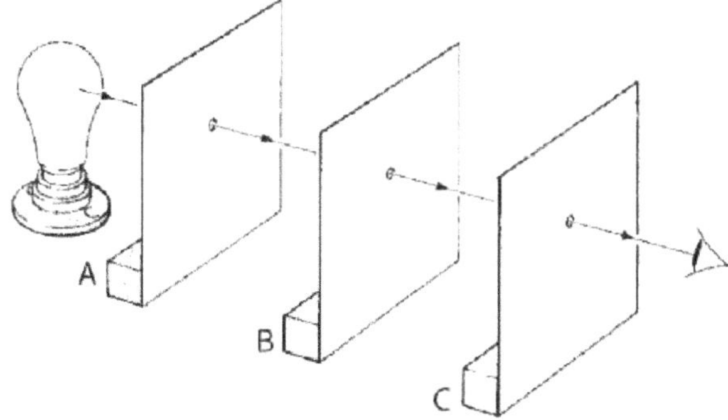

A: It indicates propagation of rays through holes duly aligned in a straight line.

B: All traces passing through holes are rays having a definite origin but no end point. Such rays can be extended endlessly in one direction.

C. Shifting cardboards forward or backward cannot alter the propagation of rays through holes.

D. Rays always propagate through a straight line and can experience an obstacle due to presence of opaque objects in the path of propagation.

E. Rays can have a definite path of propagation, one origin, no definite end point and no definite length.

F. A ray can be traced on a two dimensional surface.

Q 7. There are three sets of Abacus representing different numbers.

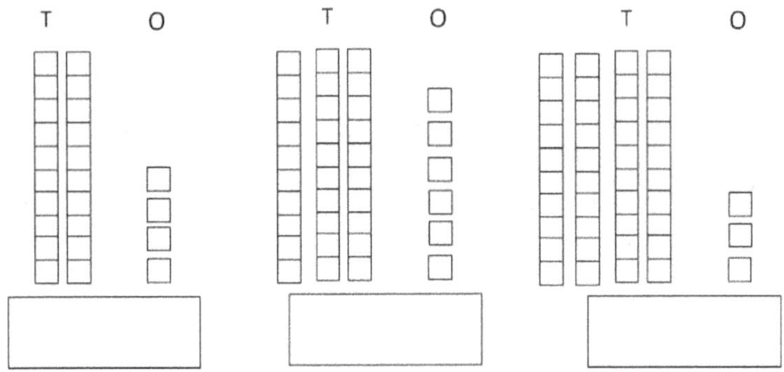

A: All numbers are two digit natural numbers.

B: All numbers can be defined as whole numbers and integers.

C: Sum of all the three numbers will be a three digit natural numbers.

D: Difference of second and third number may not return any natural number or any whole number.

E: Sum of first and second number will be greater than the third number.

F: All numbers have digits at ones and tens places, but none of the numbers have digits at hundreds place.

G: All the three numbers are decimal numbers as we use ten different digits to represent them in standard form.

Q 8. Observe the following speed time graph and strike out the statement which is not satisfied by the graph.

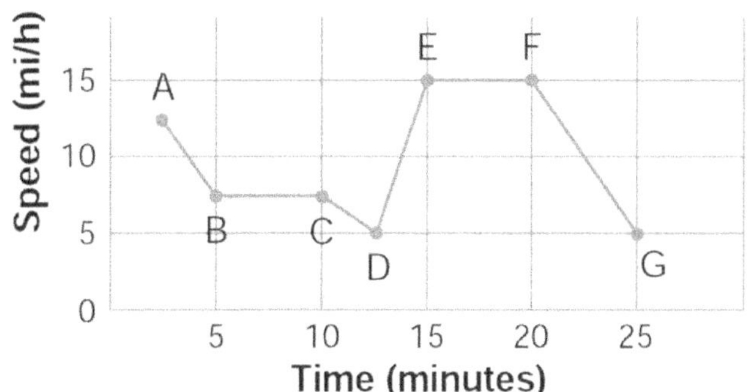

A: It represents motion of an object having acceleration, retardation and stationary state at different time interval.

B: Object was not moving in between 5th to 10th second and from 15th to 20th second.

C: Average of the speed from A to G cannot be worked out.

D: The object started at point A with a definite speed which was greater than 10 m/s, but less than 15 m/s.

E: The finished the journey at a speed of 5 m/s.

Q 9. Compare values of n in the following.

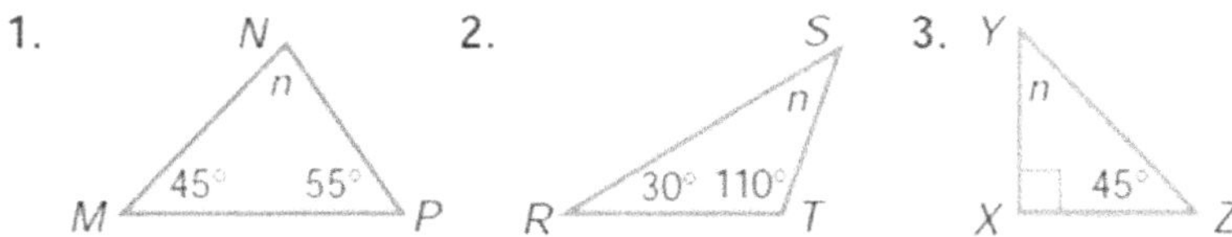

Q 10. What least number should be subtracted from greatest five digit number to obtain a smallest six digit multiple of 9?

Q 11. Sum of five consecutive number is equal to 55,0515. Find out value of the greatest number of this number series.

Q 12. Observe the following number series and complete all the steps.

11 X 11   =   121

111 X 111   =   12321;

1111 X 1111   = …………………………..

11111 X 11111   = …………………………..

Q 13. Find out values of n in the following.

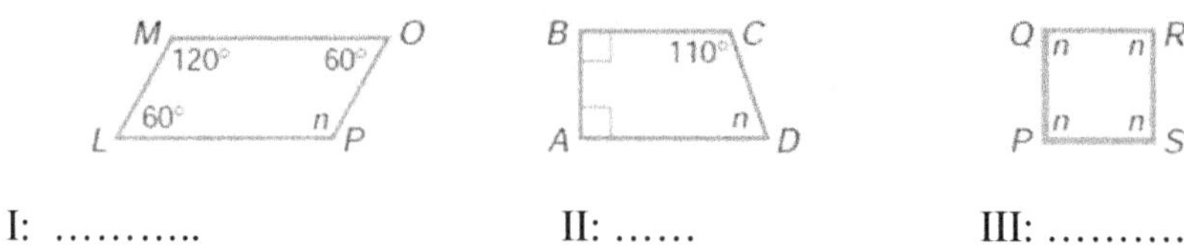

I: ………..   II: ……   III: ……….

Q 14. Work out values of variables in the following.

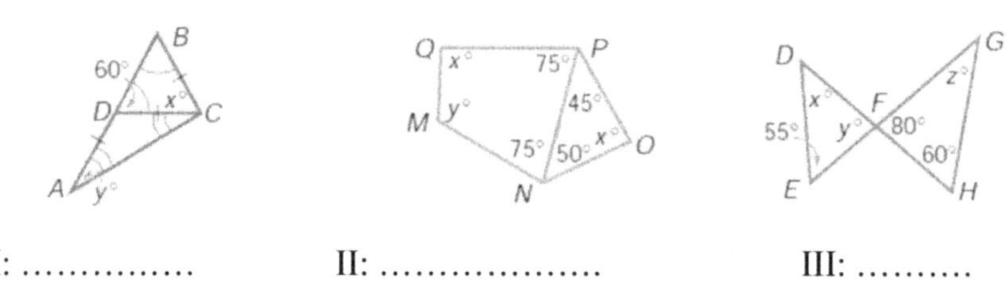

I: ……………   II: ………………   III: ……….

Q 15. Work out total area and outer boundary enclosed by both the rectangles. Rectangles are congruent to each other.

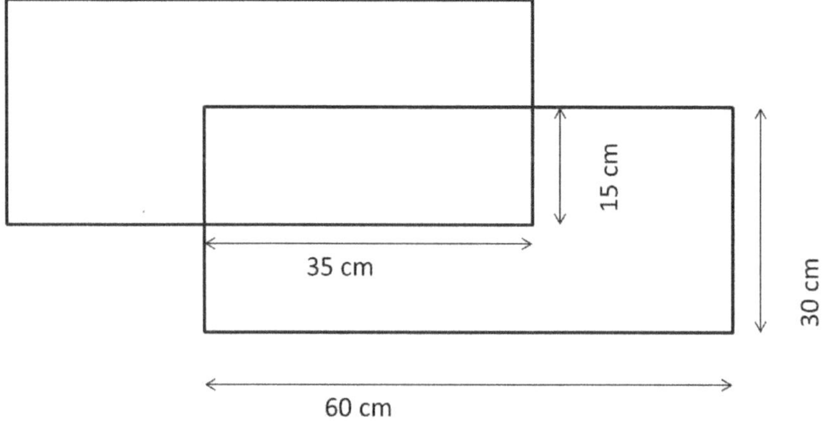

Q 16. What percentage of the following combination of grids is shaded?

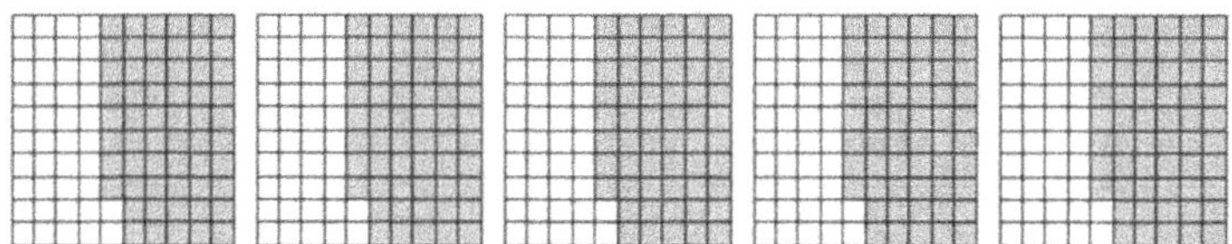

Q 17. Calculate area of the following.

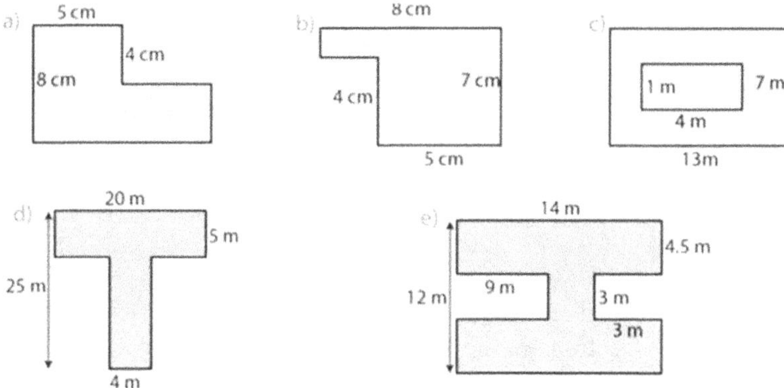

Q 18. Observe top view of the following combination to calculate dark portions enclosed by all the cans.

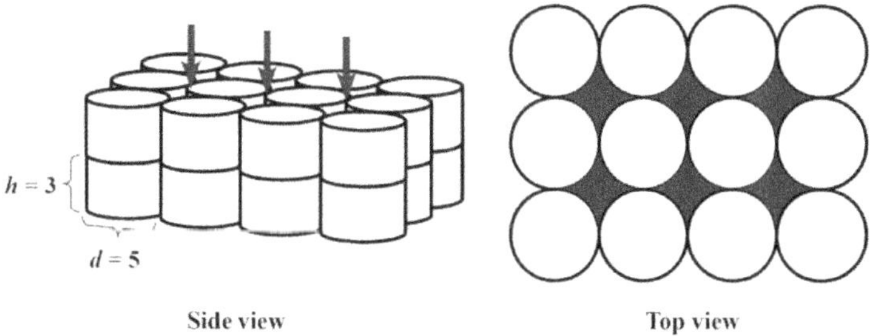

Q 19. Half of a can is filled up by sand and quarter of that can is occupied by water. Half of the empty portion can hold 200 ml of liquid. What is the total capacity of that can? How many such cans can be filled up completely by using 12 L liquid?

Q 20. What fraction of the five digit greatest number equals 11 more than 11,100?

Q 21 . Calculate outer boundary and area of the following.

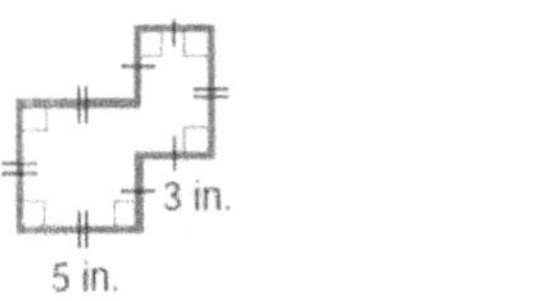
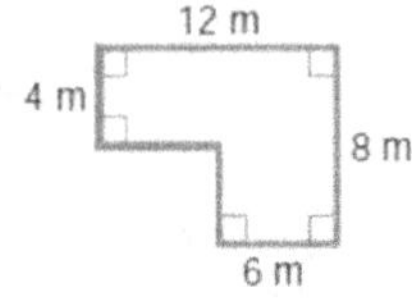
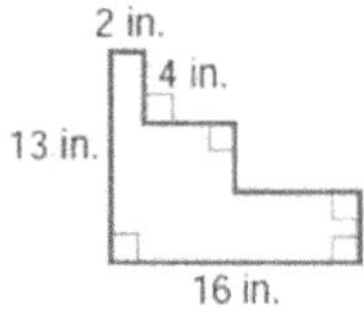

I: ....   II: III: ......

Q 22. Work out length of each of the following sides.

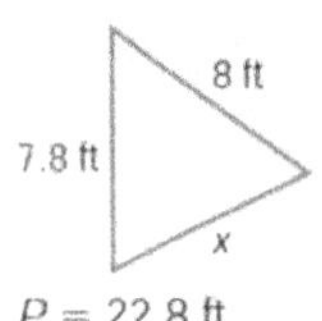
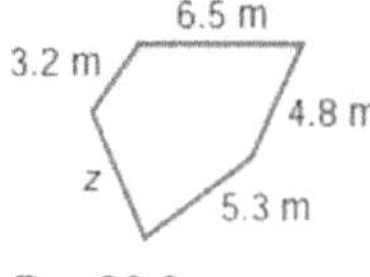

I: ....   II: ....   III: ....

Q 23. Area of a circle is equal to 3.14 X r X r; where r = radius of the given circle. What fractions of the following are shaded?

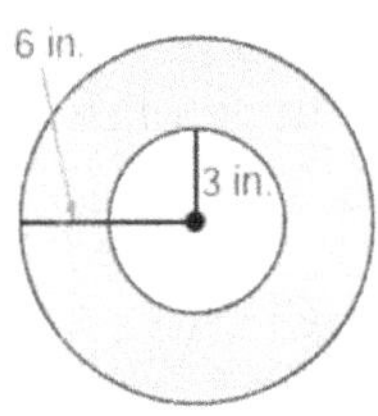
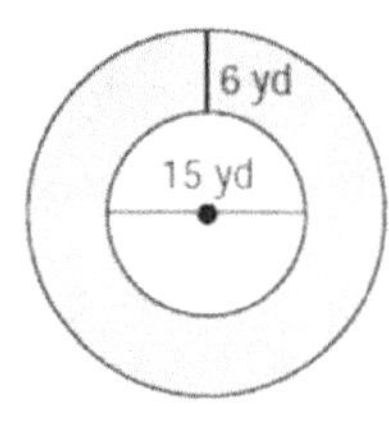

I: ....   II: ....   III: ....

Q 24. What least number should be subtracted from seven digit greatest number to obtain a greatest possible number divisible exactly by 9?

Q 25. Sum of seven consecutive numbers is equal to 7,07,0728. Find out value of the greatest number of this number series.

Q 26. Three bells toll at an interval of 5 seconds, 10 seconds and 15 seconds respectively. After what time interval all these bells toll together? How many times do all these bells toll together within an interval of one hour?

Q 27. Area of triangular faces of the following prisms can be calculated as half of the product of base and height. Area of rectangular faces can be calculated as product of length and breadth. By this process we can obtain ratio of total surface area of the following prisms. Obtain ration of all the four prisms by considering their names as I, II, III and IV.

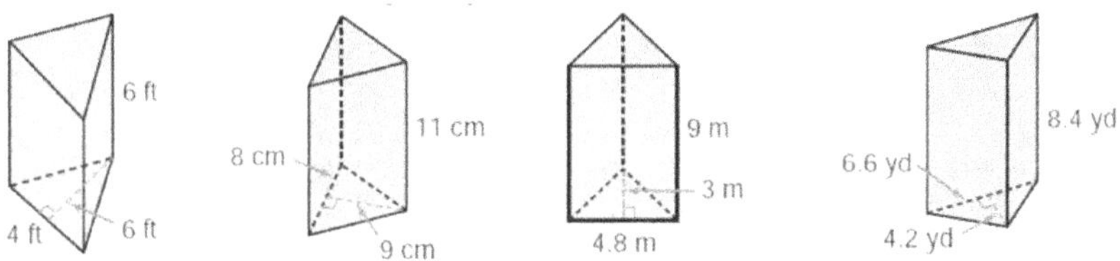

Q 28. Calculate area of the shaded portion in the following.

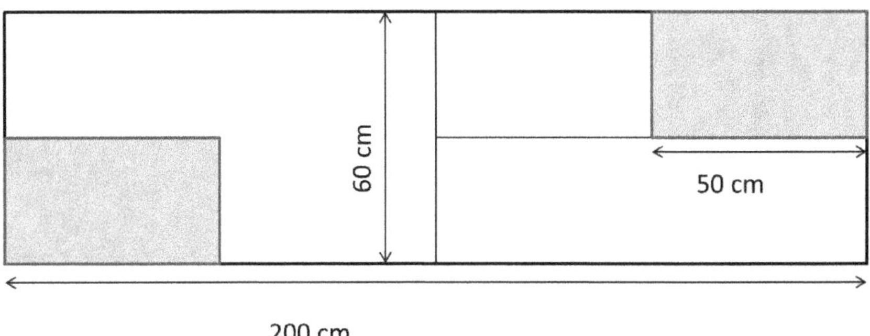

Q 29. By considering height of the liquid column in the following cans as h, which of the can is holding greatest volume of liquid?

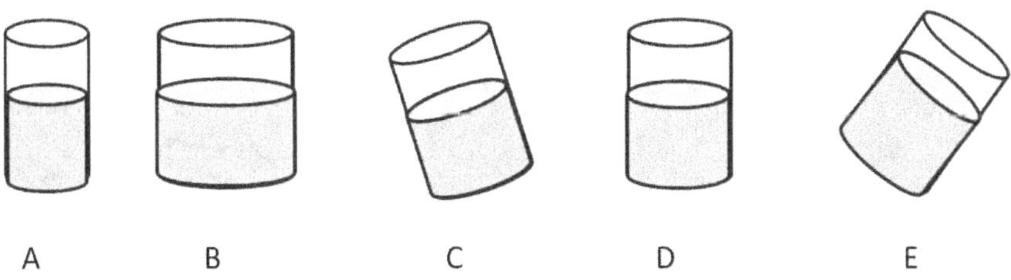

Q 30. Three angles of a triangle are of such type that angle B exceeds angle A by 30^0 and angle C is 40^0 less than the angle B. Find out complementary of angle A of that triangle.

Q 31. Find magnitude of angle A in the following.

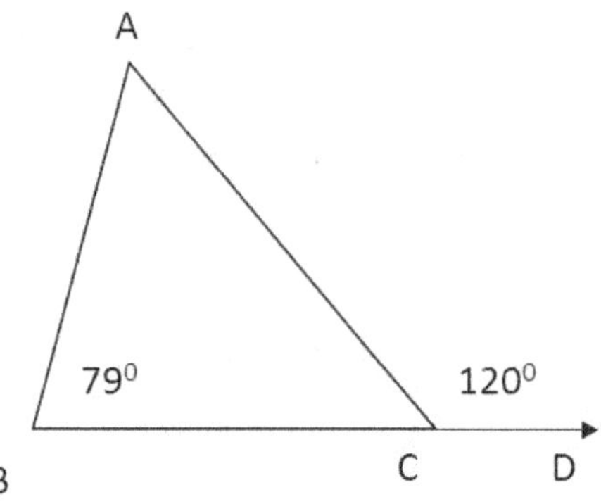

Q 32. What portions of following shapes are shaded?

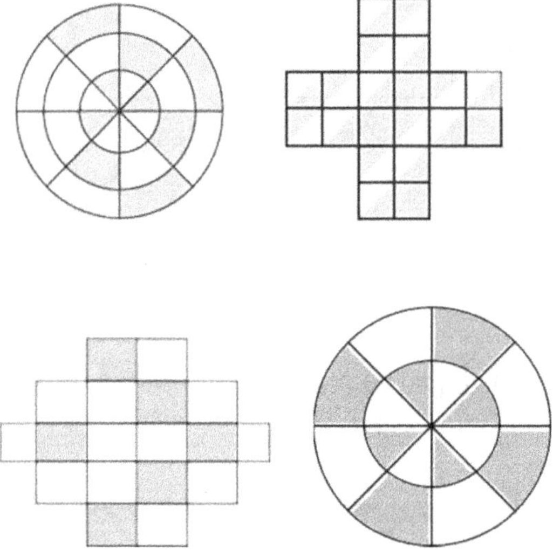

Q 33. What fraction of all the numbers from 1 to 500 are multiples of 25?

Q 34. Sum of all the interior angles of a quadrilateral is equal to sum of two straight angles. Three angles are equal to first, second and third multiple of 45^0 respectively. Find out the magnitude of the fourth angle.

Q 35. Three fourths of a given angle offers a supplementary angle, which is equal to half of a right angle. Find out the angle.

Q 36. Represent values of all the variables as displayed in the following number lines.

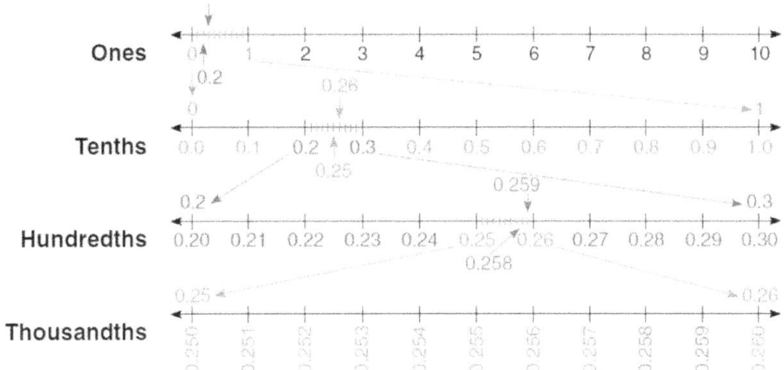

1. 

2.

3. 

4.

5.

6.

7.

8.

Q 37. What least number should be subtracted from five digit greatest number to obtain a number divisible by 6 leaving 2 as remainder.

Q 38. Jason is 136.5 cm tall. He marked this length on the ground, then did a running jump. He jumped a distance of 152.3 cm. How much longer was his jump than his height?

Q 39.

Ans 6: Option C requires modification.

Ans 7: Option D;

Ans 8: Option C; average can be worked out.

Book 2

A systematic faculty of study is the branch of science; it also encompasses different sub – branches of studies having identical alignment alongside general stream of study. This volume of publication is prepared to address some of the selected topics; principally to address increasing demand of study materials; to promote advance studies with focal attention to the need of comparative and analytical notes; to enable fellow aspirants to prepare for competitive examinations.

Main approach of this study is to provide a basic understanding of facts and figure while keeping it supplementary to the regular field of studies. Aspirants preparing for Pre- Medical entrance examinations and Olympiads can have better understanding of the materials used in this volume of publication. All the chapters have their relevant coverage to incorporate main topics (which is considered especially important for advance studies). We are also incorporating additional study materials to address feedback of fellow students who had aspirations of gaining advancement in the respective fields of study.

This publication will come in the combination of several booklets to cover up all possible topics; we are also planning to incorporate previous year questions and important questions wherever needed; such incorporations will make our effort time tested. It can be a good source material for instructors and supporters of the aspirants; as such support services will be backed up by time tested study materials; as such back up can have a fresh volume of source materials to be utiilised for addressing test papers, evaluation sheets and regular worksheets.

It cannot be claimed that this booklet series will fulfill the need of replacing regular textbook of High Schools; even it cannot be used in that way to cover up various school level contests; as the course material is designed on the basis of regular engagements duly assigned to a fellow student; as this material cannot be backed up merely to remain restricted to the realm regular studies. Higher challenges are incorporated in these booklets for the purpose addressing continuum of the prescribed Curriculum. We are also optimistic about sincere participation of teachers and instructors for the purpose of making this publication relevant and widely acceptable. Level of learning for which focus duly kept on study materials is also restricted to radial progression of the planned progress for which aspirants desire a backup. We are also planning to provide regular update to different topics duly incorporated in these volumes of publications.

Author/ Publisher

***

A Test Paper

Q 1. Represent shaded portions in the following by using a fraction.

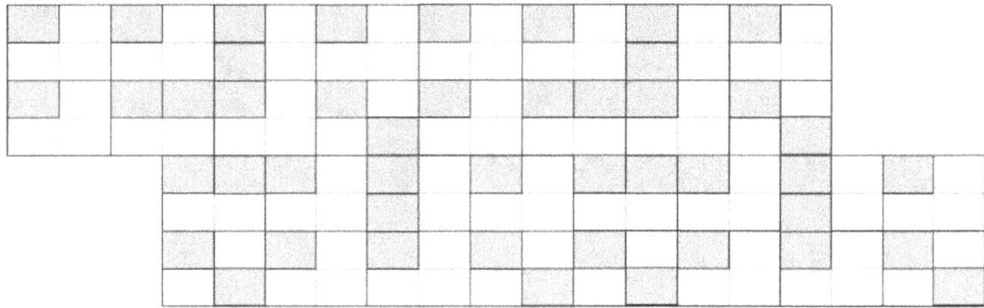

Q 2. Which of the following represents a linear triplet?

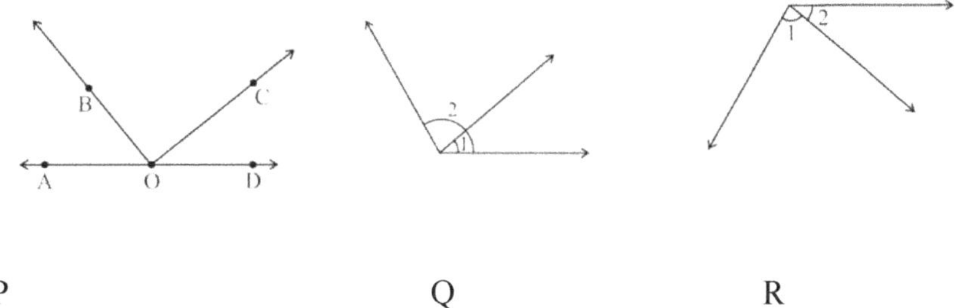

P   Q   R

Q 3. What fraction of all the numbers starting from 1 to 200 are multiples of 5?

Q 4. A passenger train spends 1m 12 seconds to cross a light post. Average speed of that train was 36 km/h. Calculate total length of that train. While moving on track a train usually covers the distance equal to its own length during crossing a narrow object having negligible thickness.

Q 5. $(1 + 2 + 3 + \ldots\ldots 21{,}000) \times (1.001 \times 10^5 - 100.1) = \ldots\ldots$

Q 6. Smallest five digit number which can be divisible by 9 leaving a remainder 5 is equal to $\ldots\ldots\ldots\ldots$

Q 6. Simplify the following.

$$\sqrt{144} = \sqrt{12 \text{ X } 12} = 12 \; ; \; \sqrt{(a+b)^2} = \sqrt{(a+b) \text{ X } (a+b)} = \cdots.$$

1. $\sqrt{900}$

2. $\sqrt{225}$

3. $\sqrt{20}$

4. $\sqrt{200}$

5. $\sqrt{32}$

6. $\sqrt{4x^2}$

7. $\sqrt{81t^2}$

8. $\sqrt{4(t+2)^2}$

9. $\sqrt{36(j-3)^2}$

10. $\sqrt{64(k+4)^2}$

11. $\sqrt{\dfrac{16}{4}}$

12. $\sqrt{\dfrac{25}{9}}$

13. $\sqrt{\dfrac{125}{16}}$

14. $\sqrt{\dfrac{50}{4}}$

15. $\sqrt{\dfrac{x^2}{36}}$

16. $\sqrt{\dfrac{200}{x^2}} , \; x \neq 0$

17. $\sqrt{\dfrac{242}{a^2}} , a \neq 0$

18. $\sqrt{\dfrac{(d-1)^2}{(f+1)^2}} , f \neq -1$

19. $\sqrt{\dfrac{(a+b)^2}{(c+d)^2}} , c+d \neq 0$

Q 7. How many bricks are there in each of the following?

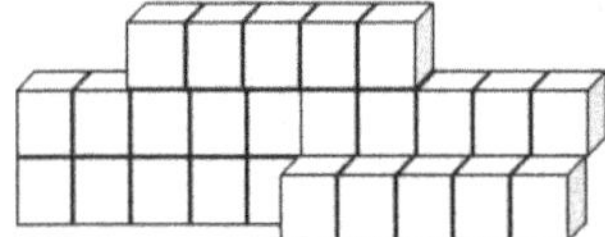 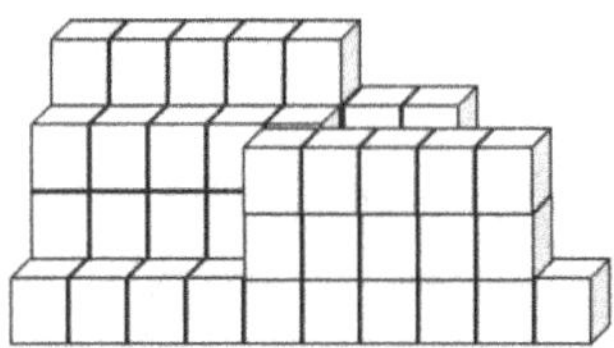

Set A   Set B

Q 8. Beat of three counters are repeated at uniform intervals of 5 seconds, 6 seconds and 8 seconds respectively. After what time interval do they beat together? How many times do they beat in a time interval of 2 hours?

Q 9. What least number should be added to the product of greatest five digit number and smallest four digit number to obtain a common multiple of 3 and 9?

Q 10. Is there any pair of natural number having LCM 169 and HCF 11?

Q 11. Sum of seven consecutive natural numbers is equal to 14,028. Find out smallest number of the seven number series.

Q 12. What is the natural number if sum of the number and its reciprocal is equal to 8.125?

System of Numeration

System of representing a number (cardinal or ordinal value) is called Number System.[1] Use of ten digits to represent numbers is the main reason for coining "Decimal System " of numeration for both Indian and International system; as they are using ten digits (0, 1, 2 , 3 … up to 9) for writing numbers in Standard form.

The decimal representation, as we use in our everyday mathematical operations, gives every nonzero natural number a unique representation as a finite sequence of digits to be placed at different places, beginning with a non-zero digit. It indicates a finite value of the given number; ensures sequence of growth; provides a definite place on a number line; confers a definite ratio to the representation. The system also satisfied basic operations having involvement of all sets of Natural Numbers, Whole Numbers, Integers and Rational Numbers. Operations related to non-rational and complex numbers is the subject of higher mathematics.

Western Arabic	0	1	2	3	4	5	6	7	8	9
Eastern Arabic	٠	١	٢	٣	٤	٥	٦	٧	٨	٩
Persian	٠	١	٢	٣	۴	۵	۶	٧	٨	٩
Devanagari	०	१	२	३	४	५	६	७	८	९

Two types of numeration systems came in focus since age old traditions to represent numerals; the arithmetic numerals (0, 1, 2, 3, 4, 5,

---

[1] *A Number System may be Indian, International or Roman System of Numeration. Representing a number in different system of numeration differ considerably; for example, there is no representation of zero in Roman Numeration.*

6, 7, 8, 9) and the geometric numerals (1, 10, 100, 1000, 10000 ...) are the system of numeration duly considered in everyday mathematics. If we use decimal system of numeration to represent a given value then the expanded form will be represented as a collection of values of exponents of 10. For example, the numeral 4327 means $(4\times10^3) + (3\times10^2) + (2\times10^1) + (7\times10^0)$, here $10^0 = 1$. Some expressions can be represented as <u>Repeating Rational</u>[2] expressions.

Rational numbers can be represented in the form of fractions having a non-zero denominator (such as $\frac{3}{7}, \frac{4}{9}, \frac{11}{13}$ etc. All such numerations can be represented in a number line. Large numbers having more than 10 digits can be converted in a definite form of exponential values by using scientific notations[3]; largest unit of distance, as we use in our day to day studies, is light year; a distance travelled by light in 1 year.

Some basic rules related to whole numbers are as follows:

1. Addition and multiplication of two whole numbers is always a whole number. (Closure Property)

2. The sum and the product of any set of whole numbers (may be three,, four, five etc.) remain the same regardless of the sequence of numbers are grouped together or arranged (Associative)

3. The sum and the product of two or more whole numbers remain the same even after interchanging the order of the numbers. (Commutative)

4. Product of any whole number and zero always returns zero. (Property of zero of a whole number)

5. Subtraction and division process cannot satisfy any of the above mentioned rules of whole numbers.

***.

---

[2] *14/11 = 1.272727272727... = 1.$\overline{27}$ or   321.3217878787878... = 321.321$\overline{78}$.*
[3] *One light year = 365 X 24 X 3600 X 3,00,000 km; speed of light = 3,00,000 km//s.*
= 365 X 24 X 3 X 10^7 km; it can be further contracted by using estimation process.

1. Daily Practice

Exercise 1

Q 1. Calculate outer boundary and area of the following.

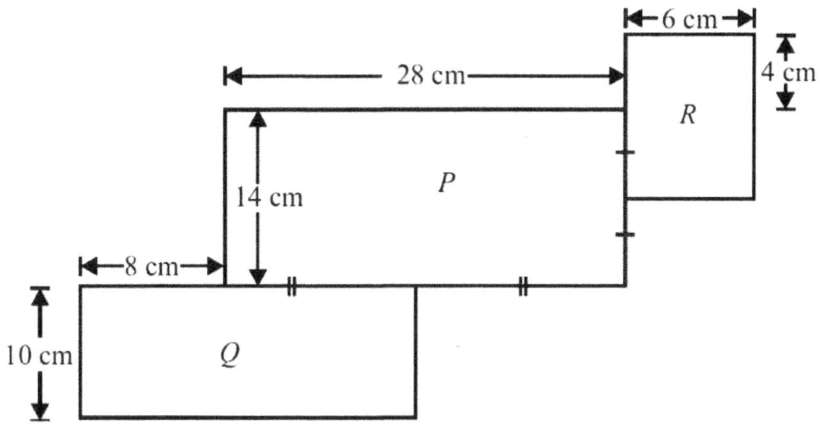

Q 2. How many bricks are there in each of the following?

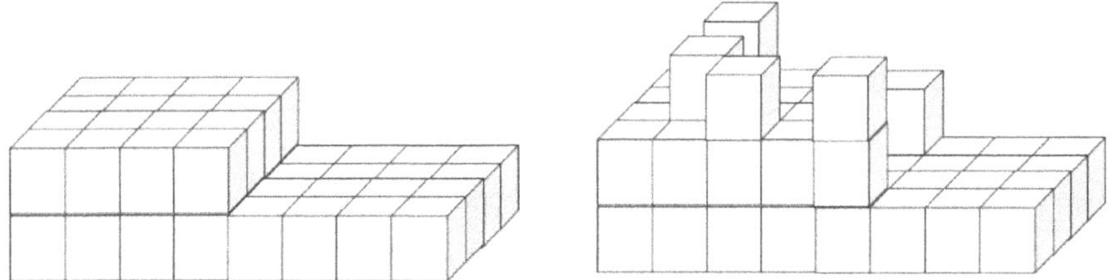

Q 3. What fraction of the following is shaded?

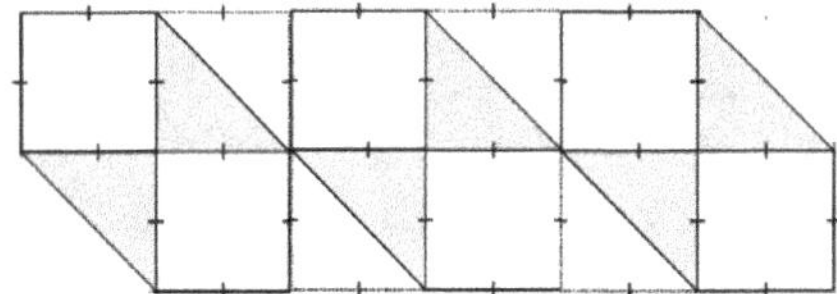

Identify the following angles as acute or obtuse types.

4. 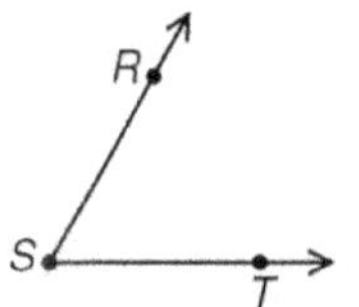

5. 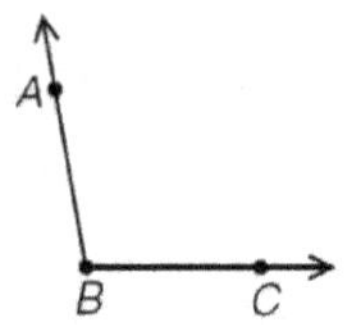

6. 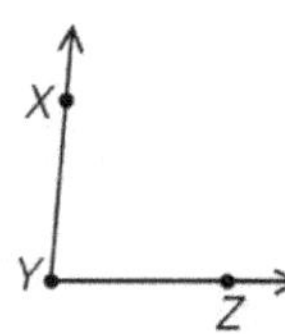

7. 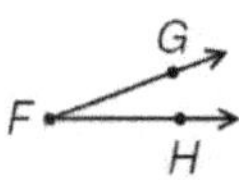

8. 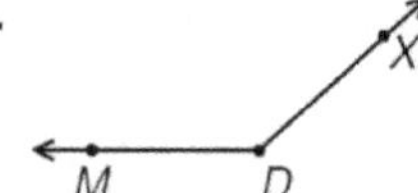

9. 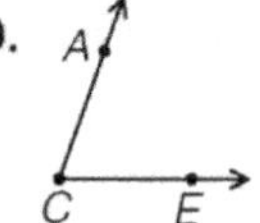

Q 10. Line l and m are parallel to each other and line n is transversal. Find out values of x.

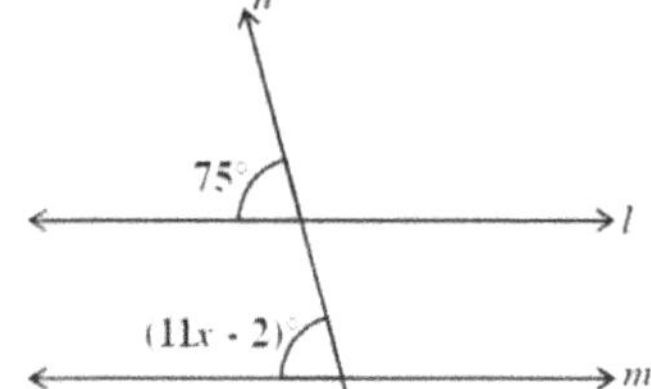

Q 11. What least number should be subtracted from the sum of greatest six digit number and smallest seven digit number to obtain a common multiple of 2, 4 and 8?

Q 12. Simplify:

$$\left(\frac{1 + 2 + 3 + \cdots\ldots 1{,}000}{500} - 1001\right) X\ 23{,}909\ X\ 125\ X\ 40\ X\ 8\ X\ 25$$

Q 13. T = 125 X 40 X 8 X 25 X 3.007 and S = 6,014 ÷ 2. Find out simplest value of (S − T) X 3.007 X 6,014 − 6,014 + 3,007.

Exercise 2

Q 1. Find out values of the variables in the following.

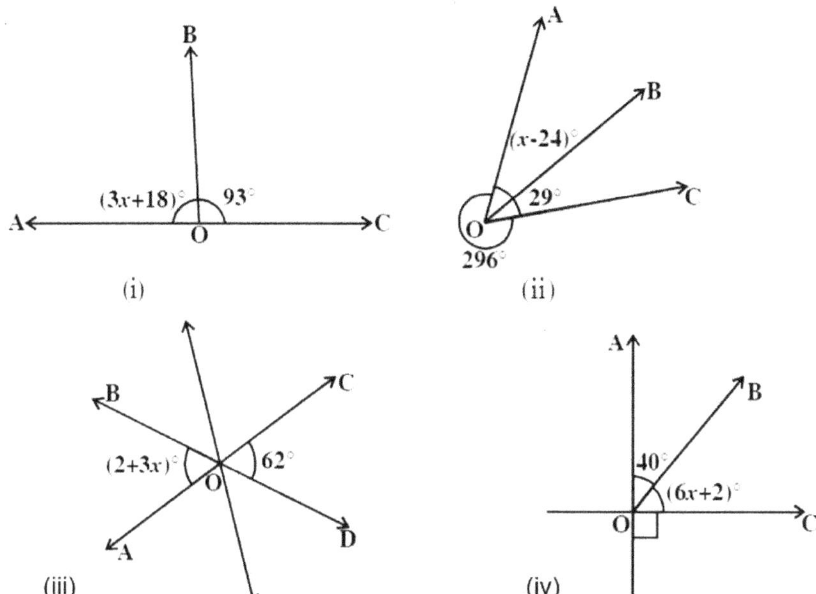

Q 2. Calculate volume.

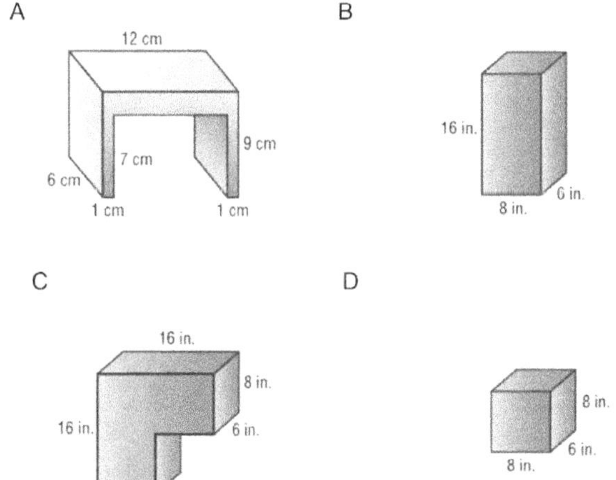

Q 3. Calculate area of shaded portions.

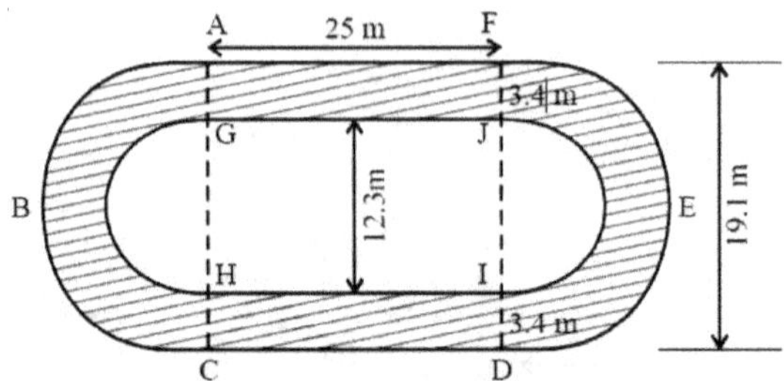

Q 4. Compare area of the following.

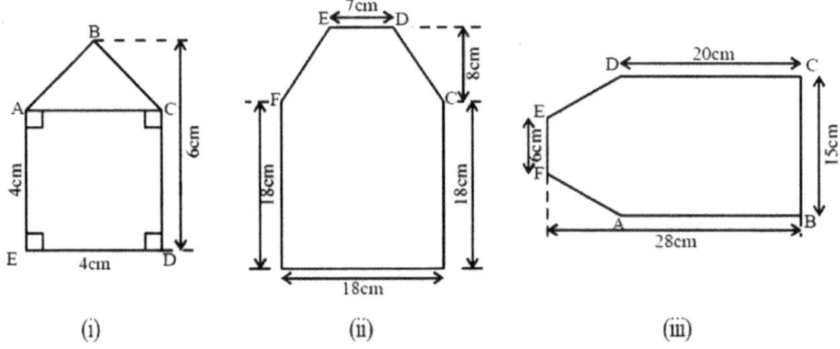

(i)   (ii)   (iii)

Q 5. Calculate area of the following.

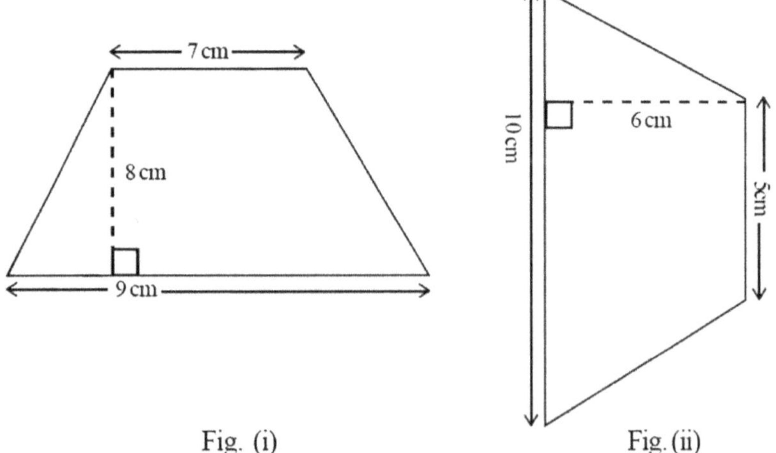

Fig. (i)   Fig. (ii)

Exercise 3

Q 1. Find out the variables in the following.

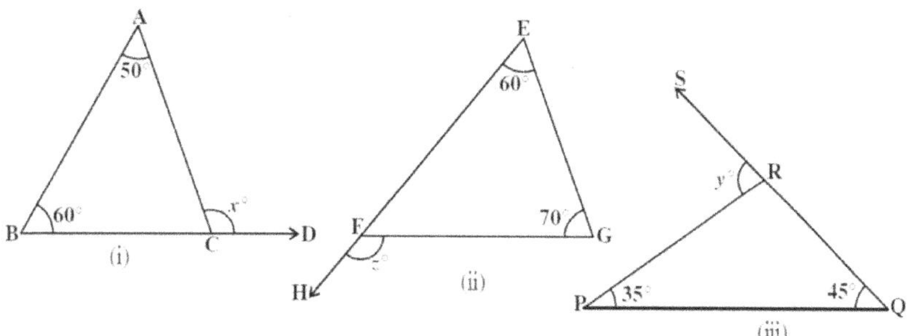

Q 2. Find out x and y in the following.

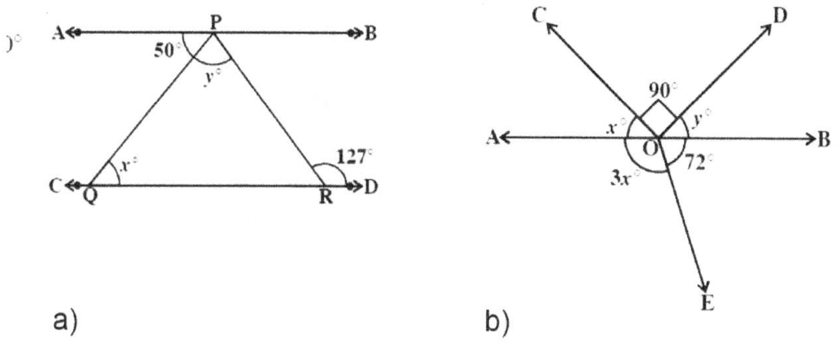

a)   b)

Q 3. Find out missing angles.

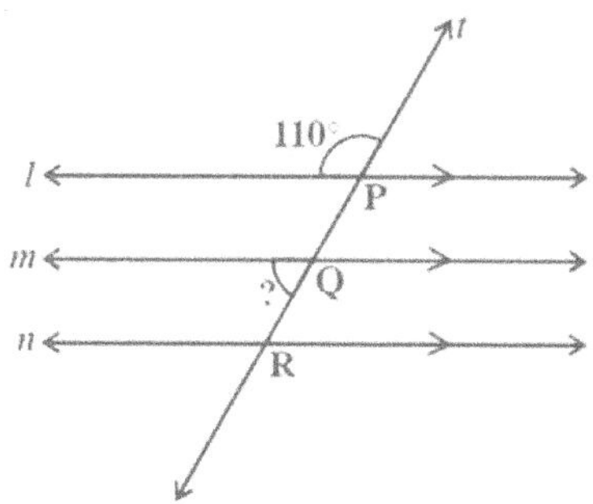

Q 4. Find out magnitude of angles represented by using variables.

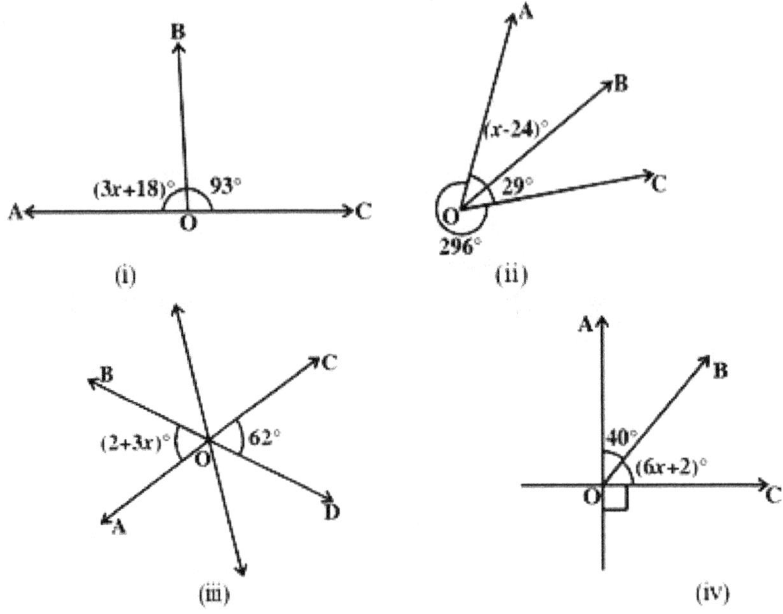

Q 5. Find out missing angles.

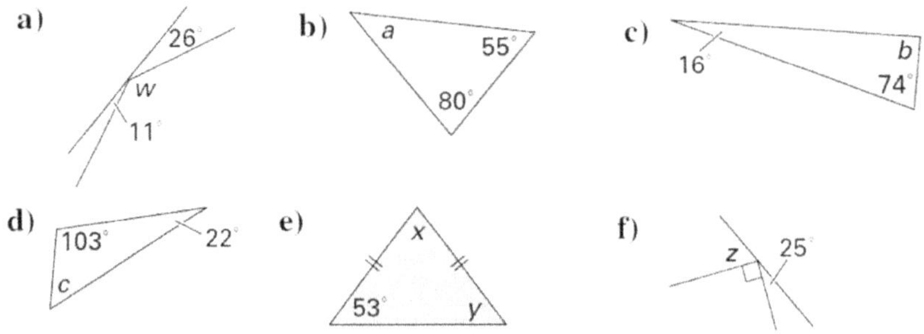

Q 6. What least number should be subtracted from the product of greatest and smallest four digit numbers to obtain a multiple of 9?

Q 7. Half of a quarter of a number is equal to 200,300,101. Find out the number.

Q 8. Seven fifth of a number exceeds seventh multiple of seven digit smallest number by 56. Find out the number.

Exercise 4

Q 1. Calculate area of shaded portions.

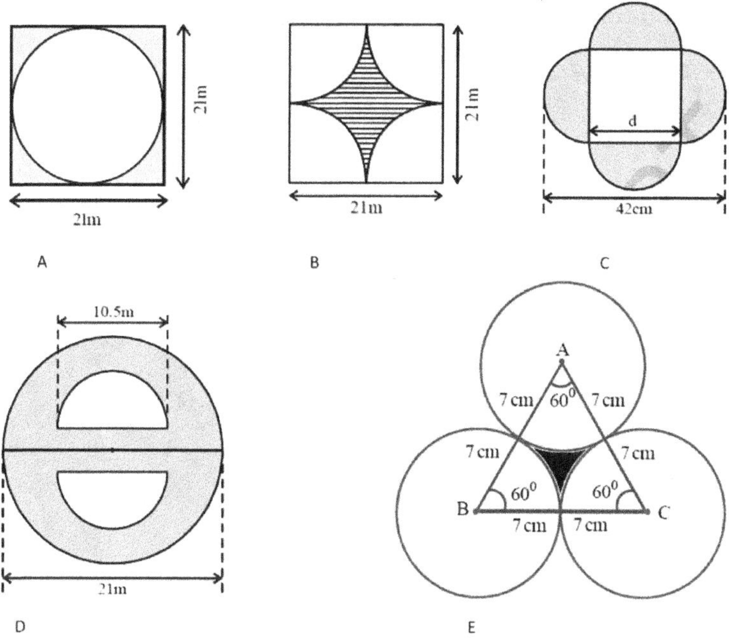

Q 2. Complete the following.

(i) $\left(\dfrac{-1}{17}\right) + (\underline{\quad}) = \left(\dfrac{-12}{5}\right) + \left(\dfrac{-1}{17}\right)$

(ii) $\dfrac{-2}{3} + \underline{\quad} = \dfrac{-2}{3}$

(iii) $1 \times \underline{\quad} = \dfrac{9}{11}$

(iv) $-12 + \left(\dfrac{5}{6} + \dfrac{6}{7}\right) = \left(-12 + \dfrac{5}{6}\right) + (\underline{\quad})$

(v) $(\underline{\quad}) \times \left(\dfrac{1}{2} + \dfrac{1}{3}\right) = \left(\dfrac{3}{4} \times \dfrac{1}{2}\right) + \left(\dfrac{3}{4} \times \underline{\quad}\right)$

(vi) $\dfrac{-16}{7} + \underline{\quad} = \dfrac{-16}{7}$

Q 3. What least number should be added to the product of smallest and greatest five digit numbers to obtain a common multiple of 3 and 9?

Exercise 5

Calculate and compare.

1.	36,587 87,943 + 13,156	2.	28,764 64,537 + 35,936	3.	65,446 1,915 + 47,291	4.	49,765 18,976 + 7,359
5.	26,542 − 17,986	6.	34,896 − 15,984	7.	41,132 − 17,545	8.	62,764 − 58,685
9.	115,609 205,399 + 411,111	10.	356,789 141,217 + 222,888	11.	471,009 180,007 + 277,777	12.	365,786 274,982 + 186,214
13.	672,244 − 456,688	14.	681,337 − 278,456	15.	524,700 − 316,672	16.	938,400 − 619,711

Q 17. Calculate simplest value.

a.
$$\frac{40^{50} - 40^{48}}{2^{96}} \times 10^{-45} =$$

(A) 20

(B) $10^3(1599)$

(C) $10^2(1601)$

(D) 200^6

(E) 200^{53}

d.
$$\frac{2^{16} - 1}{(2^4 + 1)(2^{11} + 2^3)}$$

b.
$$\frac{40^{48}(40^2 - 1)}{2^{96}} \times 10^{-45}$$

c.
If $ab \neq 0$, $\dfrac{a^8 - b^8}{(a^4 + b^4)(a^2 + b^2)} =$

(A) 1

(B) $a - b$

(C) $(a + b)(a - b)$

(D) $(a^2 + b^2)(a^2 - b^2)$

(E) $(a - b)/(a + b)$

Q 18. What least number should be added to greatest six digit number to obtain a multiple of 8?

Q 19. Three bells toll at an interval of 4 seconds, 8 seconds and 12 seconds respectively. After what time interval do they toll together?

Exercise 6

Observe the following chart of representation.

Chart	Label
1	1 whole
$\frac{1}{2}$ $\quad$ $\frac{1}{2}$	2 halves
$\frac{1}{3}$ $\quad$ $\frac{1}{3}$ $\quad$ $\frac{1}{3}$	3 thirds
$\frac{1}{4}$ $\quad$ $\frac{1}{4}$ $\quad$ $\frac{1}{4}$ $\quad$ $\frac{1}{4}$	4 fourths
$\frac{1}{5}$ $\quad$ $\frac{1}{5}$ $\quad$ $\frac{1}{5}$ $\quad$ $\frac{1}{5}$ $\quad$ $\frac{1}{5}$	5 fifths
$\frac{1}{6}$ $\quad$ $\frac{1}{6}$ $\quad$ $\frac{1}{6}$ $\quad$ $\frac{1}{6}$ $\quad$ $\frac{1}{6}$ $\quad$ $\frac{1}{6}$	6 sixths
$\frac{1}{8}$ $\quad$ $\frac{1}{8}$ $\quad$ $\frac{1}{8}$ $\quad$ $\frac{1}{8}$ $\quad$ $\frac{1}{8}$ $\quad$ $\frac{1}{8}$ $\quad$ $\frac{1}{8}$ $\quad$ $\frac{1}{8}$	8 eighths
$\frac{1}{9}$ $\quad$ $\frac{1}{9}$ $\quad$ $\frac{1}{9}$ $\quad$ $\frac{1}{9}$ $\quad$ $\frac{1}{9}$ $\quad$ $\frac{1}{9}$ $\quad$ $\frac{1}{9}$ $\quad$ $\frac{1}{9}$ $\quad$ $\frac{1}{9}$	9 ninths
$\frac{1}{10}$ $\quad$ $\frac{1}{10}$ $\quad$ $\frac{1}{10}$ $\quad$ $\frac{1}{10}$ $\quad$ $\frac{1}{10}$ $\quad$ $\frac{1}{10}$ $\quad$ $\frac{1}{10}$ $\quad$ $\frac{1}{10}$ $\quad$ $\frac{1}{10}$ $\quad$ $\frac{1}{10}$	10 tenths
$\frac{1}{12}$ $\quad$ $\frac{1}{12}$ $\quad$ $\frac{1}{12}$ $\quad$ $\frac{1}{12}$ $\quad$ $\frac{1}{12}$ $\quad$ $\frac{1}{12}$ $\quad$ $\frac{1}{12}$ $\quad$ $\frac{1}{12}$ $\quad$ $\frac{1}{12}$ $\quad$ $\frac{1}{12}$ $\quad$ $\frac{1}{12}$ $\quad$ $\frac{1}{12}$	12 twelfths

$$1 = \frac{2}{2} = \frac{3}{3} = \frac{4}{4} = \frac{5}{5} = \frac{6}{6} = \frac{8}{8} = \frac{9}{9} = \frac{10}{10} = \frac{12}{12}$$

Complete the following:

Q 1. $\frac{2}{7} = \frac{}{14} = \frac{}{21} = \frac{}{28} = \frac{}{35} = \frac{}{56} = \frac{}{63}$

Q 2. What fraction of 1331 is equal to 121?

Q 3. $1/11^{th}$ of a number is equal to 100,200,311. Find out the number.

Q 4. Seven seventeenth of a natural number exceeds smallest six digit number by 3. Find out the number.

Q 5. Sum of five consecutive natural numbers is equal to 15 more than 55,000. Find out the smallest number.

Exercise 7

Q 1. Complete the following.

Standard Form:
2,821,700,000

Expanded Form:

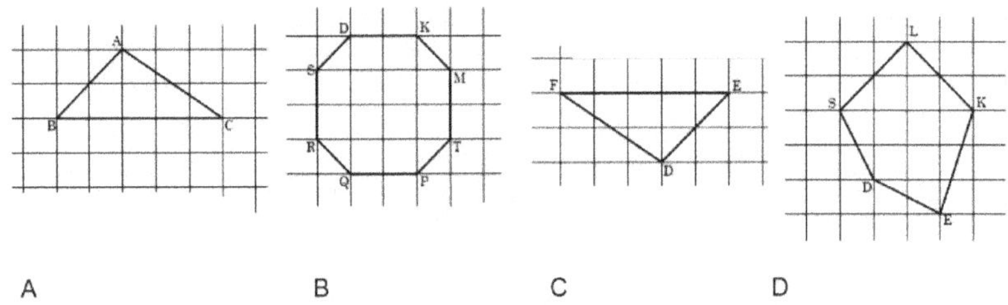

2,000,000,000 + 800,000,000 + 20,000,000 + 1,000,000 + 700,000

Word Name:

Q 2. Find out area of the following in unit square.

A	B	C	D

Q 3. Find out variables.

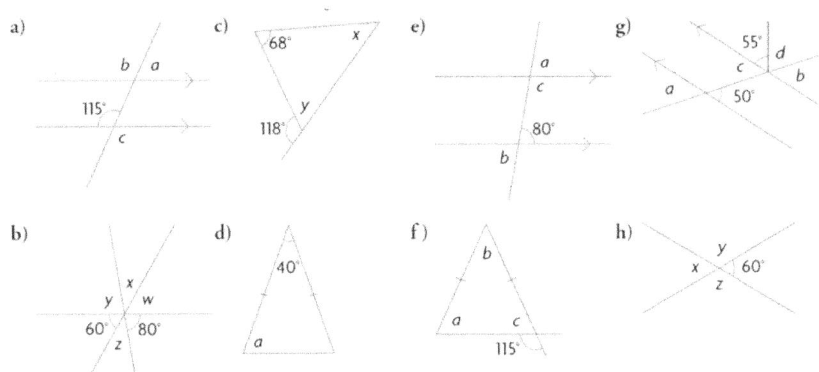

Q 4. Find out missing angles.

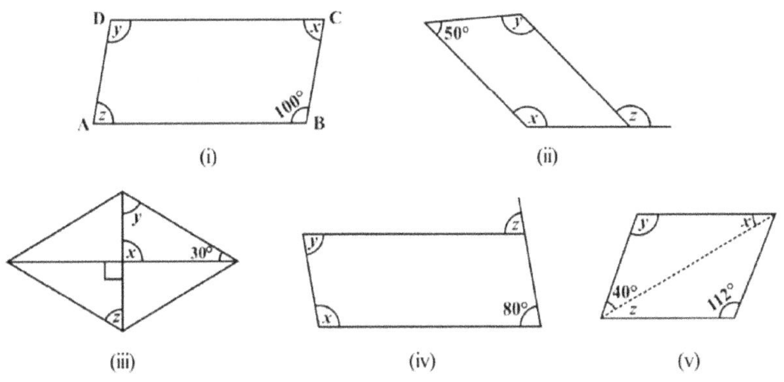

(i)

(ii)

(iii)

(iv)

(v)

Q 5. Find out area and outer boundary of the following in which side of each of the unit square is 4 cm.

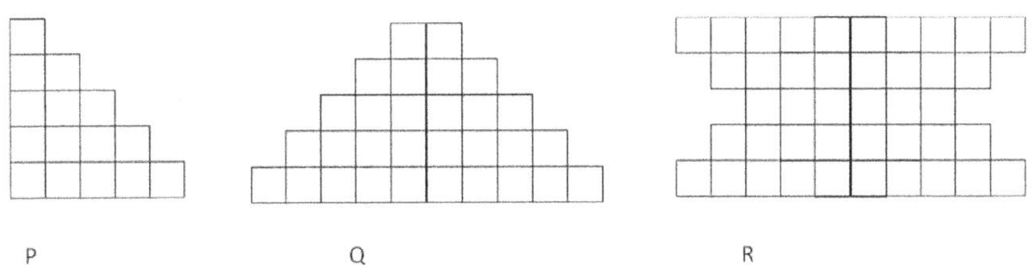

P

Q

R

Q 6. Identify following variables.

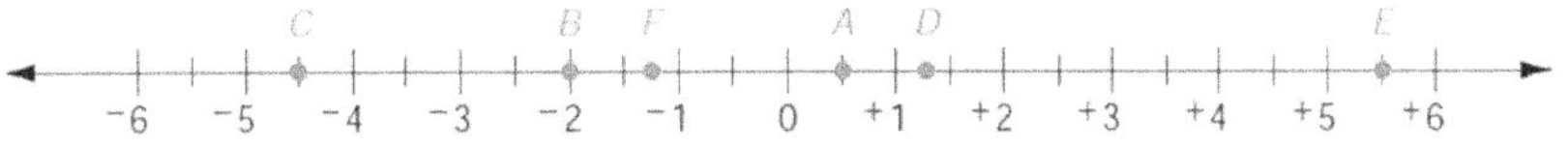

Q 7. Find out sum and difference of P and Q in the following.

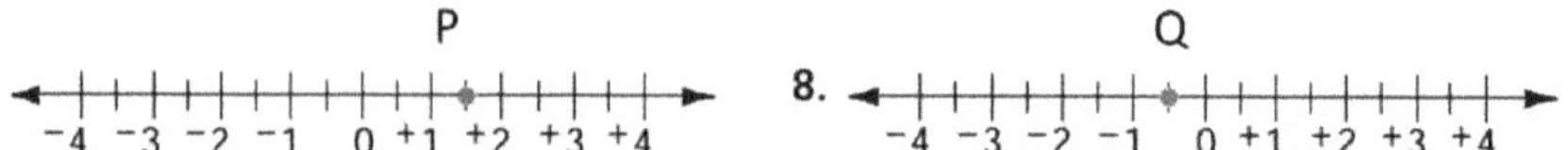

Q 8. Sum of seven consecutive natural numbers is equal to 28 more than seventh multiple of seven digit smallest natural number. Find out the smallest natural number of this number series.

Exercise 8

Divide and check your answer.

1. $2.3\overline{)6.4\,6\,3}$ quotient $2\,8\,1$

2. $0.1\,9\overline{)0.1\,7\,4\,8}$ quotient $0\,9\,2$

3. $0.9\,2\overline{)2.8\,6\,1\,2}$ quotient $3\,1\,1$

4. $0.8\overline{)4.8\,2\,4}$ quotient $6\,0\,3$

5. $0.0\,1\,1\overline{)0.0\,9\,3\,5}$ quotient $8\,5$

6. $0.0\,1\,2\overline{)0.0\,0\,1\,4\,4}$ quotient $0\,1\,2$

7. $1.5\overline{)0.0\,0\,4\,5}$ quotient $0\,0\,0\,3$

8. $0.1\,8\overline{)0.0\,3\,6}$ quotient $0\,2$

9. $0.0\,2\,4\overline{)0.0\,0\,1\,4\,4}$ quotient $0\,0\,6$

10. $0.5\overline{)7.55}$

11. $0.6\overline{)9.66}$

12. $0.4\overline{)0.76}$

13. $0.7\overline{)8.61}$

14. $92.4 \div 0.4$

15. $6.3 \div 0.3$

16. $257.2 \div 0.4$

17. $0.96 \div 0.8$

18. $2.214 \div 0.9$

19. $0.084 \div 0.3$

20. $555.6 \div 0.6$

21. $391.2 \div 0.4$

22. $0.28\overline{)4.396}$

23. $0.75\overline{)0.7725}$

24. $0.07\overline{)3.5028}$

25. $0.08\overline{)1.9216}$

26. $6.9 \div 2.3$

27. $8.93 \div 4.7$

28. $0.78 \div 0.26$

29. $0.014 \div 0.07$

Q 30. What least number should be subtracted from smallest seven digit number to obtain a factor of 9?

Q 31. A cistern takes 45 minutes to fill up half of a water tank, anther cistern takes 30 minutes to fill up quarter of the same water tank. Find out time to be taken by both the cisterns jointly to fill up the same water tank.

Q 32. Simplify:

$$\left(1+\tfrac{1}{100}\right)\left(1-\tfrac{1}{1001}\right)\left[2.002 - 2\,X\left(1+\tfrac{1}{1000}\right)\right] X\ 34.090823$$

Q 33. A water boat takes 1,5 hours to cross a stream while moving against the flow of water and it can take 30 minutes to cross the same distance while moving along with the flow of water. Find out ratio of the speed of boat and speed of the stream.

Q 34. Sum of two interior angles of a triangle is 121^{0} 32' . Find out magnitude of the third angle.

Exercise 9

Find out products.

1. 10×77 2. 30×40 3. 10×0.5 4. 10×0.0049

5. 100×13 6. 400×125 7. 100×0.7 8. 100×0.1003

9. 20×51 10. 5000×30 11. $10,000 \times 0.02$ 12. $20,000 \times 0.02$

13. 3000×50.123 14. 4000×22 15. 100×19.41 16. 1000×12.0006

17. a. 10×94 b. 100×930 c. 1000×92

18. a. 100×0.05 b. 10×0.7 c. 1000×0.94

19. a. 1000×0.0062 b. 100×0.005 c. 10×0.042

20. a. 100×0.61 b. 100×0.70 c. 1000×0.0010

Find the missing factor.

21. $b \times 1000 \times 0.0010 \times 10,000 \times 0.02 \times 45 = 900\,00 \times 0.0010$

22. $y \times 96 \times 0.0010 \times 0.0010 \times 0.0010 \times 0.0010 = 9600$

23. $300 \times 100 \times 0.05 \times 100 \times 0.05 \times 100 \times 0.05 \times a = 5100$

Q 24. Rikin went to Kolkata on a day which was Wednesday. His uncle wants to visit the same place 65 days after that day. What will be the day in which uncle planned to visit the place?

Q 25. Mohanlal wanted to visit a place which is 87 km away from the city drive. He again wants to extend his visit by 23 km to visit another city. His personal car spends 20 seconds to cross near about 189 m of distance. Calculate total time to be taken by his car drive to complete his visits and return back to home after finishing all the visits.

Q 26. A wall mount clock spends 4 seconds to ring 4 bells at 4 a.m. Calculate total time to be taken by that clock to strike 10 bells at 10 a.m.

Exercise 10

Observe the numeration chart and write given values in Standard form.

Billions Period			Millions Period			Thousands Period			Ones Period		
hundreds	tens	ones	hundreds	tens	ones	hundreds	tens	ones	hundreds	tens	ones
								8	6	3	0
							8	6	3	0	2
						8	6	3	0	2	0
					8	6	3	0	2	0	1
		8	6	3	0	2	0	1	0	0	0

A place that holds a zero may be omitted in expanded form.

(8 × 1000) (6 × 100)
(3 × 10) (0 × 1)

(8 × 10,000) (6 × 1000)
(3 × 100) (2 × 1)

(8 × 100,000) (6 × 10,000)
(3 × 1000) (2 × 10)

(8 × 1,000,000) (6 × 100,000)
(3 × 10,000) (2 × 100) (1 × 1)

(8 × 1,000,000,000)
(6 × 100,000,000)
(3 × 10,000,000)
(2 × 100,000) (1 × 1000)

Q 1. 43 million + 43 thousands + 403 hundreds + 324 tens = ...

Q 2. 39 more than 39 million + 3099 thousands = ...

Q 3. Identify the following.

1. ___ perpendicular lines

2. ___ diameter

3. ___ radius

4. ___ reflection

5. ___ ray

6. ___ equilateral triangle

a.

b.

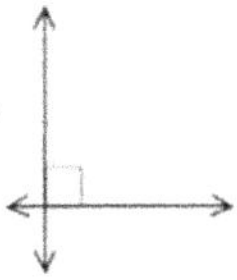

c.

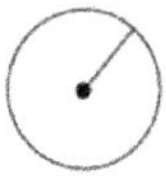

d.

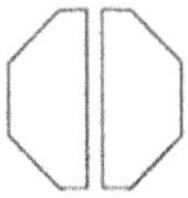

e.

f.

7. x- and y-coordinates of point C ____________

8. ____________ is located at (4, 0)?

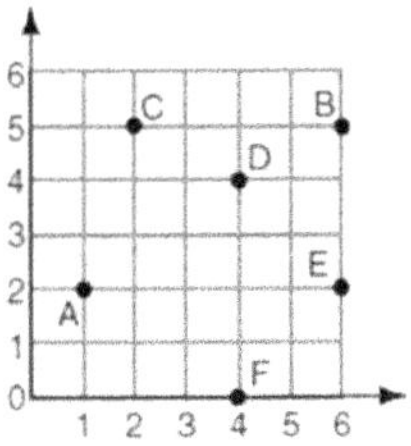

2. Revision Works

Sum of all the interior angles of a quadrilateral is equal to two straight angles..

-    *Sengupta C. S.*

1: Revision works

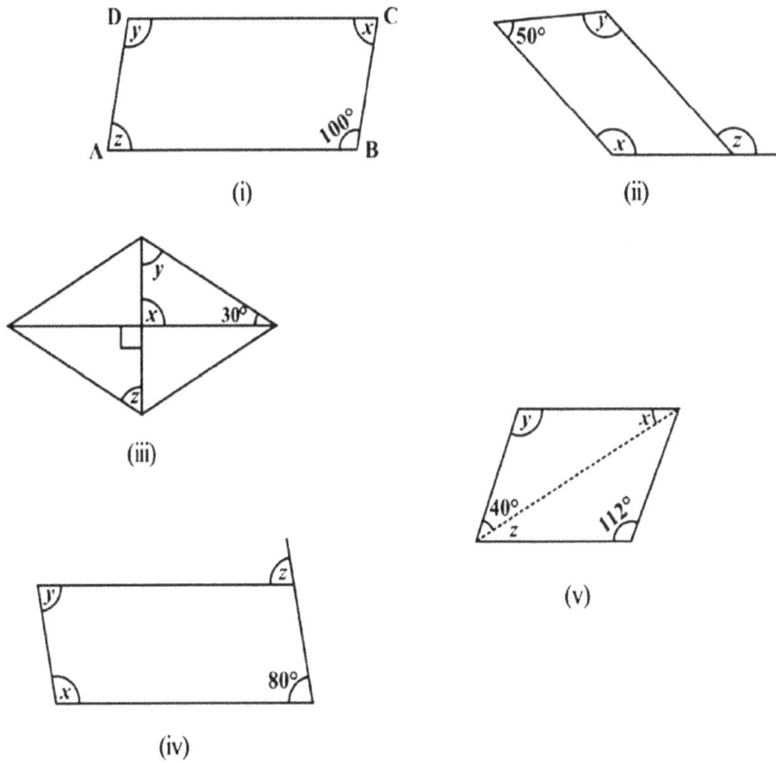

2. Sonali added 1002 to a natural number instead of subtracting it. Her result was equal to sum of five digit greatest and five digit smallest number. Find out the actual result.

3. Find out missing fractions in the following.

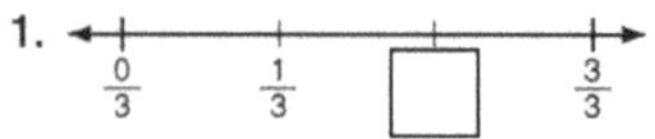

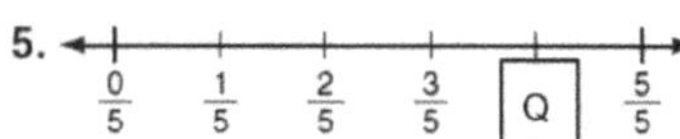

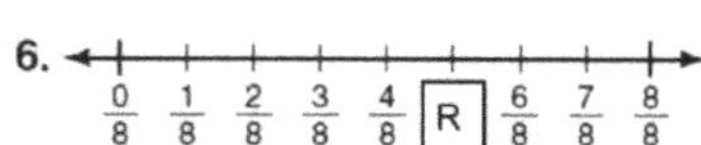

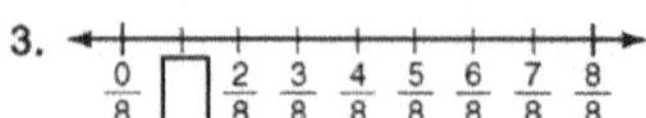

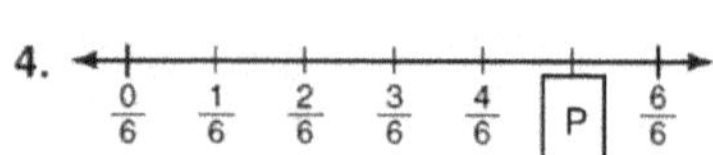

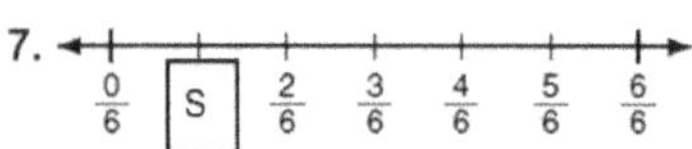

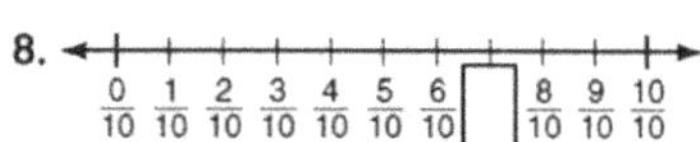

4. Compare the following numerals.

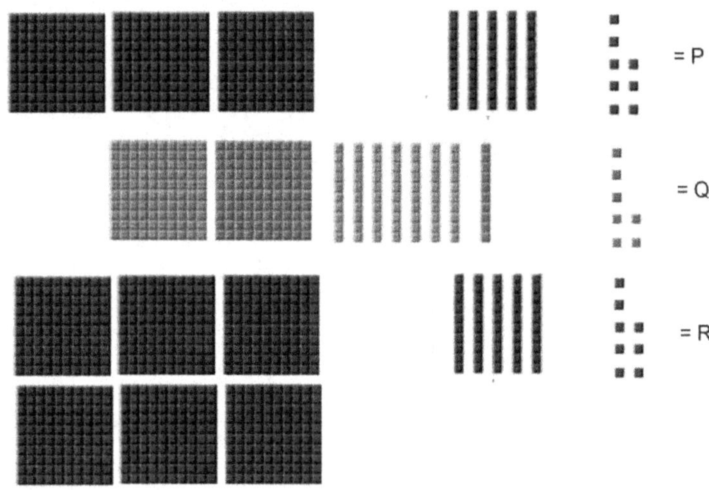

5. What least number should be subtracted from five digit greatest number to obtain a multiple of 8?

6. What digit will be there at ones place if we multiply 99, 999 and 9999?

7. P = 4,000 X 3,000 X 25 and Q = 0.1 X 0.001 X 0.0001; then find out simplest value of $(P \ X \ Q) \div \dfrac{P}{Q} + 29{,}908 \ X \ (Q - 10^8$;

3. Achievers

1: Find out value of variables in each of the following.

(i) 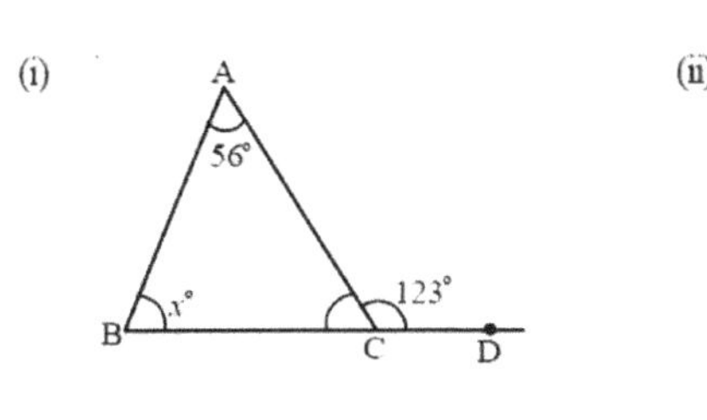

(ii) 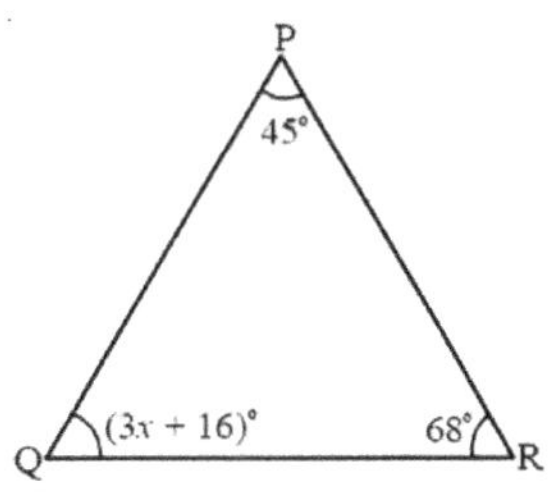

(iii) 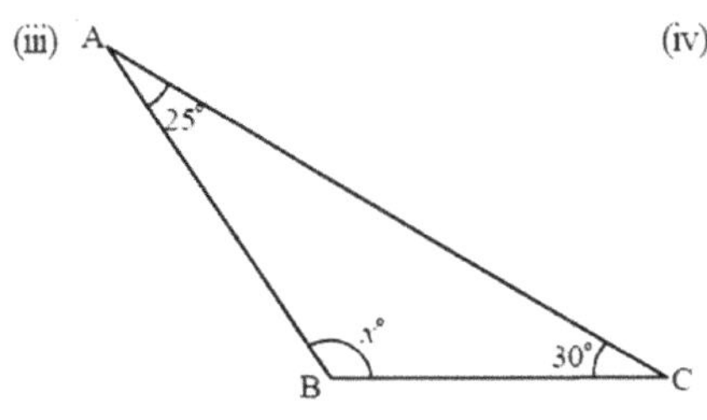

(iv) 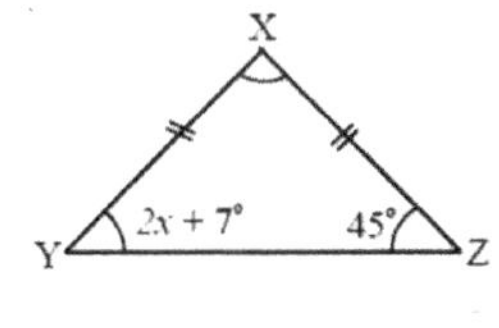

2. Complete the following:

$$\frac{2}{3} , \frac{7}{8}$$

Then $\dfrac{2}{3} \div \dfrac{7}{8} = \dfrac{2}{3} \times \dfrac{8}{7} = \dfrac{16}{21}$ which is a rational number

Check this for two more example.

$$\frac{5}{7} \div 2 = \frac{5}{7} \div \frac{2}{1} = \frac{5}{7} \times \frac{1}{2} = \frac{5}{14}$$

$$-\frac{2}{3} \div \frac{6}{11} = \underline{\hspace{3cm}} = \underline{\hspace{3cm}} = \underline{\hspace{3cm}}$$

$$3 \div \frac{17}{13} = \frac{3}{1} \div \frac{17}{13} = \underline{\hspace{3cm}} = \underline{\hspace{3cm}} = \underline{\hspace{3cm}}$$

3. What fraction of all the numbers starting from 1 to 200 are not divisible by 4?

4. February 4th was Wednesday, what day will be February 27th ?

5. Time taken by minute hand of a clock to complete a spin is ……..

6. A passenger train takes 49 seconds to cross a light post. The average speed of that train was 72 km/h. Calculate total length of that train.

7. Find out magnitude of missing angles.

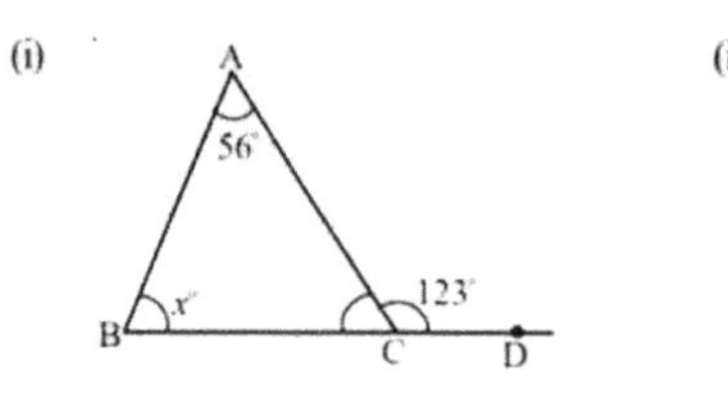

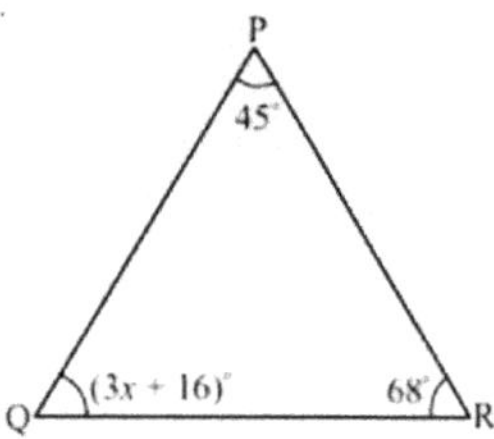

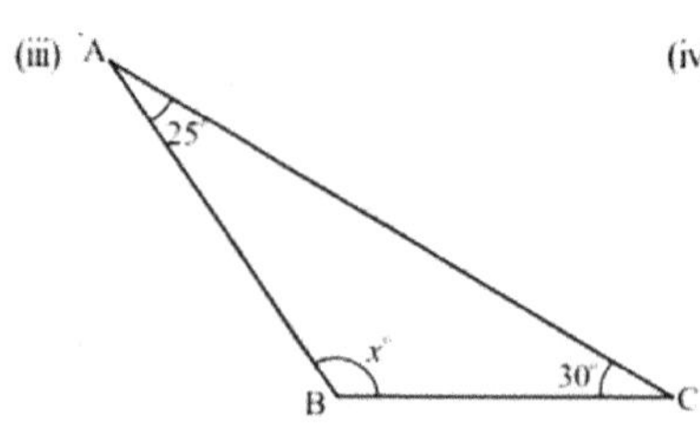

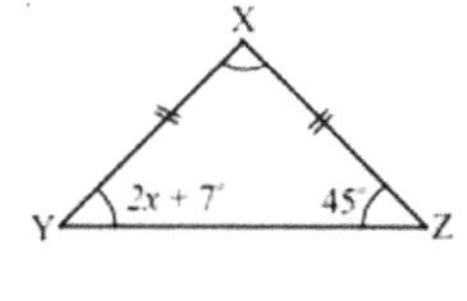

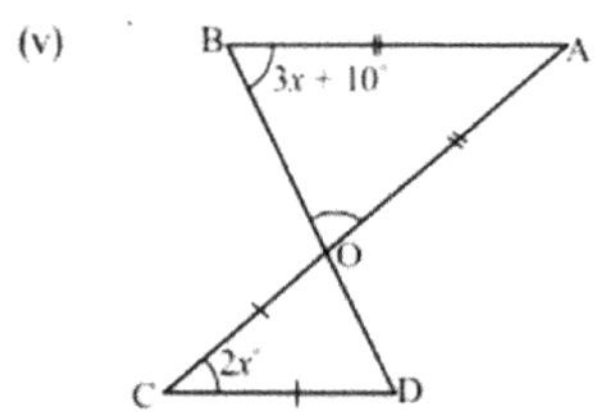

8. Half of a quarter of a natural number is equal to 100,100,101. Find out fifth multiple of that number.

9. Simplify the following:

$$\left(1.001 + \frac{1001}{9999} + \frac{209}{1009} + 2.0909 + 1.90901 + \frac{109}{9001}\right) X \left[1.0001 - \left(1 + \frac{1}{10000}\right)\right]$$

10. $(1.01 \ X \ 0.01 \ X \ 0.001 \ X \ 0.0001)$ 125 X 8 X 40 X 25 = …………

11. Find out the missing angles in the following:

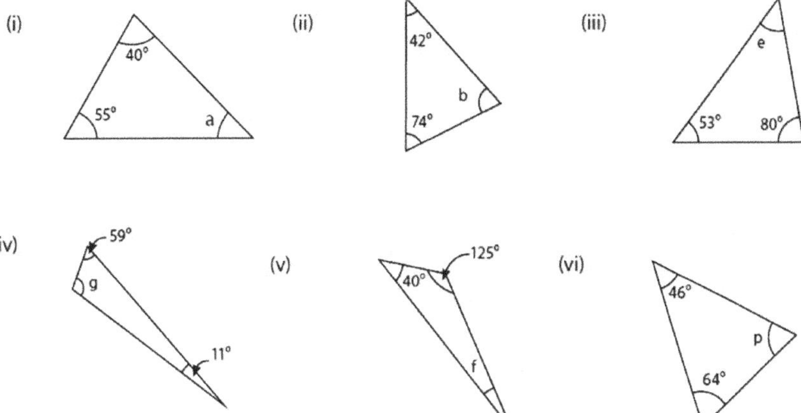

12. Find out area of the following.

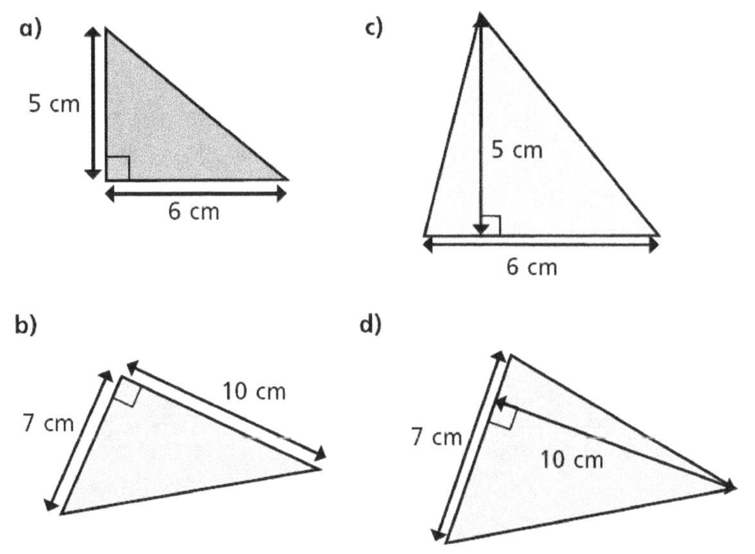

13. What fraction of all the numbers from 1 to 100 are multiples of 5?

14. P = 2.002 X 0.002 X 0.0002 and Q = 125 X 25 X 40 X 8. Find out simplest value of [(PXQ) ÷ 8].

15. Write the following representative fractions.

  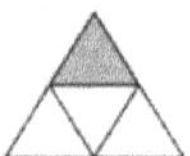 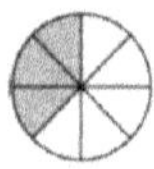 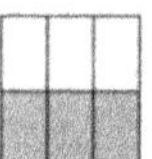 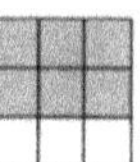

16. Find out area of shaded portions.

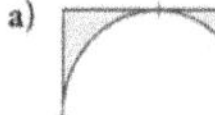 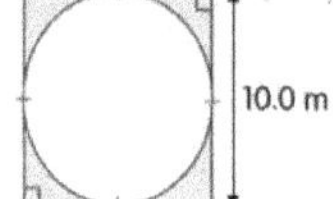 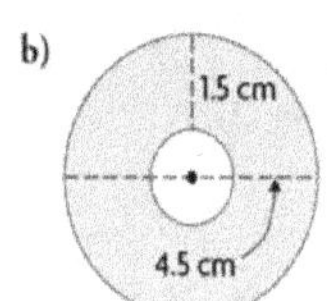 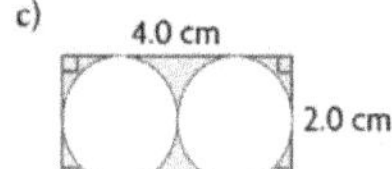 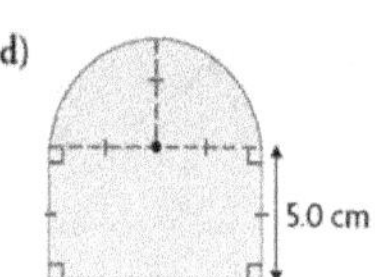

17. Here (P + Q – R) = ……………..

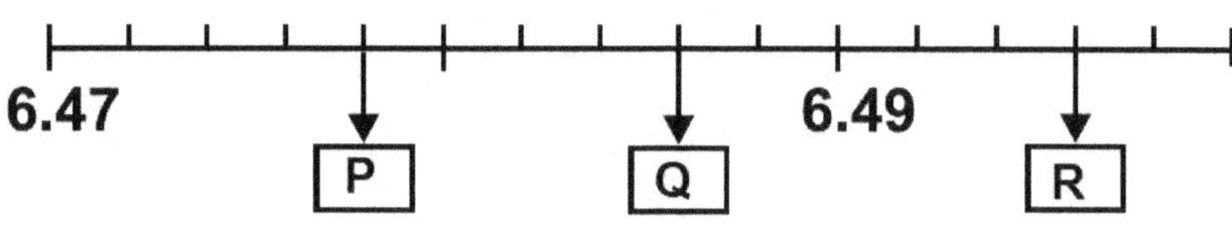

18. Find out and compare area of shaded portions.

a.
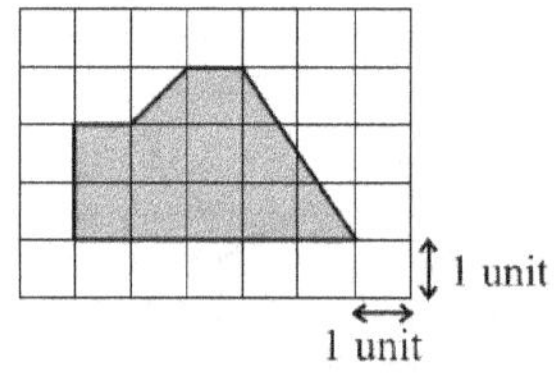

c.
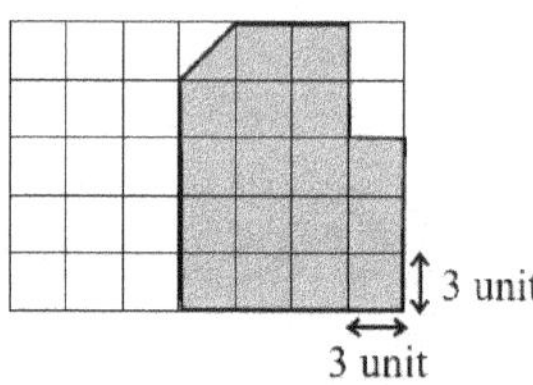

b.
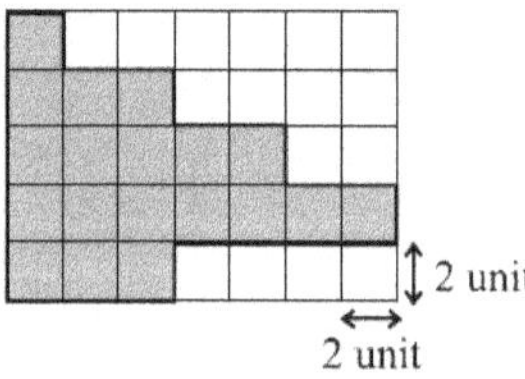

d.
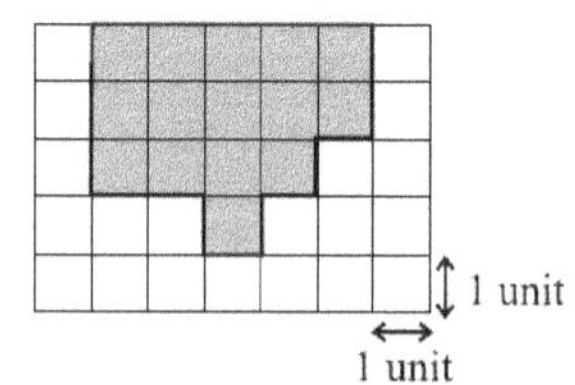

4. Evaluation II

I: Find product in each of the following:

a. 10 X 20 X 30   b. 80 X 10 X 700   c. 40 X 50 X 8000

d. 20 X 40 X 50   e. 60 X 50 X 200   f. 20 X 30 X 6000

g. 20X X 30 X 40   h. 30 X 50 X 100   i. 20 X 40 X 9000

II. Solve the following.

1. Smith made three stops during his 150-mile bike trip. He first stopped after 20 miles. His second stop was 54 miles away from the starting point, his third stop was 18 miles before the end of the trip. How many miles did he travel between his first and third stops?

2. A multiple theater complex in a shopping center has 40 rows of seats with 9 seats in each row, 50 rows having 11 seats in each row and 60 rows of seats having 12 seats in each row. Total 200 seats are reserved for VIPs. How many seats are available for non-VIP visitors?

3. How many bricks each of 16 sq. inches can be used to construct a wall of length 12 m, breadth 10 inches and height 2 m?

6. Complete the following numeration chart.

The Numbers	Places			
	Th	H	T	O
2432				
3009				
4098				

7. What fraction of all the numbers starting from 1 to 200 are multiples of 25?

8. $P = 2143 + 7856$; $Q = 21098 - 21000 + 992$; $R = 3209 + 6790$;

Calculate the value of $Q + P - R + \dfrac{R}{P} + 109{,}802 \; X \; (R - P)$

9. What fraction of all the numbers starting from 1 to 100 can be divided exactly by 5?

10. Two interior angles of a triangle are 20^0 and 40^0 respectively. Find out magnitude of the third interior angle of this triangle.

11. Simplify:

$$\left(\dfrac{121}{999} + \dfrac{1021}{9999} + 12.098 + 0.0909\right) X \left[\left(1 + \dfrac{1}{100}\right) \div \left(1 - \dfrac{1}{101}\right) - (1.01^2)\right]$$

12. Interior angles of a given quadrilateral are p, 2p, 3p and 4p. Sum of all the interior angles is equal to 360^0 . What is the value of p?

13. Find out variables in each of the following:

(i) $\dfrac{n}{5} - \dfrac{5}{7} = \dfrac{2}{3}$

(ii) $\dfrac{x}{3} - \dfrac{x}{4} = 14$

(ii) $\dfrac{z}{2} + \dfrac{z}{3} - \dfrac{z}{6} = 8$

(iv) $\dfrac{2p}{3} - \dfrac{p}{5} = 11\dfrac{2}{3}$

(v) $9\dfrac{1}{4} = y - 1\dfrac{1}{3}$

(vi) $\dfrac{x}{2} - \dfrac{4}{5} + \dfrac{x}{5} + \dfrac{3x}{10} = \dfrac{1}{5}$

(vii) $\dfrac{x}{2} - \dfrac{1}{4} = \dfrac{x}{3} + \dfrac{1}{2}$

(viii) $\dfrac{2x - 3}{3x + 2} = \dfrac{-2}{3}$

(ix) $\dfrac{8p - 5}{7p + 1} = \dfrac{-2}{4}$

(x) $\dfrac{7y + 2}{5} = \dfrac{6y - 5}{11}$

(xi) $\dfrac{x + 5}{6} - \dfrac{x + 1}{9} = \dfrac{x + 3}{4}$

(xii) $\dfrac{3t + 1}{16} - \dfrac{2t - 3}{7} = \dfrac{t + 3}{8} + \dfrac{3t - 1}{14}$

14. A cistern takes 2 minutes to fill up quarter of a water tank and one fifth of another water tank. Calculate total time to be taken by that cistern to fill up both the water tanks completely.

5. Evaluation III

I: Estimate the following.

1.	36,587 87,943 + 13,156	**2.**	28,764 64,537 + 35,936	**3.**	65,446 1,915 + 47,291	**4.**	49,765 18,976 + 7,359
5.	26,542 − 17,986	**6.**	34,896 − 15,984	**7.**	41,132 − 17,545	**8.**	62,764 − 58,685
9.	115,609 205,399 + 411,111	**10.**	356,789 141,217 + 222,888	**11.**	471,009 180,007 + 277,777	**12.**	365,786 274,982 + 186,214
13.	672,244 − 456,688	**14.**	681,337 − 278,456	**15.**	524,700 − 316,672	**16.**	938,400 − 619,711

II. Observe the following

<u>Arena</u>	<u>Seating Capacity</u>
Yankee Stadium, NY	57,545
Cleveland Browns Stadium, OH	73,200
Wrigley Field, IL	36,765
Angel Stadium, CA	45,050

A: Which arena could be preferred for accommodating near about seventy thousand viewers?

B: Arrange the given places as per their increasing seating capacity.

C: Which stadium holds minimum seating capacity?

D. Which stadium could be preferred for a mass of 35,000?

E. Average seating capacity of all the four stadium is equal to ……….

III. Earth's total surface area is about 199,560,000 square miles. Approximately 139,692,000 square miles are covered with water. About how much of Earth's surface is covered by land?

IV. Write the following in standard form.

1. CCLXIII = 100 + __ + 50 + __ + __ + __ + __ = __

2. CMXCIV = (1000 − __) + (__ − 10) + (__ − __) = __

3. XXXIV	**4.** MVII	**5.** LV	**6.** DXXI
7. CCLXX	**8.** DCCXC	**9.** XCIX	**10.** MDIII
11. XLVII	**12.** MCCLVI	**13.** CXLV	**14.** MDCCXCI
15. MMCLI	**16.** MMDCCCIII	**17.** MDCCLXXXV	**18.** MDCCCXLV

V. In the number 308,610,547,823, write the digit in the ten billions place, millions place and ten thousands place.

VI. While writing the following expanded form in standard numeration Nikhil placed digit 7 at ten thousands place. Find out difference of the actual result and result obtained by Nikhil.

1,000,000,000 + 13,000 + 1,300 + 32,098 + 28,202 + 40,000 + 80 + 3

VII. Car A travels 30 m in 4 seconds, Car B covers 76 km in 1 hour, Car C covers 600 m in a minute and Car D covers 39 m in 5 seconds. Which car is moving with fastest speed?

VIII. Arrange following numbers from least to greatest:

6,135,936;   6,315,396;   6,531,639;   6,153,693

IX. Write the following expression in standard form:

Three billion three million three thousand more than three billion two million forty-five thousand and eighty-three.

X. In May, 23,637 people attended the circus, which was 18,478 people less than the attendance in June. In July, the attendance was 5,342 more than June's. How many people attended the circus in July?

6. Model Questions

I: Rounding

Round the following to nearest hundred.

13. 158	14. 426	15. 375	16. 896
17. 719	18. 950	19. 1047	20. 3888
21. 5942	22. 6891	23. 3098	24. 8762
25. 37,405	26. 62,345	27. 88,088	28. 65,097
29. 58,706	30. 66,636		

Round the following to nearest thousand

31. 9155	32. 7983	33. 4550	34. 6237
35. 8396	36. 33,888	37. 15,942	38. 93,192
39. 87,983	40. 46,237	41. 326,150	42. 145,706
43. 357,029	44. 563,498	45. 807,476	46. 821,593
47. 450,513	48. 435,127	49. 205,120	50. 761,604

Estimate by rounding then add or subtract.

51. 215 + 687	52. 4306 − 3849	53. 6287 − 318
54. 659 − 286	55. 7583 + 2948	56. 3717 − 839

57. Three hundred seventeen less than thirteen hundred seventy nine.

58. 14th multiple of 1,002 more than 15th multiple of 5,009

59. 11th multiple of 1,002 + 12th multiple of 12,012 + 32,043

60. 309 m long track is attached to 30,0129 m long track. Total length (estimated up to) of the track will be ....

CONTENTS

II. Fraction and decimal.

Figure	Fraction	Decimal
	$\dfrac{67}{100}$	0.67
1/5th of 405 + 1/6th of 618 + 1/7th of 735		
Quarter of 636 + 1/8th of 16,424		
1.1 X 1.01 X 0.001 X 0.01 X 125 X 8		
125 X 40 X 8 X 16 X 0.004 X 0.008		
1/7th of 4,949 + 1/9th 8,181 + 1/11th of 121		
Three thousandths + 103 hundredths + 2.009		

III. Write best units of measurements which can be used for the following.

1. length of an eraser   2. width of a board

3. distance between 2 cities   4. height of a desk

5. length of a soccer field   6. width of a quarter

7. length of a pencil   a. 4 yd b. 4 in. c. 4 ft

8. height of a basketball player   9. Distance of a planet

10. distance of a star from the earth   (a. mile   b. light year)

11. Distance of the Sun from the Earth

(a. mile   b. light minute   c. light year)

12. juice in a pitcher   13. ice cream in a carton

14. paint in a can   15. water in a swimming pool

16. milk in a recipe   17. water in a bucket

18. length of a car   19. depth of the ocean

20. height of a person   21. width of a tape

22. thickness of a sandwich   24. Half of the capacity of water tank.

Answer the following.

25. A goods train spends 45 seconds to cross a light post. Speed of that train is 36 km/h. calculate length of that train.

26. Somnath jogs 1.2 m in a second while Nikita jogs at an average speed of 3.6 km/h. Who is jogging faster?

27. Namrata observed that her school bus reaches school in 38 minutes. It has five stoppages of duration 3 minutes each. Average speed of the bus is 36 km/h. What is the distance of her school ?

28. 1.9 km + 2 km 89 m + 21 km 121 m = ...

CONTENTS

Whole Number	Tenth		Hundredth
36.375	36.375	Do not write zeros to the right.	36.375
36	36.4		36.38

Ten Cents	Dollar	Ten Dollars	Hundred Dollars
$ 473.28	$473.28	$473.28	$473.28
$ 473.30	$473	$470	$500

IV. Round each to the nearest whole number, tenth, and hundredth.

1. 1.001 X 0.11 X 0.001 X 125 X 8 X 0.0001

2. $(1 + 2 + 3 + \ldots\ldots 1{,}000) \times 1001 \times \left(\left(\dfrac{125 \, X \, 8}{1001 \, X \, 1001}\right) X \, 10232\right)$

3. 1/4th of 16,0128 + 1/5th to 55,0525 + 1/6th of 1,21,212

4. Seventh multiple of 17,019 X 0.001 X 0.01

5. Half of a quarter of 2,009 + half of one fifth of 1,008

6. 11 tenths + 11 hundredths + 11 thousandths

7. 101 tenths + 1001 hundredths + 11.011 + 101.101

8. 12.012   9. 121,032   10. 324.980   11. 205.509

12. 21.12   13. 21 X 0.901   14. 134.980   15. 43.980

16. 2.1 X 2.001   17. (2.01 X 0.002 X 0.04)   18. 43 X 4.04

19. (Quarter of 104 + One seventh of 4,949 + 1.001) X 0.3

20. $\left(\dfrac{11}{19} + \dfrac{33}{38} + \dfrac{109}{190}\right) X \, 0.003 \, X \, 0.09$

21. 6.148   22. 1.792   23. 3.732   24. 24.873

25. 39.925   26. 73.159   27. 29.866   28. 548.501

29. 112.549   30. 332.532   33. 121.098   34. 32.098

Round each to the nearest dollar, ten dollars, and hundred dollars.

35. $427.89   36. $642.87   37. $792.46   38. $225.98

39. $146.72   40. $119.28   41. $542.76   42. $125.58

39. $918.92   40. $699.45   41. $15042.706

V. Solve the following:

1. There are 106 books on a shelf A, 121 books on shelf B, 98 books on shelf C and 721 books on shelf D. Nikita takes 17 books from each of the shelves. How many books are left on the shelves in all?

2. There are 11 more girls in class III and 9 more girls in class IV than the number of girls in class II, which is 17 less than the number of girls in class I, which is again 19 less than the number of girls in class V. Number of girls in class II is equal to second multiple of 11. Strength of the school is 250. How many boys are there in the school?

3. Record of rainfall of a state is displayed in the following chart. Each unit of icon is equal to 10 mm.

April	∇∇
May	∇
June	∇∇∇
July	∇∇∇∇∇∇∇∇
August	∇∇∇∇∇∇∇∇∇∇∇∇∇∇
September	∇∇∇∇∇∇∇∇
October	∇∇∇∇∇∇∇
November	∇∇

Calculate average rainfall of the state.

Which pair of months receives maximum rainfall?

4. The day Sonali left home for an outing was Saturday. She came back home after 103 days and resumed her service after 3 days. What was the day when she resumed her service?

5. In a 7-day period, Tina spends 4 h, 3.4 h, 5.02 h, 3 h 12 minutes, and 5 h 32 minutes pruning trees. Her sum exceeded 35 h mark. Duration of remaining two days estimated as a variable H. She then adds to find the total number of hours. What was the value of H? Does the order in which she adds the numbers affect the sum?

6. What least number should be subtracted from six digit greatest number to obtain a common multiple of 4 and 8?

7. Five rivers form a river system and have lengths of 513.11 miles, 247.08 miles, 211 miles, 192.09 miles and 397.03 miles. Altogether, how long are these rivers?

8. Pallavi, Richimon, Nikhil and Snehal planned to use 213, 432, 355 and 431 saplings respectively to cover one side of the roads leading to their crop fields. They kept a uniform gap of 11.5 m in between two saplings. Calculate total length of the roads used by them for the plantation works.

VI. Estimate the following.

1.	2.	3.	4.	5.
4987	6325	232	$115.27	$947.60
2526	3691	7625	372.62	25.89
+ 2844	+ 2236	+ 3475	+236.91	+ 550.09

6.	7.	8.	9.	10.
6626	7242	8934	$887.56	$932.55
− 4813	− 5759	− 812	− 259.60	− 47.28

11. 6325 + 3632 + 8422 + 1362   12. 7459 + 1359 + 813 + 5231

13.	14.	15.	16.	17.
2732	3257	4239	$ 4.67	$41.07
6146	612	624	15.08	92.53
+ 7378	+5701	+ 38	+ 41.13	+ 3.12

18.	19.	20.	21.	22.
7893	8934	9434	$83.72	$932.55
− 5421	− 819	−9251	− 8.44	− 47.48

23. 2357 + 4612 + 5318 + 675   24. 6531 + 7735 + 943 + 39

7. Book 3 : Use of Numbers

We use mathematical operations in our daily life to handle different types of calculations needed to tender business. We also use numerations to let computers work. All types of numbers we use in our daily life are decimal numbers, as ten (decim)) digits are used to represent them. We also represent numerations to count time, mass, length, area, volume and distance. Smallest unit of length in International System, for an example , is centimetre and greatest unit that we use to specify distance of celestial bodies is light year; the distance travelled by light in one year.

Triangular Numbers and Square Numbers:

Numbers which can be arranged in triangle are called triangular numbers, and numbers which can be arranged in square pattern are square numbers.

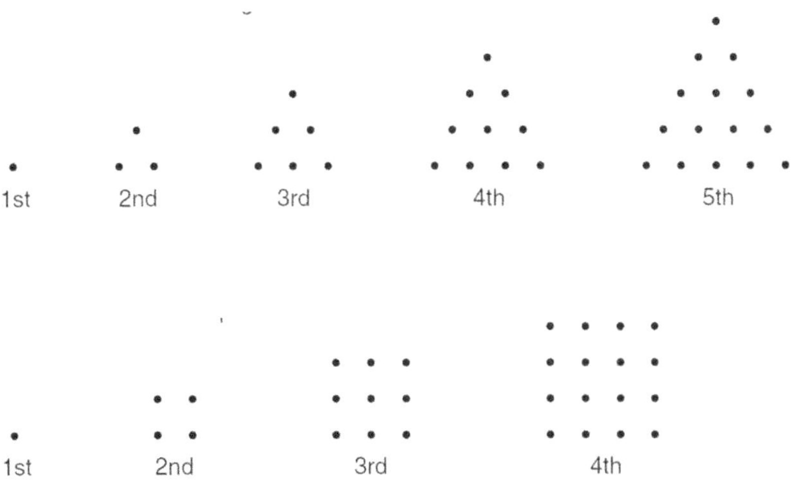

Numbers repeat its pattern in some definite fashion, that is why we have ever increasing countable numbers duly represented in numeration charts by using only ten digits. Ordinal numbers have similar pattern of representation. Numbers having only two factors are considered as prime numbers; and those having more than two factors are composite numbers. In this way 2, 3, 5, 7, 11, 13 … etc. are prime numbers as all such numbers have only two factors: 1 and the number itself. We also represent odd numbers in a series to work out square numbers. There are several other patterns of numeration which appears in our daily life.

One such example is given as follows; you can complete the same

$(1 + 3 + 5 + 7)$	$= 4 \times 4$	$= 16$
$(1 + 3 + 5 + 7 + 9)$	$= 5 \times 5$	$= …………$
$(1 + 3 + 20$ consecutive odds$)$	$= … \times …$	$= …………$

Another popular pattern we have in our daily life is product on numbers formed by using digit 1. We can work out product of any such number by following the given pattern.

11×11	$=$	$121;$
111×111	$=$	$12321;$
1111×1111	$=$	$1234321;$

Largest number of five digits without repeating any digits is 98,765. Smallest number of six digits without repeating any digit is 102,345. We use another dedicated section to explain rules related to decimals, fractions and large numbers (to be represented by using scientific notations).

Percentage is a special type of fraction having denominator 100. Decimal is a type of fraction having denominators in the form of multiples of 10.

For example: 20% of 200 = (20 X 200)/ 100 = 40;

$1/10 = 0.1;$ $1/100 = 0.01;$ $3/1000 = 0.003;$

We come across several other rules while passing through test papers and Question Banks.

***

8. Measurements

Measurement of temperature will be discussed in this section to provide better understanding of the same.

Temperature indicates state of hotness or coldness of a material medium; as we compare the same by touching the object; as we say hotness or coldness on the basis of the hotness of our body. Heat is the energy which ensures hotness or coldness of an object.

Water freezes at 0^0 C or 32^0 F; it boils at 100^0 C or 212^0 F. For that reason Freezing point of water is considered as lower fixed point and boiling point of water is considered as upper fixed point to prepare a thermometer. The length in between both the fixed points are graduated by dividing them in equal sections. Such Fundamental Intervals are 100 in Celsius scale and 180 in ^{0} F scale.

In this way 1^0 C change in temperature is equivalent to 1.8^0 F .

Therefore, 5^0 C = (5 X 1.8 + 32) ^{0} F or 41 ^{0} F

On the other hand 41 ^{0} F = [(41 – 32) ÷ 1.8] ^{0} F = 5^0 C;

Evaluation

1: The morning temperatures during the school week were 37°F, 45°F, 41°F, 21°F, and 26°F. What was the average daily morning temperature?

2. During the week the temperature each day at noon was 25°C, 23°C, 20°C, 22°C, 22°C, 18°C, and 17°C. What was the average daily noon temperature?

3. Difference of minimum and maximum temperature of a city is recorded as 10^0 C. Find the corresponding change of temperature in the ^{0}F scale of temperature.

4. While measuring temperature by using a new scale of thermometer Neha observed that it reflects 80^0 C as 64^0. Lower fixed points in both the scale are 0^0. Is it possible to work out upper fixed points of the newly developed scale?

5. We use a definite scale to measure body temperature of human beings. Such thermometer can record temperature in between 90^0F to 110^0 F. Find out the equivalent interval of temperature in Celsius scale.

6. Heat transfer during melting of ice is 80 calorie per gram. 1 g water gains a temperature of 1^0 C by consuming 1 calorie heat. 80 g ice block is placed in 100 g water having a temperature of 10^0 C. Find part of ice which will turn into water. Final temperature of the material medium will be ....

7. 20% of heating energy is used to increase temperature of the oven. If the oven throws 1000 calorie and material of oven gains 1^0 C after consuming 5 calorie heat then find out final temperature of the oven if room temperature duly recorded in 35^0 C.

8. Ice melts at 0^0 C. After mixing salt to water freezing point drops down by 3^0 C. Convert newly recorded freezing point of the given sample of salt water into ^{0}F.

***

9. Common Shapes

Shapes bounded by line segments will be considered as basic shapes; such shapes bounded by straight lines will be considered as polygons. Smallest polygon in terms of number of sides are triangles. A triangle can have three sides, three angles, three vertices and no-diagonals. Sum of all the interior angles of a triangle is equal to a straight angle.

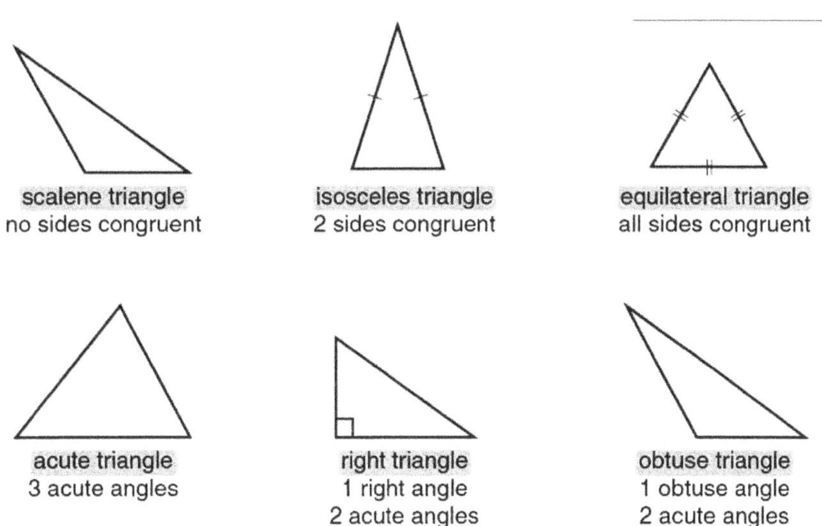

A diagonal of a polygon is a line segment that joins two vertices of the polygon but is not a side of the polygon. A quadrilateral can have two diagonals; a pentagon can have five.

We can have different types of quadrilaterals on the basis of sides and angles. A quadrilateral having all the interior angles as right angles and opposite sides parallel to each other is called rectangle. Square is a special type of rectangle having all sides equal to each other. We have regular polygons having all sides equal to each other and all angles equal to each other. To find perimeter of a polygon we work out sum of all the sides of the polygon.

Example 1: A roll of weather stripping is 24 m long and 0.9 m wide. How many rolls are needed to go around 12 square windows that are 0.9 m on each side?

Hints: $(12 \times 0.9 \times 0.9) \div (24 \times 0.9) = \ldots\ldots\ldots\ldots$ (no. of rolls)

Example 2: A field in the shape of a rectangle is 550 yd wide and 880 yd long. If Karen jogs around the field thrice, how many yards does she jog?

Hints: Total distance = $2 \times (550 + 880) \times 3$ yd.

Working out area and circumference of a circle. If radius is r then circumference will be $2\pi r$ and area will be πr^2.

Similarly you can work out circumference and area of the following.

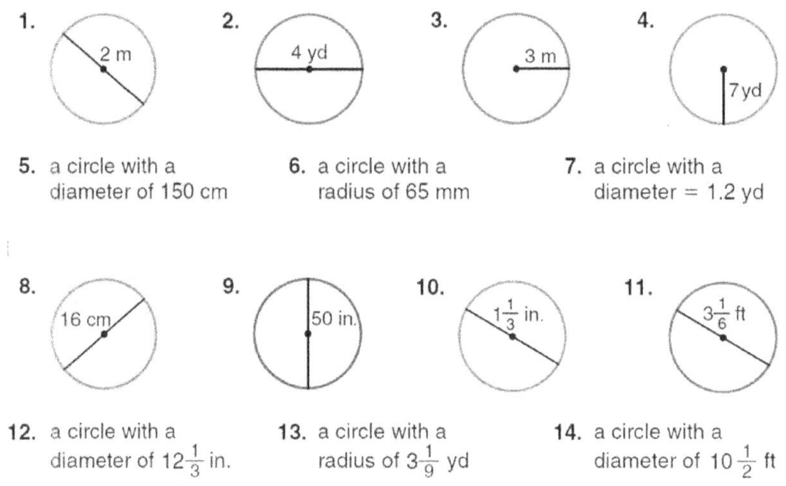

5. a circle with a diameter of 150 cm

6. a circle with a radius of 65 mm

7. a circle with a diameter = 1.2 yd

12. a circle with a diameter of $12\frac{1}{3}$ in.

13. a circle with a radius of $3\frac{1}{9}$ yd

14. a circle with a diameter of $10\frac{1}{2}$ ft

15. Wheel of a cart having diameter 1 m spins 2009 times to cover distance of village from market. Calculate distance of the market from village.

16. A 144 cm wire is used to prepare a circular ring. Find out diameter of that ring.

***.

10. Representing a Number

There are some specific rules to represent numbers (system of numeration). We can represent large numbers by using Indian System, International System of Scientific notations. Scientific notation is new to us at this level of study.

We write 100 as 10^2 ; 1000 = 10^3; 10000 = 10^4 ; and so on.

In this way speed of light can be specified as 3 X 10^8 m/s.

Similarly you can write all the following numbers by using scientific notation.

1. 400,000   2. 7,000,000   3. 50,000   4. 900,000,000

5. 9600   6. 57,000   7. 420,000,000 8. 78,000,000

9. 6760   10. 91,700   11. 48,900,000 12. 375,000,000

13. 57,510   14. 161,200,000 15. 723,400   16. 84,570,000,000

17. 121,021 X 125 X 25 X 8 X 40   18 200 times 303 million

For representing decimal values we use different types of grid. Even we can represent multiplication of two decimals by using such grids.

We can represent product of two decimal numbers as follows.

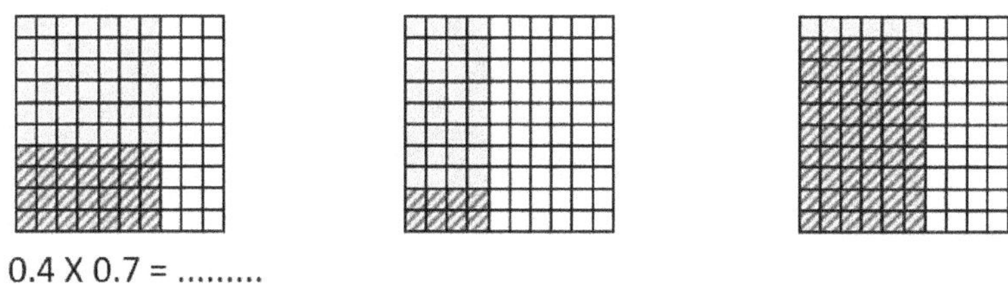

0.4 X 0.7 = ...

Similarly we can represent product of three or more decimas by using a rule of providing total decimal places to the product of numbers.

Example: 0.3 X 0.3 X 0.3 X .3 = 0.0081;

While dividing a decimal number by a whole number we apply a specific pattern to divide the number.

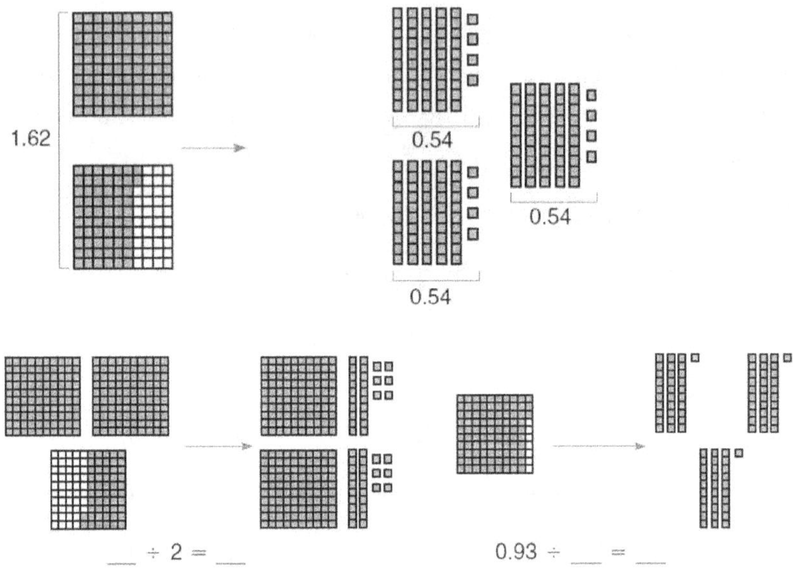

While dividing a decimal value by another decimal value we convert them in the form of representation without using decimal values.

Example : 1.25 ÷ 0.005 is equivalent to 1250 ÷ 5;

***.

11. Test Paper I

Find out surface area and volume of the following.

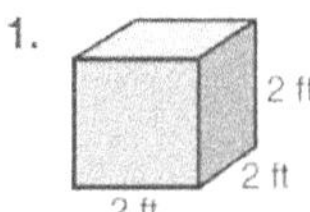
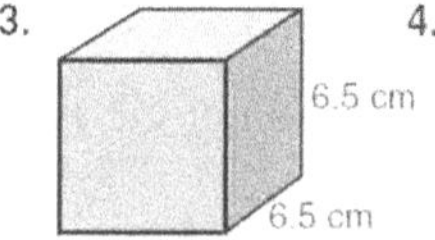

5. $s = 1.2$ dm   6. $s = 15$ in.   7. $s = 8$ m   8. $s = 1\frac{1}{2}$ yd

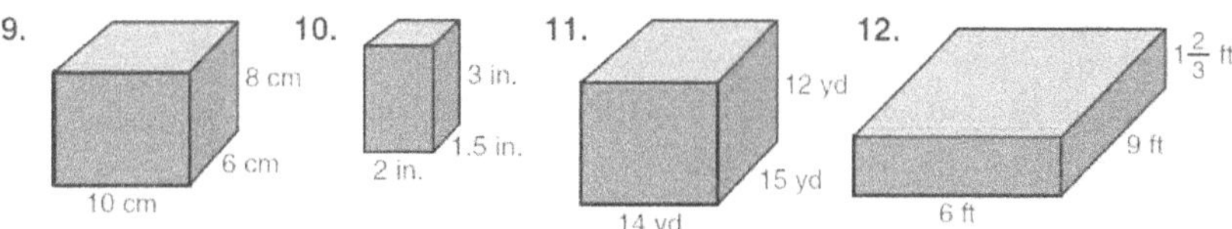

13: l = 12 cm, b = 8 cm, h = 6 cm   14: a cube of edge 12 cm

15: l = 20 cm; b = 18 cm; h = 10 cm;   16: a cube of edge 12.5 cm;

Identify missing interior angles in the following.

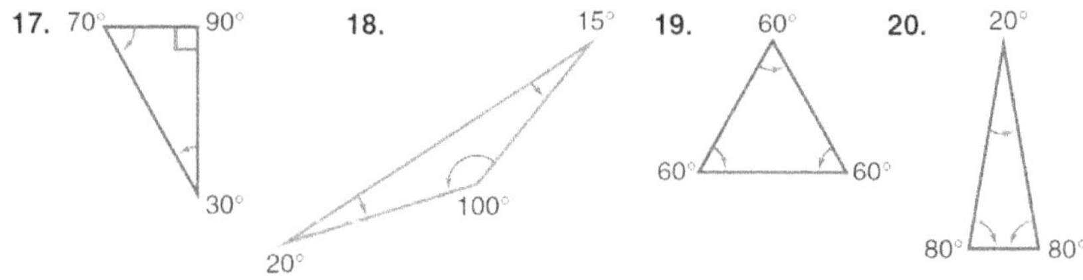

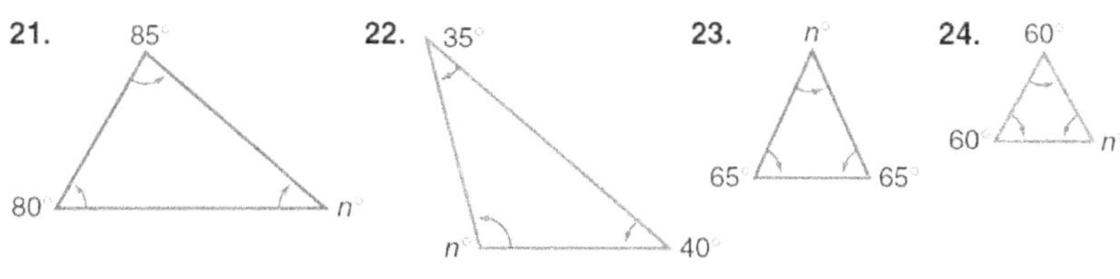

25: Three angles of a triangle are in the ratio of 2: 4: 7. Find out the angles.

26. Half of an angle is equal to quarter of its supplementary angle. Find out the angle.

27. Quarter of angle A, 3/5th of angle B and 6/19th of angle C jointly form a straight angle. Find out the angles.

28. Complementary of an angle is 39^0 32'. Find out the angle.

29. Angle A and B of a triangle jointly forms a right angle. Find out the third angle.

30. What fraction of all the natural numbers from 1 to 600 are common multiples of 30, 15 and 60?

31: What is the surface area of a utility cabinet that is 60 cm long, 46 cm wide, and 32 cm high?

32. Half of a cubical water tank of edge 1.5 m is filled with water. calculate total volume of water present in the tank. A cistern throws 200 cm^3 water in a second. Calculate total time to be taken by that cistern to fill up remaining parts of the tank.

33. What is the difference between the surface area of a cube that is 30 cm on an edge and a rectangular prism that is 40 cm long, 20 cm wide, and 10 cm high?

34. Quarter of a water tank is filled up by a cistern in 20 minutes. One fifth of another water tank is filled up by that cistern in 15 minutes. Calculate total time to be taken by that cistern to fill up both the water tanks completely.

35. Sonali and Monali jointly works to finish an assignment in 12 days. Monali alone can finish it in 18 days. Sonali alone can finish it in …. days.

***.

12. Test Paper II

All numbers are decimal numbers as we use ten digits to form all such numbers. .

Calculate volume of the following in unit cube.

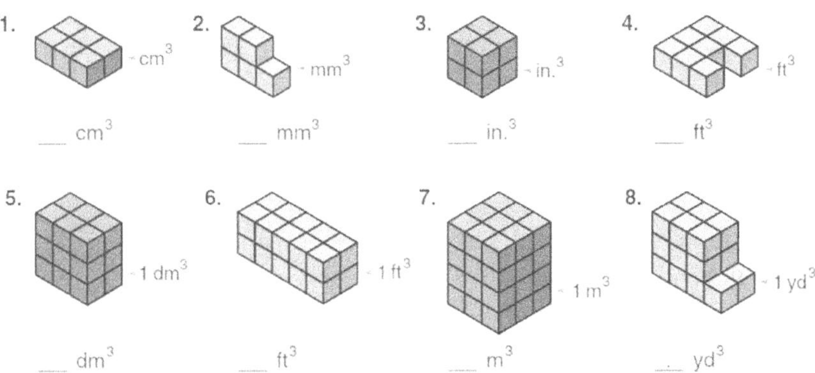

9: How many square centimeters of cardboard were used to make a cubical carton that is 3.5 cm on each edge?

10. 20% of tank A, 30% of tank B and 50% of tank C are equal to each other in terms of volume. Total capacity of all the three tanks is 4,000 m^3. Find out individual volume of the tanks.

11. Volume of a cubical tank is 1331 m^2. Find out edge of this water tank. Also find out area of the bottom.

Work out best estimation

12. crayon box	a. 500 m^3	b. 500 dm^3	c. 500 cm^3
13. tissue box	a. 90 $in.^3$	b. 90 ft^3	c. 90 yd^3
14. CD	a. 140 mm^3	b. 140 cm^3	c. 140 m^3

15. Tina made a design by pasting an isosceles right triangle in the center of a square of side 10 cm. If the length of each perpendicular side of the triangle is 5.2 cm, what is the area of the square that is still visible?

16. A special pop-up birthday card has a mass of 12.5 g. The card store sells these cards in a pack that weighs about 2.5 kg. About how many pop-up cards are in each pack?

17. A birdfeeder is 36 cm by 30 cm by 12 cm. A sack of birdseed has a volume of 14 dm3. Is this enough birdseed to fill the feeder? If there exists any difference then calculate such difference.

18. Nikita took a test paper having 45 questions. She had 21 answers correct. What is the ratio of the number of correct answers to the number of incorrect answers?

19. What percent of greatest five digit number is equal to 1250?

20. A natural number is equal to 1002 greater than third multiple of the greatest three digit number?

21. Is it possible to shade a 10 X 10 grid so that it is 15% blue, 75% red, and 20% green?

22. After selling 11 cards a shopkeeper gained an amount equal to selling price of one card. Find out total gain percentage of the shopkeeper.

23. Half of A, quarter of B, one sixth of C are equal to each other. Find out simplest value of the following:

$$\left(\frac{1}{A} + \frac{1}{B} + \frac{1}{C}\right) X \ (2A + 3B + 4C)$$

24. What least number should be subtracted from four digit greatest number and five digit smallest number to find out a common dividend which can be divided by 2, 3, 4 and 11 leaving remainder 1 in each case?

13. Test Paper III

Solve the following.

1. $n + 39 = 14$

2. $y + 327 = 522$

3. $c + 14.81 = 14.81$

4. $616 = m + 125$

5. $327 + x = 794$

6. $f + 1.018 = 3.19$

7. $n - 25 = 72$

8. $y - 319 = 105$

9. $c - 20.5 = 20.5$

10. $219 = m - 516$

11. $3.79 = x - 9.59$

12. $f - 4.08 = 19.005$

13. $x - 225 = 723$

14. $x + 749 = 4605$

15. $x - 47.9 = 1.34$

16. $58.7 = x - 9.03$

17. $8.34 = x + 0.53$

18. $4.8 + x = 6.001$

19. A number y added to 7 is equal to 12.

20. A number w decreased by 12 is equal to 22.

21. A natural number and one fifth of its reciprocal add up to 8.025. Find out value of following expression while considering the natural number as x.

$$(3 x^3 + 4x + 5 \sqrt[3]{x}) (x - 1)^2 (x + 1)^2 + (4x^2 + 4x + 1)$$

22. Three seventh of a natural number exceeds third multiple of seven digit number by 3,003. Find out the number.

23. Work out the numerical value of a in the following to make the following equations true.

A. $\frac{3}{4} + \left(\frac{1}{2} + \frac{3}{5}\right) = \left(\frac{3}{4} + \frac{1}{2}\right) + a$
B. $\frac{5}{9} + \left(a + \frac{2}{3}\right) = \left(\frac{5}{9} + \frac{1}{6}\right) + \frac{2}{3}$

C. $\frac{1}{4} \times \left(a + \frac{1}{5}\right) = \left(\frac{1}{4} \times \frac{1}{3}\right) + \left(\frac{1}{4} \times \frac{1}{5}\right)$

24. $(A + B) = 109$; $(B + C) = 207$; $(C + D) = 309$; $(D + A) = 403$; Find out simplest value of $(A + B + C + D)$.

25. 25% of a natural number exceeds 11,001 by 3001. Find out the number.

26. What fraction of 125,125,125 is equal to 125?

27. A passenger train takes 2 minutes and 45 seconds to cross a tunnel of length 1 km 300 m. Average speed of that train is 72 km/h. Find length of that train.

28. Represent the following by using percentage.

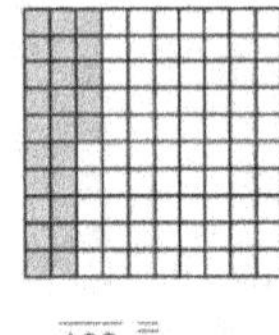 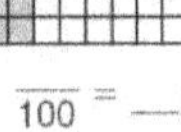 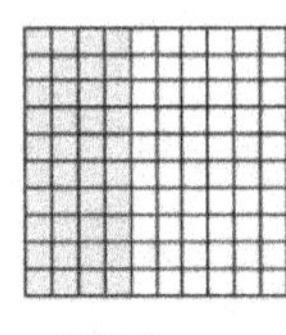  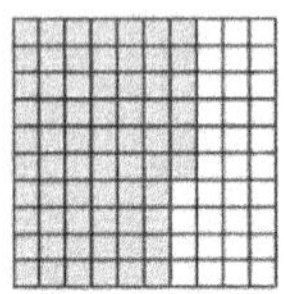

$$\frac{\quad}{100} = \underline{\quad} \qquad \frac{\quad}{100} = \underline{\quad} \qquad \frac{\quad}{100} = \underline{\quad}$$

29. Solve the following.

(i) $2 + y = 7$ (ii) $2a - 3 = 5$

(iii) $10 - q = 6$ (iv) $2t - 5 = 3$

(v) $14 = 27 - x$ (vi) $5(x+4) = 35$

(vii) $-3x = 15$ (viii) $5x - 3 = 3x - 5$

(ix) $3y + 4 = 5y - 4$ (x) $3(x - 3) = 5(2x + 1)$

30. What percentage of 125,125 is equal to 1001?

31. Is there any pair of number having LCM 2003 and HCF 198?

32. How many four digit numbers are there in all?

33. Sum of length and breadth of a rectangle is equal 25 cm. Area of that rectangle is equal to 154 sq. cm. Find out length and breadth of that rectangle.

34. Sum of an angle and one fifth of its complementary angle is equal to 54^0. Find out supplementary of that angle.

35. How many seven digit numbers are there in all?

36. What least number should be subtracted from product of greatest and smallest number of five digits to obtain a dividend which can be divided individually by 4, 6, 12 and 18 leaving remainder 3 in each case?

14. Test Paper IV

1: Following data chart shows population of birds in a city zoo.

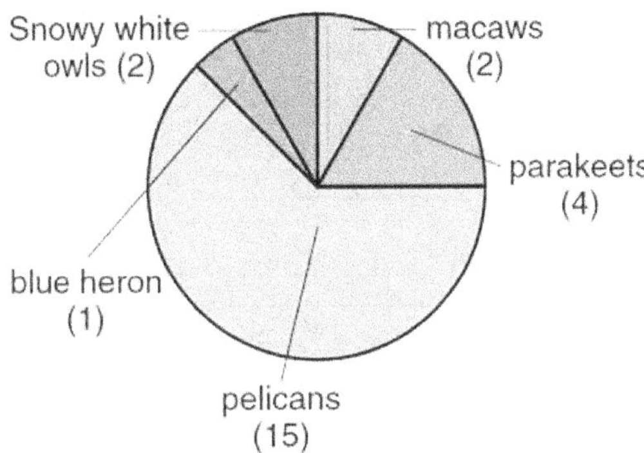

Q a. Population of which bird is recorded maximum?

Q b. What fraction of the population is occupied by macraw and parakeets?

Q c. Population of which bird is recorded minimum and by what fraction?

Q what fraction of birds in the zoo are blue herons?

2: Snehal and Rita works together to finish a work in 12 days, Rita and Anita can finish it in 14 days; Anita and Snehal can finish the same in 13 days. All the three fellow friends started working together to finish the same work together in …….. days.

3. If $\dfrac{11A}{13} = \dfrac{12B}{17} = \dfrac{13C}{19}$; $then$ $\dfrac{(A+B)(B+C)(C+A)}{3ABC} = \cdots ….$

4. What fraction of sum of one ninth of four digit greatest number and half of smallest five digit number is equal to 179?

5. What fraction of all the natural numbers starting from 1 to 5000 are common multiples of 5 and 25?

6. Is there any pair of natural number having LCM 1009 and HCF 169?

7. $(0.0121 \times 0.002 \times 0.05 \times 0.02) \times 10^5 = \ldots\ldots\ldots\ldots$

8. What digit should be there at tenths place if we multiply 1.25, 0.4, 2,5 and 0.08?

Write each of the following decimals.

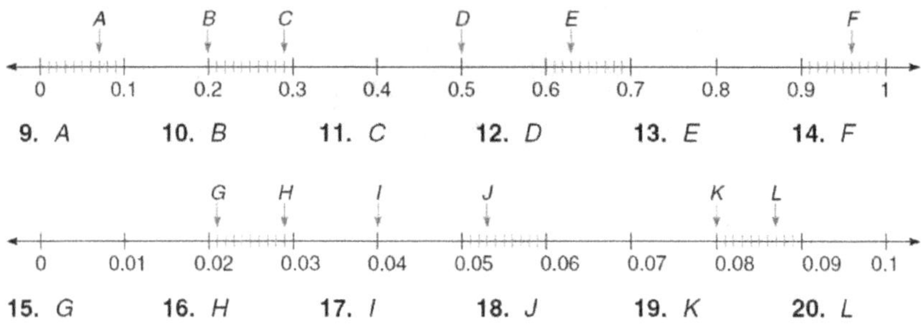

9. *A*   **10.** *B*   **11.** *C*   **12.** *D*   **13.** *E*   **14.** *F*

15. *G*   **16.** *H*   **17.** *I*   **18.** *J*   **19.** *K*   **20.** *L*

21. Sum of a natural and its reciprocal is equal to 4.25. Find out the sixth multiple of that number.

22. Three interior angles of a triangle are in the ratio of 3: 5: 8. Find out magnitude of the greatest angle of that triangle.

23. Volume of a cubical block is equal to 1331 sq. cm. Six such blocks are arranged side by side to form a cuboid. Find out length of that cuboid.

24. Elaine rode her bike 4.93 mi on Thursday, 3.45 mi on Friday, 5.38 mi on Saturday, and 6.35 mi on Sunday. About how many miles did she ride her bike in these three days?

25. What least number should be subtracted from seven digit greatest number to obtain a common multiple of 4, 8, 12 and 16?

26. $0.583 + 2.745$ .... $0.1 + 0.02 + 3.003$

27. $0.001 + 1.001 + 11.011 + 101.101 - 121 = \ldots\ldots\ldots\ldots\ldots$

***.

15. Fractions and Decimals

Exercise 1

Estimate the following.

1. $9\frac{1}{3} + 2\frac{3}{8}$ 2. $8\frac{2}{3} + 3\frac{3}{4}$ 3. $14\frac{1}{3} + 12\frac{1}{2}$ 4. $16\frac{2}{7} + 13\frac{5}{9}$

5. $11\frac{3}{5} + 4\frac{7}{8}$ 6. $16\frac{1}{4} + 4\frac{3}{8}$ 7. $19\frac{2}{9} + 15\frac{3}{4}$ 8. $15\frac{1}{8} + 14\frac{8}{9}$

9. $7\frac{1}{5} + 3\frac{4}{9} + 5\frac{1}{3}$ 10. $4\frac{2}{11} + 7\frac{1}{8} + 9\frac{3}{10}$ 11. $8\frac{3}{5} + 9\frac{4}{7} + 3\frac{5}{6}$

12. $8\frac{7}{12} - 4\frac{3}{4}$ 13. $10\frac{1}{5} - 2\frac{3}{10}$ 14. $18\frac{2}{9} - 4\frac{1}{2}$ 15. $15\frac{2}{3} - 4\frac{7}{8}$

16. $6\frac{4}{7} - 2\frac{1}{3}$ 17. $5\frac{7}{10} - 2\frac{3}{5}$ 18. $9\frac{2}{3} - 2\frac{5}{6}$ 19. $8\frac{3}{4} - 3\frac{2}{7}$

20. $12\frac{1}{8} + 3\frac{2}{3}$ 21. $9\frac{8}{11} + 7\frac{2}{9} + 6\frac{1}{10}$ 22. $9\frac{4}{5} + 8\frac{3}{4} + 4\frac{1}{3}$

23. $9\frac{5}{16} - 6\frac{1}{5}$ 24. $10\frac{3}{5} - 4\frac{2}{3}$ 25. $18\frac{7}{12} - 5\frac{2}{7}$ 26. $25\frac{1}{8} - 13\frac{11}{15}$

27. Loxy and Foxy are domesticated cats. Jointly they weigh 16 lb. Loxy weighs half lb more than Foxy, and each cat weighs more than 7 pounds. How much could each cat weigh?

28. Quarter of A, 5/9th of B, 6/11th of C, 11/13th of D are equal to each other. Find out simplest value of the following:

$$\left[\frac{(A+B)(B+C)(C+D)(D+A)}{64\,ABCD}\right] \times \left(\frac{1}{A} + \frac{1}{B} + \frac{1}{C} + \frac{1}{D}\right)$$

29. 1/13th of a number exceeds smallest number of five digits by 1001. Find out the number. Also find out seventh multiple of that number.

30. What fraction of all the natural numbers starting from 1 to 3,000 are multiples of 30?

Exercise 2

Subtract the following.

1. $\dfrac{9}{8} + \dfrac{1}{8}$ 2. $\dfrac{5}{6} + \dfrac{1}{6}$ 3. $\dfrac{7}{17} + \dfrac{15}{17}$ 4. $\dfrac{2}{5} + \dfrac{1}{10}$ 5. $\dfrac{1}{4} + \dfrac{1}{12}$ 6. $\dfrac{7}{10} + \dfrac{1}{2}$

7. $6\dfrac{7}{9} + 1\dfrac{4}{9}$ 8. $9\dfrac{7}{16} + 2\dfrac{5}{16}$ 9. $7\dfrac{1}{2} + 1\dfrac{1}{4}$ 10. $6\dfrac{1}{5} + 4\dfrac{3}{10}$ 11. $8\dfrac{5}{12} + 2\dfrac{1}{2}$ 12. $5\dfrac{3}{5} + 2\dfrac{2}{3}$

13. $\dfrac{15}{11} - \dfrac{1}{11}$ 14. $\dfrac{13}{7} - \dfrac{6}{7}$ 15. $\dfrac{7}{12} - \dfrac{1}{3}$ 16. $\dfrac{1}{2} - \dfrac{3}{8}$ 17. $\dfrac{2}{3} - \dfrac{1}{9}$ 18. $\dfrac{5}{6} - \dfrac{1}{2}$

19. $9\dfrac{3}{5} - 3\dfrac{1}{4}$ 20. $4\dfrac{2}{3} - 2\dfrac{1}{2}$ 21. $6\dfrac{1}{8} - 3\dfrac{1}{2}$ 22. $4\dfrac{1}{4} - 3\dfrac{3}{8}$ 23. $2\dfrac{7}{16} - 1\dfrac{3}{4}$ 24. $14\dfrac{1}{3} - 9\dfrac{3}{5}$

25. Rijuana came home from market at 5:45 P.M. She sent 2 and half hour in market, quarter of one hour in park and three fourth of one hour with friends. By what time did she leave home for market?

26. What fraction of all the natural numbers from 1 to 500 are common multiples of 5 and 25?

27. Which smallest number of six digits is divisible exactly by 3 and 9 leaving remainder 2 in each case. Calculate simplest value of 3/4th of that number.

28. Instead of subtracting 123.125 from a number Snehal added 125.123 to it. Find out total difference of her result and the actual result.

29. $\left[\left(1 + \dfrac{1}{2}\right)\left(1 + \dfrac{1}{3}\right)\ldots\ldots\left(1 + \dfrac{1}{10{,}000}\right) \times \left(5 - \dfrac{5}{10001}\right)\right] \times 25 \times 8 \ = \ldots$

30. What smallest number should be subtracted from smallest eight digit numbers to obtain one third of greatest seven digit number?

31. 3/7th of 7/19th of a natural number exceeds third multiple of 10,001. Find out the number.

Exercise 3

1: What fraction of all the natural numbers from 1 to 600 are common multiples of 15 and 30?

2. $\left(\frac{1}{2} X \frac{2}{3} X \frac{3}{4} X \dots \frac{9,999}{10,000}\right) X \frac{1}{10,000} X 10^p = 1$; here p = …….

3. Fractions having numerator 1 are called ………. fractions.

4. Three fourth of four eleventh of a number is equal to 30,30,303. Find out the natural number.

Write suitable number sentence for the following.

5. 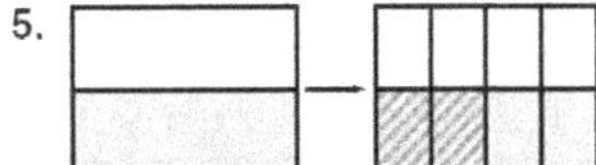   6. 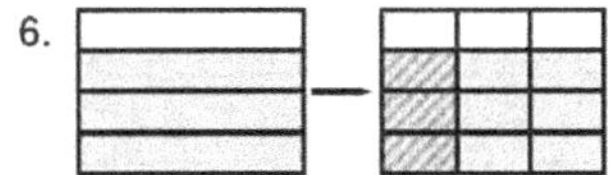

7. 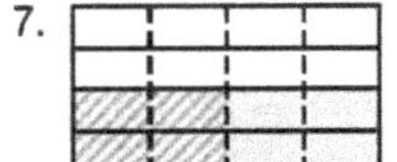   8. 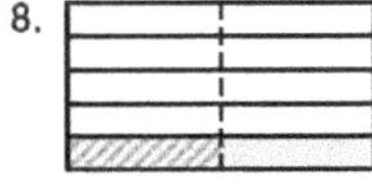   9. 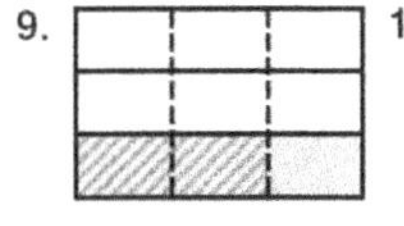   10. 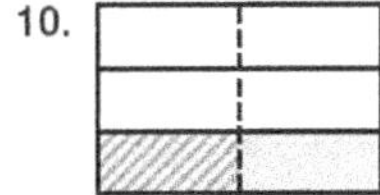

11. Represent all of the following by using suitable number sentences.

a. 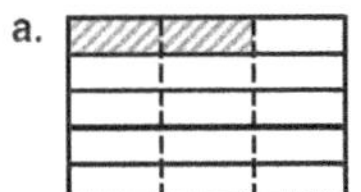   b. 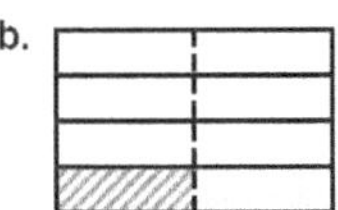   c. 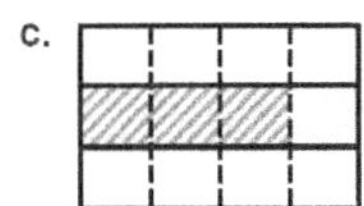   d. 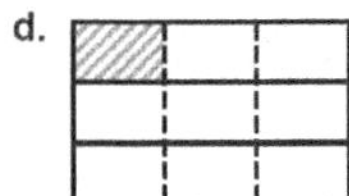

12. Namrata observed that cistern A, B and C are taking 20 minutes, 40 minutes and one hour respectively to refill $3/4^{th}$ of a water tank. If all the three cisterns kept open then time taken by these cisterns to fill up the water tank completely will be …………….

13. Anamika can finish half of a project activity in 6 days, three fourth of that work will be completed by Snehal in 8 days. If they work jointly to finish the project work then the work will be complete by them in ……. days.

Exercise 4

1: one third of angle A, one fourth of B and $1/5^{th}$ of C are equal to each other. Find out all the interior angles.

2. $7/11^{th}$ of a number is equal to $9/13^{th}$ of another number. Find out ratio of both the numbers.

Find products.

3. $\frac{1}{2} \times \frac{2}{3}$ 4. $\frac{1}{4} \times \frac{2}{7}$ 5. $\frac{2}{9} \times \frac{1}{6}$ 6. $\frac{3}{4} \times \frac{1}{9}$ 7. $\frac{4}{9} \times \frac{3}{5}$

8. $\frac{4}{7} \times \frac{3}{8}$ 9. $\frac{4}{15} \times \frac{5}{9}$ 10. $\frac{2}{3} \times \frac{3}{13}$ 11. $\frac{6}{7} \times \frac{7}{8}$ 12. $\frac{3}{10} \times \frac{7}{9}$

13. $\frac{3}{4} \times 16$ 14. $\frac{4}{25} \times 10$ 15. $\frac{7}{12} \times 24$ 16. $\frac{4}{21} \times 49$ 17. $\frac{5}{16} \times 32$

18. $32 \times \frac{5}{6}$ 19. $33 \times \frac{4}{11}$ 20. $35 \times \frac{5}{42}$ 21. $24 \times \frac{3}{8}$ 22. $25 \times \frac{2}{15}$

23. $\frac{3}{10} \times \frac{25}{27}$ 24. $\frac{8}{27} \times \frac{9}{20}$ 25. $\frac{9}{14} \times \frac{7}{15}$ 26. $\frac{7}{8} \times \frac{6}{21}$ 27. $\frac{2}{9} \times \frac{21}{26}$

28. $14 \times \frac{3}{7}$ 29. $36 \times \frac{7}{8}$ 30. $20 \times \frac{3}{25}$ 31. $\frac{5}{12} \times 8$ 32. $\frac{3}{19} \times 30$

33. $\frac{5}{8} \times \frac{4}{15}$ 34. $\frac{3}{4} \times 18$ 35. $\frac{5}{7} \times \frac{8}{15}$ 36. $72 \times \frac{5}{12}$ 37. $\frac{5}{6} \times 54$

38. Half of A, quarter of B, $4/5^{th}$ of C and $5/7^{th}$ of D are equal to each other. Find out ratio of A, B, C and D.

39. Calculate portion of grid which is not shaded.

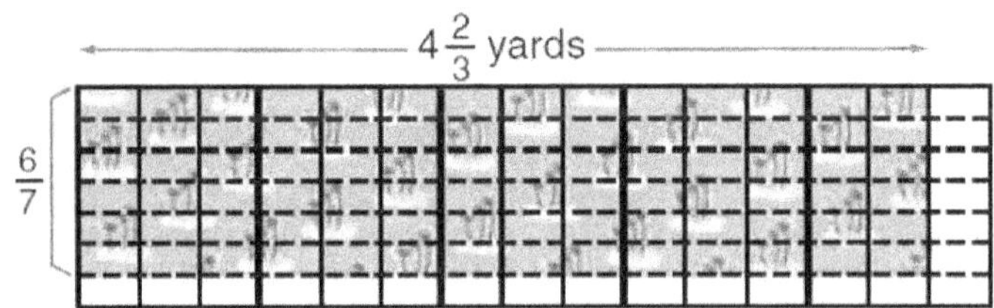

40. $\frac{1}{2}$ of $\frac{2}{3}$ of $\frac{3}{11}$ of $p = 10,20,300$. Find out simplest value of p.

Exercise 5

1: Three box pack and another three fourth of cakes are to be distributed equally amongst 15 friends. Calculate part of cakes which will be shared by each of the friends.

2. Somnath prepares a project activity in 15 days while working 4 hours a day. He preferred working 2 and half hours a day. Calculate total number of days to be taken by him to finish the project works.

3. $(1 + 2 + \dots 20{,}000) \times 10{,}000 \times (9{,}999 + 2)^{-1} = 2^p\, 5^q$; here p/q =

Divide

4. $\frac{1}{5} \div 2$ **5.** $\frac{1}{7} \div 4$ **6.** $\frac{5}{8} \div 10$ **7.** $\frac{3}{16} \div 9$

8. $\frac{12}{33} \div 4$ **9.** $\frac{9}{10} \div 3$ **10.** $\frac{6}{7} \div 4$ **11.** $\frac{15}{19} \div 6$

12. $\frac{4}{17} \div 6$ **13.** $\frac{6}{7} \div 9$ **14.** $\frac{12}{25} \div 6$ **15.** $\frac{6}{7} \div 15$

16. $\frac{4}{9} \div 36$ **17.** $\frac{5}{8} \div 40$ **18.** $\frac{9}{17} \div 27$ **19.** $\frac{9}{10} \div 81$

20. $\frac{7}{8} \div 49$ **21.** $\frac{6}{7} \div 42$ **22.** $\frac{4}{11} \div 8$ **23.** $\frac{3}{4} \div 9$

24. $\frac{3}{20} \div 21$ **25.** $\frac{2}{3} \div 50$ **26.** $\frac{5}{6} \div 20$ **27.** $\frac{7}{8} \div 14$

28. $\frac{5}{12} \div 25$ **29.** $\frac{11}{12} \div 22$ **30.** $\frac{9}{10} \div 27$ **31.** $\frac{3}{11} \div 12$

32. $\frac{6}{7} \div 8$ **33.** $\frac{4}{25} \div 12$ **34.** $\frac{12}{13} \div 16$ **35.** $\frac{10}{11} \div 15$

36. One third of the class is divided into 9 equal groups. What part of the class is each group?

37. Three fourths of a squad is divided into 12 teams. What part of the squad is each team?

38. Camilo has 3.5 hour to solve 70 math problems. If he spends the same amount of time on each problem, what part of an hour does he spend on each problem? How many problems could be solved by him in half of an hour?

Exercise 6

1: What least number should be added to 5/9th of product of greatest and smallest number of five digits to make the number divisible exactly by 9?

2. $(1 + 2 + 3 + \dots 60{,}000) \times 30{,}000 \times (59{,}999 + 2)^{-1} = 9 \times 10^{p}$; p = …..

3. What least number should be added to sum of three digit and four digit greatest numbers to obtain a common multiple of 3 and 9?

4. $2\frac{1}{2} \div \frac{5}{6}$ 5. $2\frac{1}{5} \div \frac{3}{4}$ 6. $2\frac{11}{12} \div \frac{5}{12}$ 7. $6\frac{7}{8} \div \frac{5}{8}$

8. $3\frac{1}{5} \div \frac{4}{15}$ 9. $5\frac{1}{16} \div \frac{3}{8}$ 10. $3\frac{1}{7} \div \frac{2}{7}$ 11. $7\frac{1}{2} \div \frac{5}{6}$

12. $4\frac{4}{5} \div \frac{4}{15}$ 13. $3\frac{6}{7} \div \frac{9}{14}$ 14. $2\frac{1}{4} \div \frac{9}{10}$ 15. $2\frac{8}{9} \div \frac{2}{3}$

16. $6\frac{3}{4} \div \frac{3}{5}$ 17. $2\frac{3}{4} \div \frac{5}{12}$ 18. $4\frac{1}{32} \div \frac{5}{16}$ 19. $4\frac{1}{5} \div \frac{3}{7}$

20. $4\frac{5}{8} \div \frac{3}{4}$ 21. $3\frac{7}{8} \div \frac{3}{8}$ 22. $6\frac{5}{9} \div \frac{5}{9}$ 23. $2\frac{4}{9} \div \frac{5}{6}$

Compare. Write <, =, or >.

24. $1\frac{1}{2} \div \frac{3}{4}$ __?__ $1\frac{1}{3} \div \frac{1}{3}$ 25. $2\frac{1}{2} \div \frac{1}{8}$ __?__ $3\frac{1}{3} \div \frac{1}{6}$

26. $3\frac{3}{4} \div \frac{3}{4}$ __?__ $3\frac{1}{5} \div \frac{4}{5}$ 27. $3\frac{1}{5} \div \frac{4}{15}$ __?__ $8\frac{1}{3} \div \frac{5}{6}$

28. $3\frac{1}{2} \div \frac{3}{4}$ __?__ $1\frac{1}{4} \div \frac{3}{8}$ 29. $4\frac{1}{2} \div \frac{1}{4}$ __?__ $2\frac{1}{4} \div \frac{1}{2}$

40. Tank A is filled u by cistern P completely in 40 minutes, cistern Q can take 20 minutes to fill up one fifth of the tank. Tank B is filled up completely by both the cisterns jointly in 45 minutes. Calculate total time to be taken by both the cisterns to fill up tank A and tank B completely.

41. What least number should be added to smallest odd number of six digits to make the number a common multiple of 3, 6, 99 and 12.

42. What least number should be subtracted from six digit greatest number to obtain a number exactly divisible by 8?

43. How many six digit numbers are there in all?

44. 20% of 70% of a natural number is equal to 14,28,042. Find out the number.

Exercise 7

1: Identify pair of angles in the following on the basis of their properties.

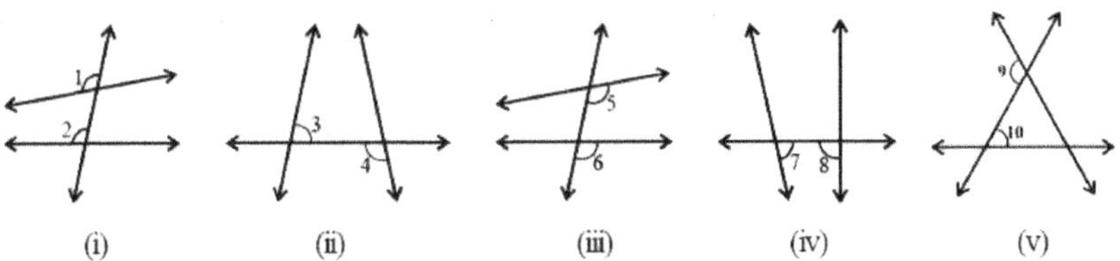

(i)   (ii)   (iii)   (iv)   (v)

2. Complete the following.

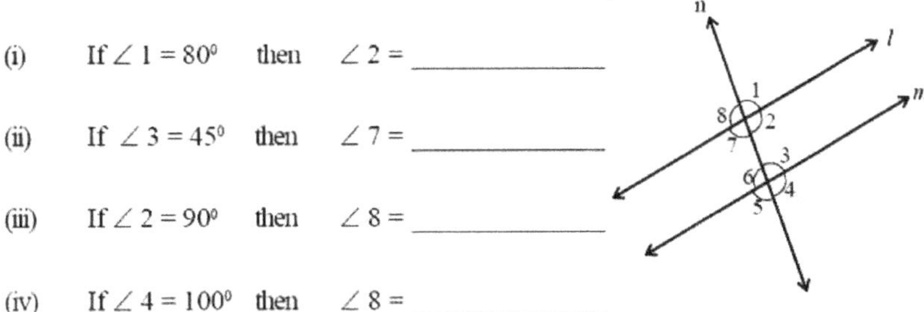

(i)   If $\angle 1 = 80^0$ then $\angle 2 =$ _____________

(ii)   If $\angle 3 = 45^0$ then $\angle 7 =$ _____________

(iii)   If $\angle 2 = 90^0$ then $\angle 8 =$ _____________

(iv)   If $\angle 4 = 100^0$ then $\angle 8 =$ _____________

3. Sum of complementary and supplementary angles of a given angle is equal to 150^0. Find out the angle.

4. Which smallest number of seven digits is divisible exactly by 9?

5. How many six digit numbers are there in all?

6. A light is placed at the top of table above 40 cm. light reaches at the edge of table by crossing a distance of 50 cm. Find out radius of the circular table.

7. In a given expression $(x^2 - x + 1) = 0$. By using this relationship find out value of x.

8. Sum of a number and three times of its reciprocal is equal to 4. Find out sum of square, cube and third multiple of that number.

9. What least number should be subtracted from fifth multiple of 10,001 to obtain a common multiple of 5 and 25?

Exercise 8

1: Find out missing angles in the following.

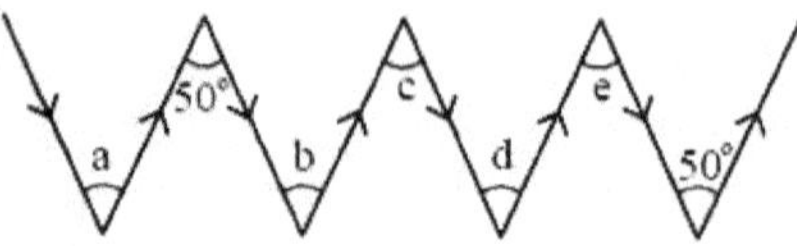

2. Find out missing angles in the following

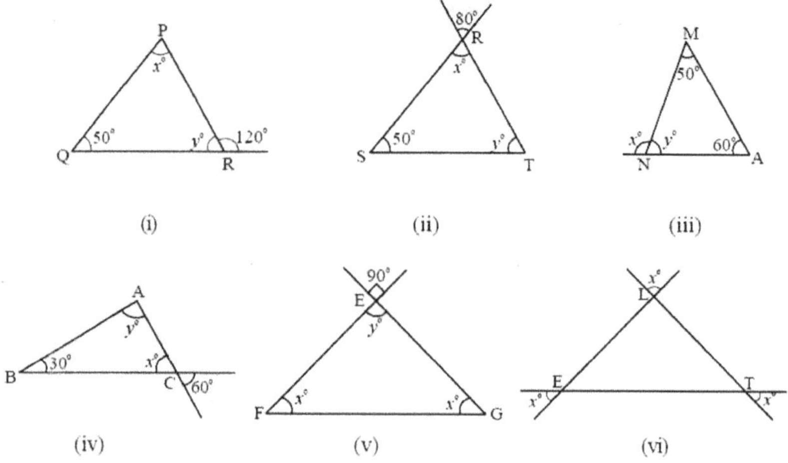

(i)   (ii)   (iii)

(iv)   (v)   (vi)

3. Find out sum of all the interior angles of a pentagon.

4. How many diagonals will be there in a pentagon which can be drawn passing through a definite vertex?

5. Is it possible to draw a triangle by using sides 3 cm, 4 cm and 8 cm?

6. Is it possible to have a quadrilateral with two reflex angles? At most how many obtuse angles could be there in a quadrilateral.

7. What least number of three digit should be added to smallest seven digit numbers to obtain a common multiple of 3 and 9?

***.

Question Bank

Set 1

1: What fraction of all the natural numbers starting from 1 to 400 are multiples of 20?

2. $\left(\frac{1}{2} \; X \frac{2}{3} \; X \frac{3}{4} \ldots\ldots\ldots \frac{9999}{10000}\right) X \; 27 = \sqrt[4]{p} \; X \; 10^q$; here p = …. and q = …

3. one tenth X 6 hundredth X 10,000 + 1.0324 = …………

4. One fifth of one sixth of 60,30,090 = ……………..

5. 3/49 of a natural number is equal to 30,30,300. Find the number.

6. Four fifth of A is equal to five sixth of B. Find simple ratio of A and B. Also represent such ratio in three equivalent fractions.

7. Five sixths of the books on the shelf are nonfiction. $1/18^{\text{th}}$ of the books are mathematics. Three fourths of rest of the books are science books. What part of the books on the shelf are science books?

Find the product. Use the Commutative Property to check your answers.

8. $\frac{7}{10} \times \frac{1}{3}$ 9. $\frac{3}{4} \times \frac{3}{5}$ 10. $\frac{3}{8} \times \frac{5}{7}$ 11. $\frac{5}{6} \times \frac{2}{9}$

12. $\frac{3}{4}$ of $\frac{2}{9}$ 13. $\frac{4}{5}$ of $\frac{4}{7}$ 14. $\frac{3}{10}$ of $\frac{2}{5}$ 15. $\frac{5}{8}$ of $\frac{4}{9}$

Find the missing fraction. Then check by multiplying.

16. $\frac{3}{4} \times n = \frac{5}{6} \times \frac{3}{4}$ 17. $\frac{6}{7} \times \frac{1}{4} = n \times \frac{6}{7}$ 18. $n \times \frac{2}{9} = \frac{2}{9} \times \frac{4}{5}$

Compare. Write $<$, $=$, or $>$.

19. $\frac{2}{5} \times \frac{1}{4}$? $\frac{1}{4} \times \frac{2}{3}$ 20. $\frac{5}{9} \times \frac{3}{5}$? $\frac{5}{6} \times \frac{3}{4}$ 21. $\frac{1}{4} \times \frac{3}{8}$? $\frac{3}{16} \times \frac{1}{2}$

22. $\frac{3}{5} \times \frac{1}{6}$? $\frac{3}{9} \times \frac{1}{2}$ 23. $\frac{3}{5} \times \frac{2}{3}$? $\frac{7}{8} \times \frac{2}{5}$ 24. $\frac{5}{6} \times \frac{9}{10}$? $\frac{1}{2} \times \frac{4}{5}$

Set 2

1: Using each of the digits 2, 3, 5, and 7 only once, find two fractions that will have a product n such that:

A: It is a product close to 1.

B: It is a maximum possible product of both the fractions.

C: It is a minimum possible product of both the fractions.

2. One third of the 24 students in class read books on sports. How many students in the class do not read books on sports?

3. What fraction of all the numbers starting from 1 to 500 are multiples of 25?

4. Seven eleventh of a natural number is equal to 70,70,707. Find out the natural number.

5. How many three digit numbers can be obtained if we use digits 2, 3 and 0 only once? What will be the product of greatest and smallest such number?

6. A passenger train takes 54 seconds to cross a light post while moving by maintaining an average speed of 18 km/h. What is the length of that train?

7. Two trains cross each other completely while moving through up and down track in 2 minutes 32 seconds. Average speed of both the trains are 18 km/h and 36 km/h respectively. Find out total length of both the trains. If ratio of both the length is 3:2 and train having greater seed is longer, then calculate length both the trains.

8. A wall mount clock spends 3 seconds for striking three bells at 3 a.m. calculate total time to be taken by this clock to strike 9 bells at 9 a. m. and 11 bells at 11 a. m.

9. What percentage of all the natural numbers from 1 to 625 are multiples of 25?

Set 3

1: What least number should be multiplied to 121,000 to make the product divisible by 1,331?

2. There are 40 members in a basketball team which is finalised for the forthcoming season. Three fifths are fifth-grade students. One tenth are class six students. Rest of the others are seniors. How many members of the basketball team are senior students?

3. $\frac{1}{2} \times \frac{2}{3}$ **4.** $\frac{1}{4} \times \frac{2}{7}$ **5.** $\frac{2}{9} \times \frac{1}{6}$ **6.** $\frac{3}{4} \times \frac{1}{9}$ **7.** $\frac{4}{9} \times \frac{3}{5}$

8. $\frac{4}{7} \times \frac{3}{8}$ **9.** $\frac{4}{15} \times \frac{5}{9}$ **10.** $\frac{2}{3} \times \frac{3}{13}$ **11.** $\frac{6}{7} \times \frac{7}{8}$ **12.** $\frac{3}{10} \times \frac{7}{9}$

13. $\frac{3}{4} \times 16$ **14.** $\frac{4}{25} \times 10$ **15.** $\frac{7}{12} \times 24$ **16.** $\frac{4}{21} \times 49$ **17.** $\frac{5}{16} \times 32$

18. $32 \times \frac{5}{6}$ **19.** $33 \times \frac{4}{11}$ **20.** $35 \times \frac{5}{42}$ **21.** $24 \times \frac{3}{8}$ **22.** $25 \times \frac{2}{15}$

Find the product in simplest form.

23. $\frac{3}{10} \times \frac{25}{27}$ **24.** $\frac{8}{27} \times \frac{9}{20}$ **25.** $\frac{9}{14} \times \frac{7}{15}$ **26.** $\frac{7}{8} \times \frac{6}{21}$ **27.** $\frac{2}{9} \times \frac{21}{26}$

28. $14 \times \frac{3}{7}$ **29.** $36 \times \frac{7}{8}$ **30.** $20 \times \frac{3}{25}$ **31.** $\frac{5}{12} \times 8$ **32.** $\frac{3}{19} \times 30$

33. $\frac{5}{8} \times \frac{4}{15}$ **34.** $\frac{3}{4} \times 18$ **35.** $\frac{5}{7} \times \frac{8}{15}$ **36.** $72 \times \frac{5}{12}$ **37.** $\frac{5}{6} \times 54$

38. A cistern can fill up half of a water tank in 15 minutes, it can fill up another water tank in 45 minutes. Calculate total time to be taken by this cistern to fill up both the tanks completely.

39. Rikin formed greatest and smallest four digit numbers without repeating any of the digits. Find out sum of both the numbers.

40. What fraction of all the numbers starting from 1 to 600 are multiples of 30?

41. Half of one seventh of a natural number exceeds seven digit smallest number by 1,001. Find out the number.

42. $1,2091 \times 125 \times 25 \times 40 \times 8 = \dots\dots\dots\dots$

Set 4

1: How many seven digit numbers are there in all?

2. (1099 X 209 X 3099X 4009X 30909) = p; if we write numerical value of p in standard form then digit at the unit place will be ....

3. Which seven digit smallest number is a common multiples of 3 and 9?

4. $3\frac{1}{2} \times \frac{1}{3}$ 5. $2\frac{1}{2} \times \frac{3}{5}$ 6. $\frac{5}{14} \times 2\frac{1}{3}$ 7. $\frac{1}{9} \times 5\frac{1}{3}$

8. $\frac{2}{3} \times 4\frac{1}{5}$ 9. $\frac{3}{7} \times 5\frac{3}{5}$ 10. $2\frac{1}{5} \times \frac{4}{11}$ 11. $1\frac{5}{7} \times \frac{5}{12}$

12. $6\frac{1}{8} \times \frac{4}{7}$ 13. $4\frac{1}{4} \times \frac{2}{3}$ 14. $\frac{9}{12} \times 1\frac{1}{3}$ 15. $\frac{3}{14} \times 2\frac{1}{3}$

16. $\frac{3}{4} \times 1\frac{2}{6}$ 17. $\frac{7}{8} \times 2\frac{2}{7}$ 18. $2\frac{1}{2} \times \frac{2}{15}$ 19. $2\frac{4}{5} \times \frac{5}{7}$

20. $\frac{6}{7} \times 4\frac{1}{3}$ 21. $\frac{6}{7} \times 2\frac{1}{3}$ 22. $2\frac{2}{5} \times \frac{5}{6}$ 23. $4\frac{1}{5} \times \frac{6}{7}$

24. Celia had 4 and half yards of ribbon in her scrap box. She used half of it for her project. Half of the remaining is given to her friend. Find out length of the ribbon which were not used.

25. Half of a number A, quarter of B and one sixth of C are equal to each other. Find out simplest ratio of A, B and C. Also find out the simplest value of $\left(\frac{A^3 + B^3 + C^3}{3ABC}\right)$.

24. What least number should be subtracted from the product of four digit greatest number and four digit smallest number to obtain a common multiple of 3 and 9?

25. Complete the following number series.

$(1 + 3 + 5 + 7)$ =   4 X 4   =   16;

$(1 + 3 + 5 + \ .... + 11)$ =   ... X ....   =   36;

(Sum of 20 consecutive odds)   =   ... X ....   = ...;

(Sum of 100 consecutive odds) =   ... X ....   = ...;

Set 5

1: Divide greatest six digit number by greatest two digit number. Add 11 to the result and again multiply 125 and 8 to it. What are the digits at ones and tens place of your result?

2. $(1 + 2 + ... + 1000) \times 500 \times 125 \times 8 \times 40 = 1001 \times 10^p$. Here p = ...

3. What fraction of all the natural numbers starting from 1 to 1000 are multiples of 125?

4. A cistern takes 15 minutes to fill up quarter of tank A, One fifth of tank B and one seventh of tank C. Calculate total time to be taken by the cistern to fill up all the tanks completely.

5. $1/11^{th}$ of $1/9^{th}$ of a number is equal to 10,10,100. Find out the number.

6. A shopkeeper gains an amount equal to SP of 1 apple by selling 11 apples. Find out total gain percentage made by the shopkeeper.

7. $7\overline{)350}$	**8.** $9\overline{)720}$	**9.** $3\overline{)1800}$	**10.** $8\overline{)6400}$
11. $80\overline{)240}$	**12.** $60\overline{)420}$	**13.** $50\overline{)300}$	**14.** $30\overline{)120}$
15. $50\overline{)2000}$	**16.** $40\overline{)2800}$	**17.** $60\overline{)3600}$	**18.** $20\overline{)18,000}$
19. $40\overline{)16,000}$	**20.** $700\overline{)49,000}$	**21.** $800\overline{)480,000}$	**22.** $300\overline{)270,000}$

Use basic facts and patterns to find the value of _n_.

23. $720 \div 9 = n$	**24.** $60 \div 3 = n$	**25.** $800 \div 2 = n$
26. $2400 \div 6 = n$	**27.** $1200 \div n = 40$	**28.** $3500 \div n = 70$
29. $2800 \div n = 40$	**30.** $6300 \div n = 90$	**31.** $4200 \div 60 = n$
32. $30,000 \div 50 = n$	**33.** $64,000 \div 80 = n$	**34.** $45,000 \div 90 = n$
35. $54,000 \div 60 = n$	**36.** $630,000 \div n = 900$	**37.** $560,000 \div n = 8000$

Compare. Write $<$, $=$, or $>$.

38. $3600 \div 6$ _?_ $4000 \div 8$	**39.** $4200 \div 70$ _?_ $4800 \div 80$
40. $70,000 \div 7$ _?_ $80,000 \div 2$	**41.** $45,000 \div 90$ _?_ $25,000 \div 5$

42. 20% of 30% of a number is equal to tenth multiple of 1,001. Find it.

Set 6

Complete the following.

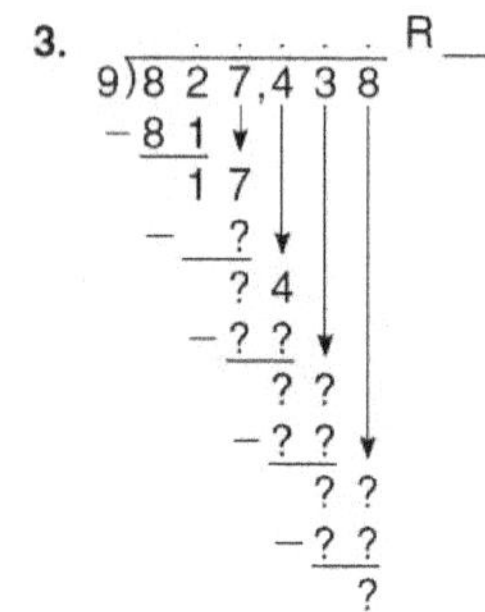

4. Divide 1,33,11,331 by 11 and check your answer.

5: The Art Guild has 4338 flyers to give out. If 5 members of the Guild share the job equally, how many flyers will each give out? How many flyers will be left over?

6. If we multiply 199, 109, 909, 189 and 139 then digit at the unit place will be ....

7. If we divide 121,121,121 by 33 them digit at the unit place of the result will be ....

8. If we divide a six digit greatest possible number by 3 then remainder is 2, if it is divided by 4 then the remainder is 1. Find out the number.

9. What fraction of all the natural numbers starting from 1 to 400 are multiples of 16?

10. Rikin jogs a yard in 2 seconds, Snehal walks 4 ft in 3 seconds, Pintu jogs a couple of yard in five seconds. Who jogs fastest. Arrange their names as per the increasing speed of jogging.

11. Mohini prepared a painting work in 5 days while working 3 hours a day. She can take ..... days to finish a couple of such paintings while working 6 hours a day.

Set 7

1: A scanner (along with scanning operator) requires six mnths to scan 198,198 books completely. Equal books are scanned Everyday by the scanner. What number of books is scanned in a month?

2. While dividing a number by 121 a student obtained 100,100,100. There was no remainder. What was the number?

3. There were 20,172 tickets sold for a 3-game tournament series. If the same number of tickets was sold for each game, then find out how many tickets were sold for each of the games?

4. Mohini collected Rs 625 from her class to promote a charity show. Each of the students contributed amount equal to the student strength of that class. How many students are there in the class?

5. There are 378 people going on a field trip. Nine buses are hired for the trip. There will be two passengers extra in sixth bus and a couple of passengers less in fifth bus. If the same number of people rides in rest of the other buses, then find out total people ride in each bus?

6. $(A + B) = 2002$; $(B + C) = 2003$; $(C + A) = 3009$; Find out simplest value of $(A + B + C)$.

7. Somalika can finish her assignments in 16 days while working three hours a day. She can finish all her assignments in ….. days while working 4 hours a day.

8. Three bells toll at an interval of 3 seconds, four seconds and six seconds respectively. How many times do all the three bells toll together in 2 h 24 minutes?

9. Speed of car A is 18 km/h and speed of car B is 10 m/s. car B was 2 km away from car A. Smita started her stop watch to record total time taken by car A to overtake car B while moving through the same road. Find out reading of the stop watch.

10. 30% of 50% of 10,20,300 = ………………………

Set 8

Estimate.

1. 1758 ÷ 4   2. 3951 ÷ 5   3. 7453 ÷ 8   4. 8326 ÷ 9

5. 9875 ÷ 23   6. 4282 ÷ 34   7. 63,792 ÷ 59   8. 84,796 ÷ 78

Estimate the quotient.

9. 1957 ÷ 4   10. 4893 ÷ 5   11. 6397 ÷ 8   12. 3319 ÷ 9

13. 2679 ÷ 83   14. 8529 ÷ 92   15. 4813 ÷ 68   16. 7945 ÷ 94

17. 83,592 ÷ 94   18. 39,125 ÷ 58   19. 61,958 ÷ 75   20. 38,958 ÷ 49

Estimate to compare. Write <, =, or >.

21. 27,903 ÷ 7 _?_ 35,903 ÷ 9   22. 5798 ÷ 3 _?_ 11,938 ÷ 6

23. 2829 ÷ 23 _?_ 4173 ÷ 13   24. 12,636 ÷ 24 _?_ 15,296 ÷ 32

25. 46,879 ÷ 18 _?_ 49,362 ÷ 19   26. 69,135 ÷ 27 _?_ 56,238 ÷ 16

29. Sonalika prepared three counters which produce beats at uniform intervals of 5 seconds, 10 seconds and 15 seconds. After what time intervals do they produce beats together? How many times joint beats will be generated by them in time interval of a couple of hours?

30. 30 men works together to finish a work in 380 days. 27 additional men joined the team to finish the work as early as possible. Calculate total number of days saved by them in this way.

31. A boat moves down the stream in 39 minutes and returns back while moving up-stream in 1 h 21 minutes. Calculate ratio of the speed of the boat and speed of the stream.

32. Equal numbers of square sized tiles are used for the floor of 1331 sq cm. find out maximum possible size of all such square sized tiles.

33. Alhan observed that sound of a fighter plane reaches him after six seconds of its visibility in sky. By ignoring speed of light calculate altitude of the fighter plane by considering speed of sound in air as 340 m/s.

34. $(1 + 2 + \ldots\ldots 50{,}000) \times 25{,}000 \times 16 = (50{,}000 + 1) \times 10^{p}$.

Set 9

1: What least number should be added to the product of four digit greatest number and four digit smallest number to obtain a common multiple of 3 and 9?

2. 12,43,405 X 125 X 25 X 8 X 40 ÷ 10,000 = ...

3. Fifth multiple of 5,005 + 6th multiple of 6,006 = ...

4. Half of 2,002 + quarter of 4,004 + $1/6^{th}$ of 6,006 = ... X (999 + 2)

Check divisibility of the following by 11.

5. 133,100`   6. 121,121,121   7. 134,431,000

Check divisibility of the following by 9. Also work out least number to be added to the numbers to make them divisible by 9.

8. 324,543,654   9. 430,435,003   10. 999 X 1001

11. 2 more than the product of greatest and smallest 5 digit numbers.

12. $19\overline{)1578}$	**13.** $17\overline{)1462}$	**14.** $18\overline{)1693}$	**15.** $15\overline{)1159}$
16. $18\overline{)3427}$	**17.** $17\overline{)2869}$	**18.** $14\overline{)3609}$	**19.** $13\overline{)3921}$
20. $12\overline{)10,512}$	**21.** $18\overline{)16,038}$	**22.** $17\overline{)13,243}$	**23.** $19\overline{)18,981}$
24. $14\overline{)73,501}$	**25.** $12\overline{)13,732}$	**26.** $13\overline{)13,296}$	**27.** $15\overline{)16,438}$
28. $11\overline{)115,932}$	**29.** $13\overline{)148,732}$	**30.** $14\overline{)193,475}$	**31.** $16\overline{)167,652}$

32. What least number should be subtracted from six digit greatest number to obtain a common multiple of 2, 3, 6 and 9?

33. Half of water tank A, Quarter of B, $1/5^{th}$ of C and $1/6^{th}$ of D are filled up individually by a cistern in 20 minutes. Calculate total time to be taken by that cistern to fill up all the water tanks completely.

34. Three interior angles of a triangle are in the ratio of 2: 3: 6. Find out magnitude of the greatest angle.

35. (1 + 2 + ...40,000) X 20,000 X 250 = (39,999 + 2)) X 10^{p} ; p = ...

Set 10

1: Half of p, quarter of q and $1/7^{th}$ of r are equal to each other. Find out simplest possible ratio of $(p^3 + q^3 + r^3)$ and 3pqr.

2. Sohanlal prepared a project activity in 6 gays while working 5 hours a day. He preferred working 4 hours a day to complete a couple of such project. Find the number of days needed to finish that project.

3. There are 720 students enrolled in VKV Valley School. If there are 18 classrooms in the school, what is the average number of students in each classroom?

4. $32\overline{)96}$	**5.** $22\overline{)88}$	**6.** $41\overline{)205}$	**7.** $17\overline{)153}$
8. $61\overline{)854}$	**9.** $43\overline{)688}$	**10.** $34\overline{)680}$	**11.** $27\overline{)621}$
12. $51\overline{)358}$	**13.** $65\overline{)201}$	**14.** $82\overline{)331}$	**15.** $46\overline{)283}$
16. $35\overline{)1019}$	**17.** $76\overline{)3733}$	**18.** $44\overline{)1456}$	**19.** $63\overline{)3792}$
20. $59\overline{)1193}$	**21.** $36\overline{)2884}$	**22.** $43\overline{)3886}$	**23.** $72\overline{)4332}$
24. $45\overline{)9542}$	**25.** $62\overline{)6905}$	**26.** $81\overline{)9729}$	**27.** $76\overline{)9884}$

28. Rikin divided 133,112,100 by 11. Find out the quotient.

29. Smita divided 3 and half cakes amongst her 14 friends. Find out fraction of the slice obtained by each of her friend.

30. Pallavi, Snehal, Kamalika and Niharika joined a project activity to complete the same in three days. If they prefer working individually then calculate number of days required to finish their individual projects.

31. By selling 22 apples a shopkeeper gained an amount equal to SP of 2 apples. Calculate percentage of profit gained by the shopkeeper.

32. Roy feeds the birds in the zoo 10,400 ounces of birdseed in one year. How many ounces of birdseed does he feed the birds each week?

33. $(1 + 2 + \ldots\ldots 60,000) \times 30,000 = 540,009 \times 10^p$; here p = ……..

Set 11

Divide (by estimation)

1. $63\overline{)31{,}550}$	**2.** $34\overline{)32{,}200}$	**3.** $57\overline{)22{,}850}$	**4.** $72\overline{)56{,}890}$
5. $62\overline{)29{,}145}$	**6.** $43\overline{)42{,}145}$	**7.** $54\overline{)37{,}841}$	**8.** $92\overline{)82{,}890}$
9. $27\overline{)553{,}529}$	**10.** $16\overline{)521{,}613}$	**11.** $29\overline{)884{,}560}$	**12.** $21\overline{)430{,}629}$
13. $42\overline{)193{,}242}$	**14.** $32\overline{)876{,}821}$	**15.** $27\overline{)105{,}595}$	**16.** $26\overline{)174{,}590}$
17. $58\overline{)349{,}334}$	**18.** $64\overline{)493{,}444}$	**19.** $91\overline{)364{,}460}$	**20.** $82\overline{)582{,}692}$
21. $77\overline{)273{,}080}$	**22.** $47\overline{)991{,}985}$	**23.** $39\overline{)928{,}210}$	**24.** $53\overline{)483{,}651}$
25. $90\overline{)63{,}000}$	**26.** $39\overline{)45{,}164}$	**27.** $80\overline{)32{,}320}$	**28.** $41\overline{)12{,}500}$
29. $56\overline{)420{,}810}$	**30.** $45\overline{)180{,}000}$	**31.** $27\overline{)101{,}520}$	**32.** $17\overline{)170{,}006}$

33: Find out a number A number between 2700 and 2800 when divided by 25 has a quotient that contains three odd digits and has no remainder.

34. A number p is in between 130 and 140 when divided by 12 has a quotient that contains the same two digits and has no remainder. Find out simplest value of p.

35. Sum of a natural number and its multiplicative inverse is equal to 8.125. Find out cube root of that number. Consider the natural number as a positive integer.

36. What least number should be subtracted from the product of three digit greatest number and four digit smallest numbers to obtain a multiple of 11?

37. Half of a bucket p, quarter of bucket q, one eleventh of bucket r holds equal volume of water. Compare volume of all these three buckets.

38. Roshanlal jogs at a speed of 18 km/h. Sohanlal accompanies him and moves 12 forward in 24 seconds. Find out the speed maintained by Sohanlal.

39. 29% of a natural number is equal to 101,001. Find out the number.

Set 12

1: While moving from city to village Pallavi travelled half of total distance by bus, half of rest of the distance by auto, half of the remaining distance by city drive and remaining 870 m by walking. Calculate total distance travelled by her.

2. Anand kumar is 28 cm taller than Rikin and 9 cm shorter than Neha. Height of Neha is 14 cm less than her sister Sneha. Sneha recorded her height 21 cm less than 2 m. Find out height of all the fellow partners of the team.

3. Half of p, $3/5^{th}$ of q, $4/7^{th}$ of r, $7/9^{th}$ of s are equal to each other. Find out simplest ratio of p, q and r. Also find out simplest value of $(p^2 + q^2 + r^2)$ and $2(pq + qr + rq)$.

4. 4)$15.12	**5.** 3)$6.27	**6.** 8)$159.60	**7.** 7)$107.10
8. 54)$14.04	**9.** 47)$39.95	**10.** 67)$62.31	**11.** 24)$13.68
12. 19)$114.00	**13.** 26)$208.00	**14.** 15)$139.50	**15.** 42)$153.30
16. 28)$157.92	**17.** 31)$186.62	**18.** 53)$365.70	**19.** 85)$177.65
20. 34)$173.06	**21.** 47)$325.24	**22.** 32)$322.56	**23.** 11)$250.25
24. 17)$402.05	**25.** 23)$530.15	**26.** 19)$1179.71	**27.** 21)$1997.10

28. Smallest six digit number which is divisible by 9 leaving remainder 7 exceeds smallest six digit number by ………

29. $(1+ 2 + 3 + …6000) \times 3,000 \times 125 \times 8 = 54,009 \times 10^{p}$; here p = ….

30. Quarter of a number exceeds product of greatest four digit number and smallest four digit number by 201. Find out the number.

31. Total distance travelled by Nikhil in 100 minutes is equal to 300 m. Find out total time to be taken by him to cover 54 km of distance.

32. Namrata, Sohanlal and Vineet preferred working together to finish a work in 4 days. They work with equal capacity. Find out time taken by Namrata alone to complete the same work.

Set 13

Simplify the following:

1. $8 \times 2 \div 4$
2. $4 \times 6 + 3$
3. $2 \times 7 - 4$
4. $81 \div 9 - 3$
5. $64 \div 8 + 5$
6. $8 + 3 \times 4 - 5$
7. $9 + 45 \div 5 - 3$
8. $9 \times 4 \div 6 + 7$
9. $48 \div 6 \times 3 - 5$
10. $27 - 16 \div 4 + 2$
11. $18 - 3 \times 2 + 9$
12. $81 \div 9 - 2 \times 3$
13. $4 - 9 \div 3 - 1$
14. $16 \div 4 + 2 \times 6$
15. $(3 \times 7) + (64 \div 8)$
16. $(18 - 9) \div (1 + 2)$

17. $(1 + 2 + \ldots\ldots 3{,}000) \times 1{,}500 \div 3{,}001$

18. 2001 times $5 + 4{,}002$ times $6 + 8{,}004$ times $7 = \ldots\ldots \times 2001$

19. $18 \times (11 - 6)$
20. $7 + (19 - 2) \times 3$
21. $3 + 5 \times 10 \div 2 + 8$
22. $17 + 63 \div 3 \times 6 - 9$
23. $59 - 45 \div 5 \times 3 + 41$
24. $134 - 8 \div 4 \times 2$
25. $10 \times 4 + (49 \div 7) \times 2$
26. $(35 \div 5) \times 2 + 3 \times 6$
27. $18 - 3 \div 3 + (63 \div 3) - 6$
28. $19 - 4 \times 2 + (19 - 3) \div 4$
29. $(28 \div 7) + 5 - 3 + (7 \times 2)$
30. $4 + (29 - 2) \div 9 + (16 + 2)$
31. $(4 \times 8) - 5 + (0 \div 6)$
32. $(24 \div 6) - 3 + (2 \times 4)$
33. $2 + (3 \times 6) + n$ when $n = 10$
34. $(12 + 72) \div n$ when $n = 6$
35. $(28 + n) \times 4$ when $n = 32$
36. $(9 \times 8) - (n \times 6)$ when $n = 3$
37. $n \times 2 \div 2 + 24$ when $n = 8$
38. $6 + n - 3 \times 6 \div 9$ when $n = 2$

Use parentheses to make the following true.

39. $25 - 5 \times 10 \div 2 = 0$
40. $19 - 4 + 3 \div 7 = 18$
41. $3 \div 6 \times 5 + 5 = 50$
42. $9 - 5 \times 2 \div 6 = 14$
43. $8 + 24 \div 14 - 8 = 12$
44. $27 - 5 + 4 \div 3 = 24$
45. $9 + 5 \div 2 - 4 = 3$
46. $4 \times 3 + 5 - 2 = 30$
47. $y + 48 \div n$ when $n = 6; y = 12$
48. $a \times b - 12$ when $a = 13; b = 29$
49. $4 \times (a + b) + 2$ when $a = 6; b = 3$
50. $(n - y) \div (2 \times y)$ when $n = 200; y = 40$

Set 14

1: Nancy bought a bag of red, white, and blue balloons for the birthday party. There were total number of 49 balloons in the bag. If there are 2 times as many red as blue and half as many white as blue baloons, how many of each color balloon are there in the bag?

2. There are 12 mail carriers in Tundon Town. Monday, they delivered 24,780 letters. Letters being delivered on Tuesday was 36,720. Each carrier delivered the same number of letters. How many letters did each carrier deliver in two days?

3. Three fourth of a number exceeds third multiple of smallest five digit number by 309. Find out the number.

4. $(1/5^{th}$ of $5,005 + 1/6^{th}$ f $6,006 + 1/7^{th}$ of $7,007$) $\div 1,001 = $ ....

Divide and check.

5. $\quad 63 \div 9$	**6.** $\quad 54 \div 6$	**7.** $\quad 35 \div 7$
$630 \div 9$	$540 \div 60$	$350 \div 70$
$6300 \div 9$	$5400 \div 600$	$3500 \div 70$
$63,000 \div 9$	$54,000 \div 6000$	$35,000 \div 70$

8. $64,000 \div 80 = n$ **9.** $150,000 \div n = 3000$ **10.** $n \div 60 = 400$

11. $9\overline{)3027}$ **12.** $8\overline{)5866}$ **13.** $24\overline{)49}$ **14.** $41\overline{)984}$

15. $31\overline{)1836}$ **16.** $15\overline{)945}$ **17.** $86\overline{)68,906}$ **18.** $73\overline{)78,146}$

19. $28\overline{)\$56.56}$ **20.** $17\overline{)\$35.02}$ **21.** $26\overline{)\$286.26}$ **22.** $64\overline{)\$204.80}$

23. What fraction of all the natural numbers starting from 500 are multiples of 25?

24. Which natural number of six digits will be the smallest multiple of 9?

25. $(1.001 \times 0.001 \times 0.01 \times 12,904) \times 10^{5} = $ ....

26. Half of $1/7^{th}$ of $14,28,510 = $ ....

Set 15

1: Find out smallest four digit number which is divisible by 4, 5, 6 and 7 leaving remainder 3 in each case.

2. In her coin book, Sylvia wants to arrange 18 French coins and 24 Spanish coins and 36 Asian coins in equal rows on the page. What is the greatest number of Spanish, French or Asian coins she can arrange in each row? How many rows will she have in this way?

3. What least number should be subtracted from greatest six digit number to obtain a common multiple of 3, 6, 9 and 18?

4. Provide missing values.

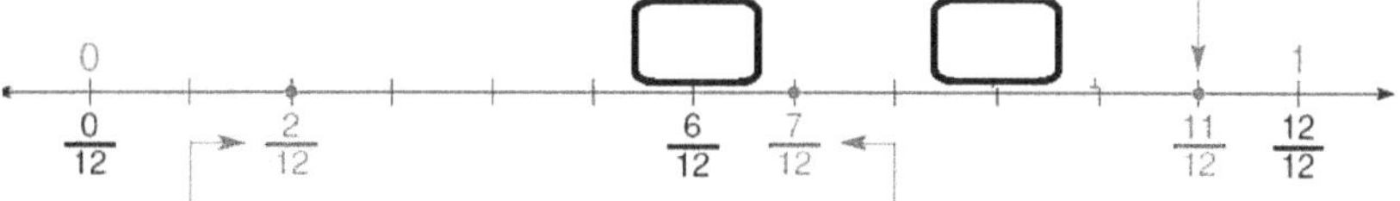

5. Find out value of n in the following.

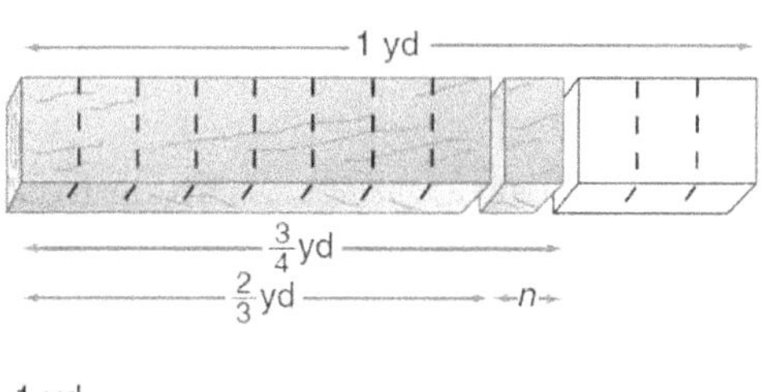

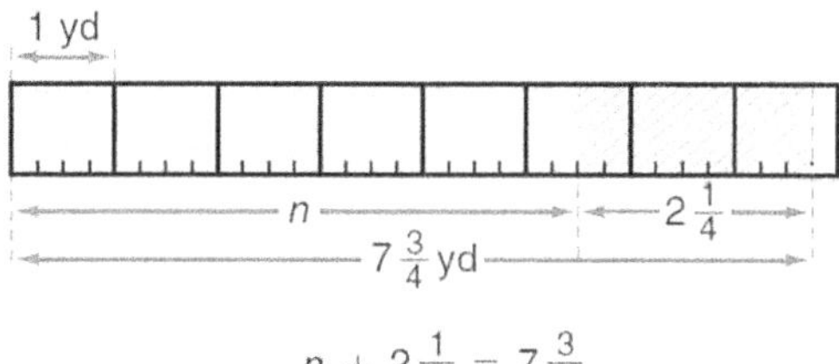

$$n + 2\frac{1}{4} = 7\frac{3}{4}$$

6. Half of 1/11th of a natural number is equal to 10,20,300. Find out the number. Also find out sixth multiple of that number.

7. 20% f 70% of a natural number exceeds 14th multiple of smallest number of four digits by 56. Find out the number.

8. What least number should be subtracted from greatest number of six digits to obtain a number which can be divided by 6, 12 and 18 leaving remainder 5 in each case?

9. Sonalika prepares three toys in 3 days while working 3 hours a day. Find out number of days needed to 12 toys while working 4 hours a day.

10. Write when the fractional part of the difference of two mixed numbers is equal to zero; also write when the whole-number part of the difference is equal to zero. Use models to explain your answers.

11. What digit will be there in the product of greatest and smallest number of five digits?

12. Train A moves 20 m in 1 second and train B covers 36 km in 1 hour. They started moving towards each other through up and down tracks respectively. When there was a gap of 108 km a bird started flying to and fro in between both the engines. The bird continued flying until and unless both the engines started crossing each other. The bird covers 54 km in 1 hour. Calculate total time taken by the bird to fly to and fro in between both the engines, also find out total distance travelled by the bird while flying so.

13. What fraction of all the natural numbers starting from 1 to 1000 are multiples of 20?

14. Is there any pair of natural number having LCM 1331 and HCF 121?

15. Three ringing bells toll together at an interval of 3 seconds, 5 seconds and 8 seconds. How many times do all these bells toll together in a span of a couple of hour?

16. 37th of $5/9^{th}$ of a natural number is equal to 125,125,075. Find out the number.

***

Book 4

We can draw three lines passing through two out of three non-collinear points. A ray can have only one origin and can be extended endlessly in any one direction.

Practice time: Calculation of area of trapezium.

Area of a triangle = half of height and base. Area of parallelogram = height X base.

Calculation of area of triangle and parallelograms.

A line segment can have two end points and a definite length. Light travels nearly three lakh km in a second by following a straight line; the distance covered by light in one minute is considered as 1 light minute; light minute, light hour, light day, light uear etc. are units of length used for representing large values of distance. Light 8 minutes to reach a planet from a star. It indicates the intermediate distance of star and planet equal to distance covered by light in eight minutes.

Percent is a special type of fraction having denominator 100. Fractions can be represented into equivalent decimal by taking denominators as multiple of 10. Decimals can be represented into fractions by taking representative unit fractions: one tenth = 1/10; one hundredth = 1/100; and so on. Repeated addition is equivalent to multiplication and repeated subtraction stands for division. Basic shapes bounded by three or more line or line segments are called polygons. Smallest possible polygon is a triangle. Sum of all the interior angles of a polygon is equal to a straight angle.

For finding out area and outer boundary of complex figures we divide complex figures in sections of basic shaes and then work out area and perimeter.

Area of trapezium = sum total of parallel sides X half of height.

Area of a parallelogram can be calculated by multiplying base and height.

Area of a rectangle will be obtained by multiplying length and breadth.

A triangle having two right angles or two obtuse angles is not possible.

A quadrilateral having all the four angles as obtuse angles is not possible.

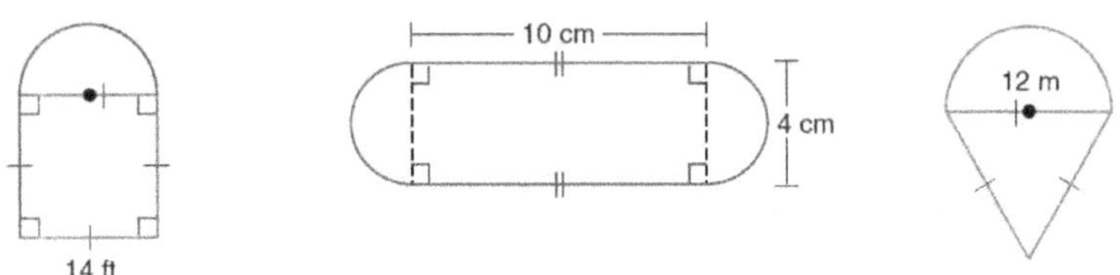

We use mathematical system of numeration to denote a number by using digits. Involvement of ten digits in the system of numeration is the reason due to which the term "Decimal (Decim)" is coined for the system of numeration in which ten digits (such as 0, 1, 2, 3, 4, 5, 6, 7, 8 and 9) are used.

Roman numerals used to denote some special purpose of numerations in the field of Science and Technology. Basic chart of such numeration exhibits uses of different symbols.

I	II	III	IV	V	VI	VII	VIII	IX	X
1	2	3	4	5	6	7	8	9	10
V	X	XV	XX	XXV	XXX	XXXV	XL	XLV	L
5	10	15	20	25	30	35	40	45	50
X	XX	XXX	XL	L	LX	LXX	LXXX	XC	C
10	20	30	40	50	60	70	80	90	100
C	CC	CCC	CD	D	DC	DCC	DCCC	CM	M
100	200	300	400	500	600	700	800	900	1000

We use symbols V, L, D and M without repeating. An Example: DCX = 500 + 100 + 10 = 610.

Multiplication is a repeated addition.

To calculate area of a circle: we multiply square of radius of the circle by value of pi (22/7 or 3.14). Area of a circle having radius 7 cm will be:

$$2\,\pi\,r^2 = 2 \, X \frac{22}{7} \, X \, 7 \, X \, 7 \; cm^2 = 44 \, X \, 7 \; cm^2 = 308 \; cm^2 \; .$$

The number system which deals with 10 different digits is called decimal system.

324,432,232 is the number represented by using digits from the collection of 10 different digits, such as 0,1,2,3,4,5,6,7,8 and 9.

Expanded form of 213,324,543 can be expressed as follows:

$$213,324,543 \quad = \quad \_\_\_ \text{ X } 1,00,000,000$$

$$+ \quad 1 \text{ X } 10,000,000$$

$$+ \quad 3 \text{ X } 1,000,000$$

$$+ \quad \_\_\_ \text{ X } 100,000$$

$$+ \quad \_\_\_ \text{ X } 10,000$$

$$+ \quad \_\_\_ \text{ X } 1,000$$

$$+ \quad \_\_\_ \text{ X } 100$$

$$+ \quad \_\_\_ \text{ X } 10$$

$$+ \quad \_\_\_ \text{ X } 1$$

We can write place value to represent position of a digit in expanded form of a given number.

Example: Represent place value of underlined digits.

1. 85,990	2. $94.20	3. 549,218	4. $651.99	5. 56,843
6. $429.28	7. 825,053	8. $10.56	9. 742	10. 36,987,301
11. 12,634,087	12. 221,034	13. $6.42	14. 3198	15. $54.04

Place value of 9 in example 1 is 900. Smilarly we can work out other place values.

Example 2: Write in standard form: 201 tens + 3,009 hundreds + 21,009 tens + 1,012

Solution: 2010 + 300900 + 210090 + 1012 = ...

Practice Set I

Heat and Temperature

    a.   Ice melts at …….. and water boils at …………………

    b.   We use ……………………….. to measure our body temperature.

    c.   We use ……………….. to use quantity of heat.

    d.   Difference of upper and lower fixed point divided by 100 is called ……………………………

    e.   Only ………………… heat can be measured by using a thermometer. We cannot measure latent heat by using a thermometer.

    f.   Reading of a thermometer remains unchanged during …………… ……………… Of a matter; during such transition ice melts, water boils, steam condenses.

    g.   Light travels …………… Km in 10 seconds.

Practice Set II

1: 20% of $1/4^{th}$ of 400,800,600 = ……………….

2. Half of a quarter of 80,16,096 + $1/9^{th}$ of 81,72,099 = …………..

3. Four fifth of five million five hundred fifteen = ……………

4. Ratio of three interior angles of a triangle is 8:1:9. This is a …….. triangle.

5. What least number should be subtracted from three digit greatest number to obtain a common multiple of 2, 4 and 8?

6. 1.021 + three hundredths + fifteen thousandths = ……………….

Rename each of the following unit of time

7. 9 min = …….. s

8. 4 d = …….. h

9. 2 y= …….. mo

10. 400 y = …….. cent.

11. 42 d = …….. wk

12. 260 min = …….. h

13. 192 min = …….. h min

14. 300 wk = …….. y ………… wk

15. 7 y 5 mo = …… mo

16. 220 s = …………. min = …….. s

Things to Remember

1. We can construct 6 different three digit numbers by using digits 2, 4 and 8 only once.

    Six such numbers constructed by using digits 3, 6 and 9 are:

    369, 396, 639, 693, 963 and 936

2. There are two different types of numeration, one is Indo-Arabic system of numeration and the another one is International system of numeration. All numbers can be expressed in any of the given system of numeration.

    The given number   : 125894534
    Indo- Arabic Numeration   : 12,58,94,534
    Twelve crore, fifty-eight lakh ninety four thousand five hundred and thirty four
    The given number   : 125,894,534
    One hundred twenty five million, eight hundred ninety –four thousand five hundred and thirty four.

3. Sum total of all the interior angles of a triangle is 180^0.

4. Hour hand, minute hand and second hand of a clock complete one rotation by forming a complete angle at the center (360^0).

5. The greatest five digit number without repeating any digit twice is 98,765.

6. The smallest five digit number without repeating any digit twice is 10,234.

7. 3 must be subtracted from the greatest five digit number to make the value divisible by 4.

    $$[\ 99,999 - 3 = 99,996\ ;\ \frac{99,996}{4} = 24,999\ ;]$$

8. Numbers having only 2 factors, 1 and the number itself, are

called prime numbers. 1 is not a prime number. 2 is the smallest and only even prime number.

9. Any natural number and whole number can be represented in a number line.

10. All basic shapes having length and breadth are called 2 dimensional shapes.

11. All basic shapes having length breadth and height are called 3 dimensional shapes.

12. All basic shapes occupy a definite space.

13. All 2 dimensional shapes lie on a definite plane.

14. Two planes meet through a straight line.

15. Decimals are special types of fractions having denominators in the form of a multiple of 10.

16. Percentage is a special type of fraction having denominator 100.

17. All decimal numbers (continuing repeating types and terminating types) can be placed on the number line. Continuing non-repeating types of decimals cannot be placed on number line.

18. Clinical thermometer is graduated by using Fahrenheit (^{0}F) scale, but laboratory thermometers are graduated by using ^{0}C (Celsius) scale.

19. We can accommodate three non-overlapping triangles inside a pentagon.

20. Sum of all the interior angles of a quadrilateral is equal to two straight angles.

21. Sum of first 50 natural numbers is equal to $(50 + 1) \times \frac{50}{2}$.

22. We can draw three lines passing through two out of three non-collinear points.

Revision Works

1: Find out missing lengths: a) area $= 15$ cm^2 b) area $= 12$ m^2

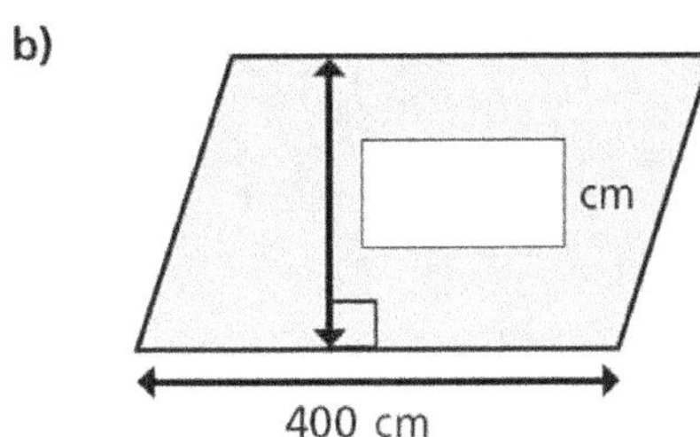

2: Calculate area of the following.

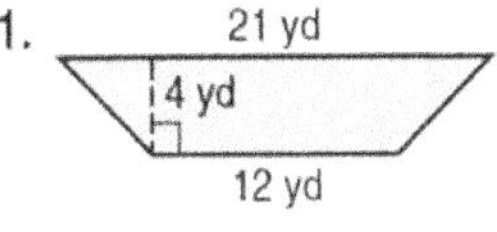

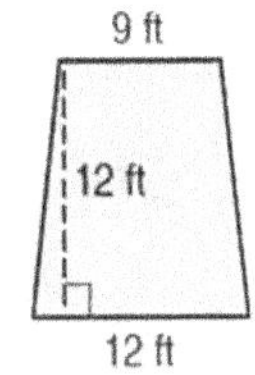

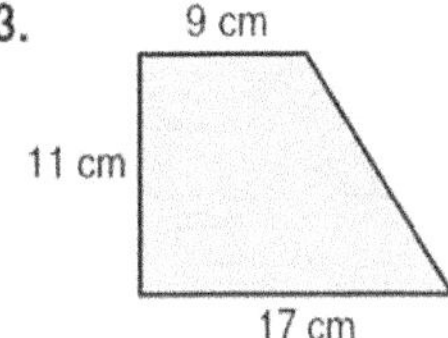

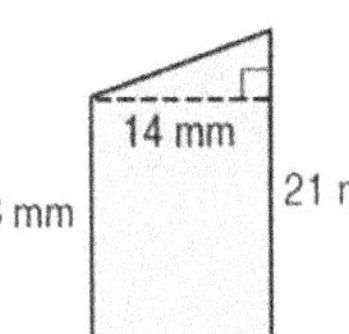

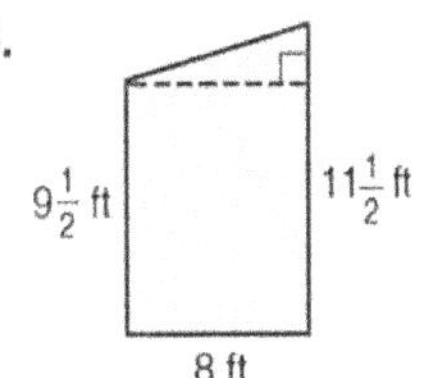

3: Rikin observed that a passenger train takes 55 seconds to cross a light post. It moves while maintaining an average speed of 36 km/h. Calculate total length oof the train.

4: Total 22 children attended a birthday paprty. Each girl drank two glasses of juice and each booys drank three glasses of juice. Boys took 31 more glasses of fruit juices than girls. How many girls attended the birthday party?

5: Half of 20,032 + quarter of 40,064 = ……………….

6: What least number should be added to smallest odd number of seven digits to obtain a common multiple of 3, 6 and 9?

7: Represent shaded parts by using fractions.

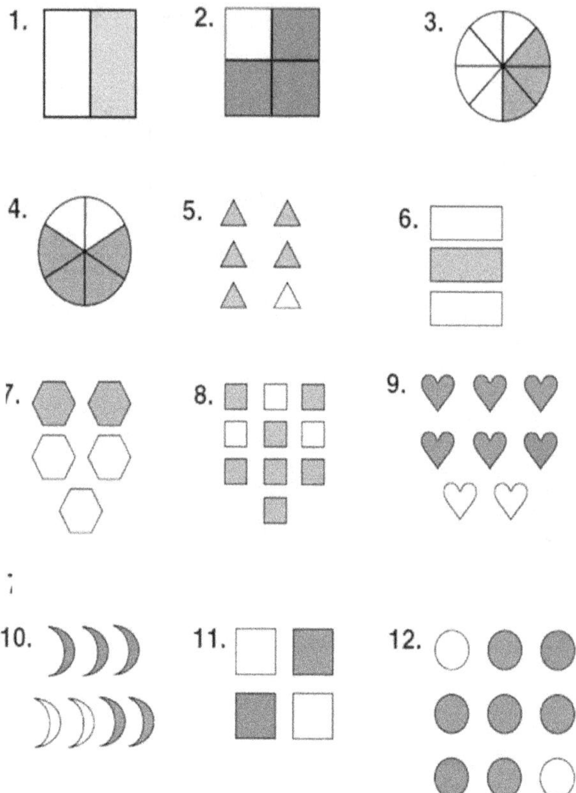

8. How many bricks each of edge 12 cm can be made by melting a cuboid of dimensions 24 cm X 30 cm X 60 cm?

9. A wall mount clock spends 2 seconds in striking 2 bells. It will spend .... seconds in striking 12 bells.

10. $1/11^{th}$ of 220,330,440 + $1/13^{th}$ of 260,390,520 = ...

11. How many edges and corners are there in a pentagonal prism?

Revision Works 2

I: Simplify the following.

1. 10% of 120   2. 50% of 46   3. 25% of 224

4. 75% of 48   5. 20% of 325   6. 30% of 80% of 2,00,000

7. 80% of 240   8. 15% of 180   9. 60% of 30% of 100,100

10. 40% of 300   11. 90% of 200   12. 35% of 50% of 120

II. Compare:

13. 29% of 2,00,000 ….. 39% of 1,02,000

14. 50% of 400 ….. 60% of 300

Solve the following:

15. Half of a quarter of a given numbers is equal to 202,303,404. Find out the number.

16. Choice of students of a school is recorded: Fine Arts (25%), French (30%), Japanese (20%), Italian (10%) and rest of the other 45 students prefer music. How many students are there?

17. In a box of 60 different cards, 12 were birthday cards, 20 were anniversary cards, 16 were teacher's day cards, and the rest were normal cards. What percent of the box of cards were normal cards?

18. After selling six boxes of fruits a shopkeeper makes a profit equal to selling price of a box. What is his gain percentage?

19. What percentage of all the natural numbers starting from 1 to 100 are multiles of 20?

20. Ananthika collected few playing cards from different sources. Half of her collection came from different friends, half of the remaining cards were from her playmates, half of the remaining gifted ones and rest of 36 cards contributed by parents. How many cards were there in her stock?

21. Piskilla forms a 2-digit number. The sum of the digits is 15 and the difference between them is 3. What are the possible numbers?

III. Calculate value of a in the following.

22. $(1\,a + 2\,a + 3\,a + \cdots \ldots \ldots 1{,}000\,a)\ X\ \left(1 - \dfrac{1}{1{,}001}\right) X\ 250\ =\ 10^{\,11}$

23. $\left(\dfrac{1}{a} + \dfrac{2}{a} + \cdots \ldots \dfrac{5{,}000}{a}\right) X\ 8\ X\ 100\ =\ 10^{10}$; here a stands for ……..

24. Sum total of three consecutive number exceeds 12,009 by 24. Find out the number.

25. (a + 2 a + 3 a + 4 a …… 2,000 a) = 2,001 X 1,000 X 21,0987.

Here $a^2 + 2a + 1 - (a - 1)^2 + 16\,a^3 =$ ……….

26. Sum total of a natural number and decimal form of its reciprocal is equal to 8.125. Find out the number.

27. Select perfect time frame for the following. (seconds, minutes, hours, days, weeks, months etc.)

a. Baseball season lasts about 7 ……..

b. Jane exercised for 15 . ……..

c. The lightning flashed for about 3 . ……..

d. Leo's cold lasted 1 . ……..

e. The circus performed 263 ? last year. ……..

f. The movie was about 2 ………… long.

28. Half of a quarter of a couple of day means ……………….. hours.

29. Hour hand of a clock moves ……. times completely around the dial in a couple of days.

30. A polygon has six sides 2 m 2 cm, 3 m 3 cm, 4 m 14 cm, 4 m 15 cm, 4 m 9 cm and 4 m 11 cm respectively. Calculate outer boundary of that polygon.

31. Diameter of a semicircular park is 210 m. Calculate outer boundary of the park; also calculate cost of fencing at the rate of Rs 320 per meter.

32.

Few Words

This book is for aspirants looking for some more practices to enhance their mathematical skills and competence. It can be used only after completing the text books and reference books recommended by the school of the fellow learner. This book accommodates all possible streams of curriculum prescribed for the students belonging to the age group of 09 to 13 years. It can even help them in gaining skills of tackling composite mathematical problems duly coined for addressing more than three and more basic skills.

Answers of individual problems are not included in this booklet. There exists a separate collection for fulfilling such purposes. Due to this reason this handbook can be used by teachers and fellow parents for assessing achievement levels of their aspirants.

This handbook provides ample scope of skill enhancement through offering series of test materials in which aspirants have to use more than one skill at a time. It will also improve the ability to think and work out own strategies of resolving mathematical problems.

There are mathematical problems which require knowledge of more than one thematic area. Such problems are incorporated in the collections of Composite worksheets. In this workbook such composite worksheets are more in number.

For all students it would be better if they acquire such skills in advance before moving through the composite worksheets.

The curriculum recommended by CBSE and ICSE are on the same format like those developed and implemented by different state level educational organisations. After integrating all such streams a common core of the curriculum is duly obtained for making the book a widely applicable one. Some of the mathematical problems are from past test papers. In some papers there may remain some questions of identical format. All such questions will be addressed only after proper understanding of the relevant theories.

Some of inter related areas are converged to bring compactness in the representation of the content areas. There may exist some types of questions in more than two places with an aspiration of exhibiting its composite nature.

This book can be followed after completion of basic studies as per the prescribed curriculum and content areas of a textbook. Additional study materials and related study notes can be taken up from this book for Olympiads and talent search examinations. Higher challenges are there for the type of questions often framed by different schools during test examinations.

Before moving through the collection of worksheets and related fields of activities it is recommended for all the students that one should go through the content areas duly provided by the authority of examinations. Students can follow this book on a regular basis to gain mastery in mathematical skills. It is also equally important for aspirants having eagerness to gain pace and momentum in the field of mathematics.

Other books in this series are as follows:

1. Handbook of Mathematics

2. Creative Mathematics Book 4 Part 1

3. Olympiad and Talent

4. Aspirations of Mathematics

5. My Own Book of School Mathematics.

6. NCERT mathematics Workbook, Class 4

Combined Worksheets

All the worksheets are prepared by taking sample questions from different content areas.

Worksheet 1

1: Convert the following expression into an equivalent fraction.

a: 20 tenths + 203 hundredths + 2,005 thousandths + 12 tenths

b: $15/19^{th}$ of 19,019 + $11/13^{th}$ of 13,013 + $16/33^{rd}$ of 33,033 = ...

c: Half of 500 multiplied by 625 and again multiplied by 1,000

2: Sum total of a number and its reciprocal is equal to 8.125. Find the number.

3: Somalia converted six digit greatest multiple of 4 into a common multiple of 5, 10 and 15 by subtracting .... from it. (Consider it as a smallest possible number.).

4: Is there any pair of number having LCM 12321 and HCF 1690?

5: What least number can be subtracted from the greatest even number of six digits to obtain a multiple of 6?

6: Sum total of five consecutive numbers is equal to third multiple 150,005. Find sum total of smallest and greatest numbers of this number series.

7: Rohit can finish half of a wall painting in 12 days and Mohan can finish quarter of the same painting in 4 days. They started working jointly to finish 7 such wall paintings. They can finish their works in ……….. days.

8: A train can cross a light post in 1 m 4 seconds while moving with a uniform speed of 72 km/h. Find time to be taken by this train to cross a tunnel of length 5 km 60 m.

9: Sneha reduced her consumption of fuel by 20% to balance price rise of fuel. Calculate the percentage increase of cost of fuel by using the above data.

10: After incorporating Joseph in a team of 11 students of average height 1 m 6 cm the average age is increased by 12 cm. Find height of John.

11: Half of a quarter of 16,064 + one seventh of 14,056 + 1/11th of 22,088 = ...

12: Simplify: $\left(1 + \frac{1}{11}\right)\left(1 + \frac{1}{12}\right) ... \left(1 + \frac{1}{1,000}\right) \div 2,002 \, X \, 121 - 101 =$ ....

13: Fifty times 5,050 divided by one fifth of 175 = ...

14: Half of one seventh of 560,070 − 400,005 = ...

15. What least number should be subtracted from five digit smallest multiple of 18 to obtain a common multiple of 3 and 9?

16. (n + 2 n + 3 n + ... 50,000 n) X 5,000 X 8 = 50,001 X 10^{12} X 12.009 ; here n = ...

17. A train takes 400 seconds to cross a light post while moving at an average speed of 72 km/h. Find out length of that train.

18. What least number should be subtracted from greatest six digit number to obtain a common multiple of 2, 4 and 8?

19. Two interior angles of a triangle are 54^0 and 43^0. Find supplementary angle of the third interior angle.

20. Quarter of 144 + half of 3,408 + one third of 3,939 = ...

21. [(1 + 2 + .. +10) ÷ 11] X 1,001 = ...

Worksheet 2

1: What fraction of all the numbers starting from 1 to 1,000 are multiples of 25?

2: Write three fractions which can be placed in between 1/3 and ¼ on a number line.

3. Half of a quarter of a number exceeds eighth multiple of 300,003 by 72. Find the number.

4: Radius of a square sized playground is equal to 21 m. Mohini completes her daily practice of jogging by encircling around it for four times. Find total distance covered by Mohini during her daily jogging.

5: A cistern can fill up a water tank in 45 minutes another cistern takes 1 h 30 m to fill up the same water tank. Both the tanks kept open to fill up the water tank. Time taken by both the cisterns jointly to fill up the water tank will be …………………..

6: Simplify: [(5.5 + 5.05 + 5.005 + 5.0005 + 5.00005 + 5.000005) − 25] ÷ 5 = ………………..

7: Cost of half a dozen banana is equal to Rs 40. Cost of 50 bananas will be Rs. ………………

8: Rijuana travels 20 m in a couple of seconds by using her car. Mohini travels by using her car with an average speed of 76 km/h. They started jointly from the origin and a gap developed in between them after half an hour. Calculate the gap developed in between them as they were travelling in the same direction.

9: Calculate the least possible time interval after which three bells toll together. These bells toll at an interval of 10 seconds, 15 seconds and 20 seconds respectively.

Write each decimal as a fraction in simplest form.

| 10. 0.9 | 11. 0.07 | 12. 0.43 | 13. 0.77 |
| 14. 0.003 | 15. 0.127 | 16. 0.45 | 17. 0.36 |

Worksheet 3

1: What least number should be added to a six digit smallest multiple of 3 to obtain a common multiple of 4, 6, 8 and 12?

2: Simplify: (1.111…+2.222… + 3.33…..+ 4.444…) 10 = ………..

3: Anthony emptied his coin bank and made a bar graph of the numbers of each type of coin. The interval he chose was 5 coins. If the graph showed 5 intervals of quarters, 2 intervals of dimes, 3 intervals of nickels, and 10 intervals of pennies, what was the total amount of money in his bank?

4: The floor of a room a hotel is 12 m long and 10 m wide. 45 tiles of 1 m square was in stock. Tiles come in market in pack of ten tiles. How many more 1m square tiles does the manager need to completely cover the floors of three such rooms?

I: 15 tiles more than 30 full pack

II: 5 tiles more than 31 full pack

III: 25 tiles more than 29 full pack

IV: 50 tiles more than 25 full pack

Select your answers

A: Only I   B: Only II   C: I, II and III   D: Only IV

5: Average of ten consecutive even numbers is 20. Is it possible to work out values of all the numbers? Find the average of first six such numbers.

6. Instead of adding 108, Ravi subtracted 100.81 from a collection of 50 find the difference of the desired result and wrong result.

7: Sum total of all the even numbers starting from 2 to 10,000 is ______

8. half of 2,626 + quarter of 3,636 + 1/7th of 1,414 = ………..

9. Ratio of three interior angles of a triangle is 2: 3: 5. Find out supplementary angle of the greatest angle.

Worksheet 4

1: Arrange the following shapes as per their increasing number of faces.

Cylinder, Sphere, Cuboid, Triangular Prism, Rectangular Pyramid.

2. A train is running at an average speed of 80 km per hour. It is covering up 4 km 4 m more in every interval of 10 minutes than that of a car. Find the average speed of the car.

3. A half filled oil container is used to store residue oil of capacity 125 liters. After filling the residue three eighth of the container remained empty. Find the capacity of the container.

4. One tenth of a container is equal to 16 cans of capacity 8 liters each. The entire container can hold ___________ liters of oil.

5. What least number must be subtracted from 219.376 to make the result exactly divisible by 219?   [Ans: 0.157]

6. A train, moving at the speed of 15 m per second, is taking 20 seconds to cross a telephone post. This train can take ________ seconds to cross a 1.5 km long platform. [Ans : 2 minutes]

7. Roshanlal can finish a work in 16 days while working 5 hours a day. He can finish the same work in ……….. days while working 4 hours a day.

8. Rani is buying light bulbs for her Christmas decorations. She buys 1020 but when she gets to the cash, she has to put back 3 hundred 13 because they are broken. How many light bulbs does Marie buy?

9. There are two combinations of packs containing pens and pencils. Packet one containing 6 pens and 5 pencils costs Rs 128. Packet B containing 5 pens and 6 pencils costs Rs 103. Calculate the cost of a new pack containing 10 pens and 10 pencils of such type?

A: Rs. 250   B: Rs. 120   C: Rs. 135   D: Rs. 210

Worksheet 5

1. $P = 515.15 - 15.51 - 1.51 - 5.11 - 1.11.$
   Find the value of $2P + 1$

2. If $a = (7.5 \times 7.5 + 37.5 + 2.5 \times 2.5)$, then find the value of
   $$\frac{a^2 + 1}{a^2 - 1} - \frac{a^2 - 1}{a^2 + 1}$$

3. A began a business with Rs 45000 and B joined after wards with Rs 30000. At the end of a year, the profit is divided in the ratio 2:1. When did B join ?

4. An employer reduces the number of his employees in the ratio 7: 5 and increases their wages in the ratio 15 : 28. State whether his bill of total wages increase or decrease and in what ratio.

5. In three vessels, the ratio of water and milk is 6 : 7, 5 : 9 and 8 : 7 respectively. If the mixtures of the three vessels are mixed together, then what will be the ratio of water and milk ?

6. A drum contains 20 liters of a paint. From this, 2 liters of paint is taken out and replaced by 2 liters of oil. Again 2 liters of this mixture is taken out and replaced by 2 liters of oil. If this operation is performed once again, then what would be the final ratio of paint and oil in the drum ?

7. If $a : (b + c) = 1 : 3$ and $c : (a + b) = 5 : 7$, then $b : (a + c) = $ __.

8. 15 men, 18 women and 12 boys working together earned Rs 2070. If the daily wages of a man, a woman and a boy are in the ratio 4 : 3 : 2, the daily wages (in Rs) of 1 man, 2 women and 3 boys are ___________________.

9. Ratio of the incomes of A, B and C last year was 3 : 4 : 5. The ratio of their individual incomes during the last year and this

year are 4 : 5, 2 : 3 and 3 : 4 respectively. If the sum of their present incomes is Rs 78800, then find the present individual income of A, B and C.

10. 10% of A = 20% of B = 30% of C. Find the value $\frac{AB+BC+AC}{ABC}$.

11. $\frac{1}{10}$ of a number x exceeds $\frac{1}{15}$ of another number y by 5. Find the value of P.

$$P = \frac{3x-2y}{3x+2y} + \frac{3x+2y}{3x-2y} .$$

12. Tap A can fill a tank in 30 minutes and tap B can fill the same tank in 40 minutes. Both the tap can fill the tank jointly in _____ mins.

13. In two alloys, copper and zinc are related in the ratio of 4 : 1 and 1 : 3. 10 kg of 1st alloy, 16 kg of 2nd alloy and some of pure copper are melted together. An alloy was obtained in which the ratio of copper to zinc was 3 : 2. Find the weight of the new alloy ?

14. Railway fares of 1st, 2nd and 3rd classes between two stations were in the ratio 8 : 6 : 3. The fares of 1st and 2nd class were subsequently reduced by $\frac{1}{6}$ and $\frac{1}{12}$ respectively. If during a year, the ratio between the passengers of 1st, 2nd and 3rd classes was 9 : 12 : 26 and the total amount collected by the sale of tickets was Rs 1088, the collection from the passengers of 1st class was ______________.

15. Salary of Mark is increased by 16%. His previous salary was _____ % less than that of the increased salary.

16. Solve   the   following   equation   :
$$\frac{11}{144} X \frac{12}{169} X \frac{13}{121} X \frac{132}{341} X \frac{682}{1001} X \frac{13}{19} =$$

Worksheet 6

1. How many different possible solutions can satisfy the following equation?

$$(x^2 - 5x + 5)^{(x^2 - 12x + 45)} = 1$$

2. A three digit number is such that the number N = 100a + 10b + c. Again the number is a product of two factors b and 10c + b. Find the number.

3. An integer is a palindrome when the same number is obtained when digits are reversed. 121,253, 132 etc. are all palindromes. Find a number in such that n^2 will be a palindrome with 6 digits.

4. Sum of the digits of a smallest possible number N is 18. Sum total of all the digits of 2N is 27. Find out the value of N.

5. What least number must be added to a six digit smallest number to make the number 1210214 divisible by 74.

6. Evaluate the following.

$$(\sqrt{2} + \sqrt{11} + \sqrt{13})(\sqrt{2} + \sqrt{11} - \sqrt{13})(\sqrt{2} - \sqrt{11} + \sqrt{13})(-\sqrt{2} + \sqrt{11} - \sqrt{13})$$

7. Each interior angles of a heptagon is obtuse. Angles are multiples of 9. Find the degrees of sums of the two largest angles.

8. A three digit number is multiplied by 3 and 1 added to it, then the result is a reverse of the original number. Find the original number.

[Hints: (100 a+ 10b + c)X3 +1 = 100c + 10b + a   100 a+ 10b + c = ?]

9. If $ab = a^b$ and $\dfrac{a}{b} = a^{3b}$, find b^{-a}

10. $0.33 < \dfrac{m}{n} < \dfrac{1}{3}$. Find the smallest possible value of n to satisfy the above mentioned relationship.

11. Find the smallest seven digit number which is divisible by 11. What are the two digits will be there in tens and ones place of that number?

12. Mark deposited $ 23,500 in his savings bank account which was offering 4% simple interest per year. Find the amount that Mark will obtain after a tenure of 4 years and 5 months.

13. -4.5 + 5.64 + _______ = 0. Make this equation true.

14. Solve the following

    a. $7 \times 20 - 2 \times 4 + 3^2 + 12 \div 4$

    b. $\dfrac{\left(\sqrt[3]{0.125} + \sqrt[2]{.0064}\right)}{\sqrt[3]{1.331} - \sqrt[2]{0.0081}}$

    c. If $x + \dfrac{1}{x} = 9$ then find the value of

    d. $(2x - 9)^2$

15. A shopkeeper purchased 16 dozen bananas at the rate of Rs 24 per dozen and found that 5% of his stock became non sellable. Rest of his stock was sold at the rate of Rs 30 per dozen. Find out the rate percent of his gain or loss incurred in this business.

16. Simplify the following: $7[120 - 2(4 + 3)^2 + 12] \div 2$

17. What fraction of all the natural numbers from 1 to 200 are multiples of 25?

18. Write a smallest five digit number which is a common multiple of 2, 4, 6 and 8.

19. Ratio of 5 m 5 cm and 2 m 2 cm = ………………

20. 11th multiple of 1,001 + 9th multiple of 2,002 = …………

Worksheet 7

1. $X = 0.3333... + 0.4444 + 0.9999..$ Find the value of $\dfrac{x+1}{x-1} + \dfrac{x-1}{x+1}$

2. Shweta joined a Yoga Centre and her body weight was reduced from 76 kg to 65.6 kg. Find the percentage weight loss that she made during the tenure of her exercises.

3. Base of a triangle is reduced by 5% and its height is increased by 5%. Find the total percentage increase or decrease in the area of the triangle.

4. All the five sides of a regular pentagon is 12 cm each and apothem is 8 cm. find the area of this pentagon.

   [Hints: The apothem of a regular polygon is a line segment from the center of the polygon perpendicular to a side.]

5. A ___________ angle is an angle with its vertex at the center of a circle whose sides are radii.

6. Calculate the total surface area of a cuboidal room of dimension 8mX6mX5m.

7. Arrange the following values in ascending and descending order:

8. What is the next number in the following sequence: 2, 4, 8, 16, ______, _______ ?

9. Write 3/7 and 5/9 in their corresponding decimal form. What are the common things in both the decimal form?

10. The cost of a camera is reduced by 10% to make it equivalent to another camera having a selling price calculated on the basis of 10% profit on the cost price of 21,850. Find the original cost price of the first camera.

11. 3% of 600 is __________ less than 5% of 500.

12. A college offers 25% of all seats of the Graduate programme to local candidates. Last year 125 local candidates got admission in that college. Find the total seat capacity available in that college for Graduate programmes.

13. A shopkeeper offers two discounts of value 5% and 8% on an item. Calculate the equivalent discount of two such consecutive discounts.

14. Population of a city increases at the rate of 10% of previous year's population. Calculate the population of a city in which population before two years was 125,000. Also calculate the population of that city after two year.

15. Parking lot of a school is represented by an expression: $\frac{3}{4}\left(2(2 + 4k) + 2\left(3 + \frac{5}{6} k\right)\right)$

Convert this expression in simplest form.

16. 30% of a number is equal to 40% of another number. Calculate the ratio of both the number.

17. $P = \sqrt{20} - \sqrt{20} + \sqrt{20} - \sqrt{20} \dots\dots\dots \infty$. Find the value of $P^2 + 3P -20$.

18. $\sqrt{15} = 3.88$. Find the value of $\sqrt{\frac{5}{3}}$.

19. A person moved on towards countryside at 6 O'Clock. He travelled certain distance at an average speed of 4 km/h, and then another distance at 3 km/h and again a distance at an average speed of 6 km/h. After reaching he turned back and reached the place from where he had started. That time it was 12 noon in his wrist watch. Find the distance travelled by him. [Ans: 24 km]

Worksheet 8

1. A 500 m long train crosses a telephone post in 20 seconds. The same train crosses a platform in 90 seconds. Find the length of that platform.

   [Ans: 1 km 750 m]

2. Two trains of length 200 m and 400 m respectively. They cross each other in 15 seconds while moving in opposite direction and 75 seconds while moving in the same direction. Find speed of both the train. [Ans: 24 m/sec. and 16m/sec]

3. Normally Nikita performs her morning walk at an average speed of 12 km/h. Today her speed was $5/6^{th}$ of the average. Because of this reason she was late by 10 minutes. Find the normal time that she spends daily for morning walk. [Ans: 50 minutes]

4. Speed of a train was reduced from 65 km/h to 50 km/h. Earlier this train was taking 1.5 hours to cover certain distance. Now it will take __________ minutes more to cover the same distance.

   [Ans : 27]

5. In a kilometer race A beats B by 100 meters, B beats C by 100 meters. A beats C by ____ meters. [Ans : 190 meters]

6. A bus moves a distance without stoppage at an average speed of 420 km/h. With stoppages the same distance is covered by that bus at an average speed of 28 km/h. find the hourly stoppage time of that bus.

   [Ans: 20 minutes]

7. A 300 m long car is running at an average speed of 90 km/h. another car of length 200 m is running in the same direction at an average speed of 60 km/h. Find the time taken by the first car to overtake the second one.

   [Ans: 50 seconds]

8. Length of a train is half that of a km long bridge. A train clears this bridge in 2 minutes. Find the speed of that train.

   [Ans: 45 km/h]

9. A train of length 110 m passes a man, who is walking against it at an average speed of 6 km/h, in 6 seconds. The speed of this train is

   __________.

[Ans: 60 km/h]

10. A boat running upstream takes hours 48 minutes to cover certain distance. It takes 4 hours to cover the same distance running downstream. Find the ratio between the speed of the boat and speed of the stream.   [Ans: 8:3]

11. What fraction of numbers in between 1 and 50 are prime numbers?

12. What least number must be added to 1029.1016 to make it exactly divisible by 1029?

13. Third multiple of a prime number which is greater than 90 and less than $100 =$ ______.

14. Find the value of $\dfrac{m^2+1}{m^2-1} - \dfrac{m^2-1}{m^2+1}$,

$$\text{if } \sqrt[3]{m} = \left(1 - \tfrac{1}{2}\right)\left(1 - \tfrac{1}{3}\right)\cdots\left(1 - \tfrac{1}{1000}\right)$$

15. If $\dfrac{2}{1 + \dfrac{1}{1 + \dfrac{x}{1-x}}} = 1$, then find the value of
$$\left(\dfrac{x+1}{x-1}\right)^2 + \left(\dfrac{x-1}{x+1}\right)^2 .$$

16. Find the value of x if $x^2 + x + 1 = 0$.

17. Capacity of three cans is in the ratio of 1:2:3. Smallest can holds 200 ml less than a liter of any liquid. Find capacity of all the cans.

18. Find the two largest numbers of four digits having 531 as their HCF.

19. Quarter of a natural number exceeds five digit smallest number by 201. Find the number.

20. Three seventh of 14,084 added to fourth multiple of 10,001. Find out the number.

21. 30% of $1,010 + 40\%$ of $2,020 + 50\%$ of $1,010 = \ldots\ldots\ldots\ldots$

22. Ratio of two interior angles other than right angle of a right triangle is 3:5. Find out magnitude of both the angles.

Worksheet 9

1. 15 men, 18 women and 12 boys working together earned Rs 2070. If the daily wages of a man, a woman and a boy are in the ratio 4 : 3 : 2, the daily wages (in Rs) of 1 man, 2 women and 3 boys are ___________ .

2. Bolton started business investing Rs 8000. Three months later John joined him investing Rs 6000. If they make a profit of Rs 5100 at the end of the year, how much should be John's share ?

3. The employer reduces the number of employees in the ratio 9 : 8 and increases their wages in the ratio 14 : 15. If the previous wage bill was Rs 189000, what is the amount by which the new wage bill will increase or decrease ?

4. Rs 2010 are to be divided among A, B and C in such a way that if A gets Rs 5, than B must get Rs 12 and if B gets Rs 4, then C must get Rs 5.50. The share of C will exceed that of B by ___________ .

5. Find the ratio of 12% 0f 12 and 15% of 15.

6. What least number must be added to 1968 to make it divisible by 11?

7. A bottle is full of spirit. One-third of it is taken out and then an equal amount of water is poured into the bottle to fill it. This operation is done four times. Find the final ratio of spirit and water in the bottle.

8. The students in three classes are in the ratio 2 : 3 : 5. If 40 students are increased in each class, the ratio changes to 4 : 5 : 7. Originally the total number of students was ___________ .

9. Find the least number which when divided by 12, 24, 36 and 40 leaves a remainder 1, but when divided by 7 leaves no remainder.

10. A drum contains 20 l of a paint. From this, 2 l of paint is taken out and replaced by 2 l of oil. Again 2 l of this mixture is taken out and replaced by 2 l of oil. If this operation is performed once again, then what would be the final ratio of paint and oil in the drum ?

11. 100 ml 80% alcohol and 150 ml 90% alcohol mixed up properly to make a new combination having strength _______ %.

12. Concentrations of three solutions A, B and C are 20%, 30% and 40% respectively. They are mixed in the ratio 3 : 5 : x resulting in a solution of 30% concentration. Find x.

13. Ratio of incomes of A, B and C last year was 3 : 4 : 5. The ratios of their individual incomes of last year and this year are 4 : 5, 2 : 3 and 3 : 4 respectively. If the sum of their present incomes is Rs 78800. Find the present individual income of B.

14. Ravi earns 25% more than Nisha, gut his earning is 18% less than that of Faquir. Find the ratio of their earnings.

15. The cost of manufacturing a TV set is made up of material costs, labour costs and overhead costs. These costs are in the ratio 4 : 3 : 2. If materials costs and labour costs rise by 10% and 8% respectively, while the overhead costs reduce by 5%, what is the percentage increase in the total cost of the TV set ?

16. A number is increased by 20% and then again by 20%. By what per cent should the increased number be reduced so as to get back the original number ?

17. The number of employees working in a farm is increased by 25% and the wages per head are decreased by 25%. If it results in x% decrease in total wages, then the value of x is ___________ .

18. A candidate who gets 20% marks in an examination fails by 30 marks but another candidate who gets 32%, gets 42 marks more than the pass marks. The percentage of pass marks is _________ .

19. In the expression xy2 , the values of both variables x and y are decreased by 20%. By this the value of the expression will be decreased by ___________________ .

20. In an examination Nancy obtained 20% more marks than Hary but are 10% less than Della. If the marks obtained by Hary are 1080, find the percentage of marks obtained by Nancy, if the full marks are 2000.

21. A student took five papers in an examination, where the full marks were the same for each papers, this marks in these papers were in the proportion 6 : 7 : 8 : 9 : 10. In all the papers together, the candidate obtained 60% of the total marks. Then, the number of papers in which he got more than 50% marks is equal to ___________________ .

22. A tax payer is exempted of income tax for the first Rs 100000 of his annual income but for the rest of the income, he has to pay a tax at the rate of 20%. If he paid Rs 3160 as income tax for a year, his monthly income is _________________

23. A house-owner was having his house painted. He was advised that he would require 25 kg of paint. Allowing for 15% wastage and assuming that the paint is available in 2 kg cans, what would be the cost of paint purchased, if one can costs $ 2 ?

24. By receiving 5% less vote than the winner of a by-election a candidate received only 12% of the total vote. Find the ration of votes received by both the candidate.

25. In an election, 10% of the people in the voter's list did not participate. 60 votes were declared invalid. There are only two candidates A and B. A defeated B by 308 votes. It has found that 47% of the people listed in the voters' list voted for A. Find the total number of votes polled.

26. Prices register an increase of 10% on food grains and 15% on other items of expenditure. If the ratio of an employee's expenditure on food grains and other items be 2 : 5, by how much should his salary be increased in order that he may maintain the same level of consumption as before, his present salary being Rs 2590.

27. What per cent is the least rational number of the greatest rational number, if $\frac{11}{12}, \frac{2}{3}, \frac{3}{4}, \frac{5}{9}$ and $\frac{17}{18}$ are arranged in ascending order ?

28. If$\frac{1}{891}$ = 0.001122334455667788 99... Then what is the value of $\frac{198}{891}$?

29. If$\frac{p}{q}$ = 2.525252525 …… then find the value of $\frac{p^2+q^2}{pq}$.

30. A flower garden is 22.50 m long. Sheela wants to make a border along one side using bricks that are 0.25 m long. How many bricks will be needed?

31. The time taken by Rohan in five different races to run a distance of 500 m was 3.20 minutes, 3.37 minutes, 3.29 minutes, 3.17 minutes and 3.32 minutes. Find the average time taken by him in the races.

Worksheet 10

1. Anuradha can do a piece of work in 6 hours. What part of the work can she do in 1 hour, in 5 hours, in 6 hours?

2. Ravi can do half of a work alone in 12 days, Munish can do quarter of the same work in 18 days and Roushan can complete one tenth of the work in 2 days. If they all join hands to complete the same work then by what time the entire work will be finished?

3. What is the ratio of two numbers whose difference is 45, and the quotient of the greater number by the lesser number is 4 ?

4. Raj travels 360 km on three fifths of his petrol tank. How far would he travel at the same rate with a full tank of petrol?

5. It takes 17 full specific type of trees to make one tonne of paper. If there are 221 such trees in a forest, then what fraction of forest will be used to make; (a) 5 tonnes of paper. (b) 10 tonnes of paper? To save $7/13^{th}$ part of the forest how much of paper we have to save?

6. 23% of a number is equal to the thousandth multiple of 92. Find three fifth of that number.

7. All the multiples of 9 are also multiples of ______, but all the multiples of ______ are not necessarily a multiple of 9.

8. Sum total of digits of ones and hundreds place is equal to the digit located at tens place. Number formed by last two digits is a greatest possible multiple of 4. Find the reciprocal of that number.

9. Municipal Corporation of a city has decided to organize plantation works beside a 25 km long road by placing trees beside both the sides of the road at an interval of 50 m. find the total number of trees that can be planted. Also find the cost of maintaining those plants at a rate of $ 2 for every 5 plants.

10. Half of a quarter of 98 = _______.

11. Three bells toll at an interval of 12 seconds, 36 seconds and 45 seconds. After what time interval do they toll together? How many times do they toll together in a gap of three hours?

12. A train moving with a uniform speed of 72 km/h took 2.5 minutes to cross a light post. Find the time taken by it to cross a 1.8 km long platform.

13. Find the value of $\sqrt{272^2 - 128^2}$

14. The square root of 0.4444…. is ____________.

15. 4320 X p is a perfect cube value. Find the value of $p^2 + 3p + 9$

16. $\sqrt[3]{4\frac{12}{125}}$ = x. Find the value of $3x^2 + 4x + 5$

17. $x^3 - 2mx\,2 + 16$ is divisible by x + 2. Find the value of m.

18. $2x^4 - px^3 + 3x^2 + 3x - 2$ is exactly divisible by $x^2 - 3x + 2$.

    Find the value of $p^2 + 3p + 17$.

Worksheet 11

1. Three athletes completed their rounds in 18 seconds, 24 seconds and 44 seconds, respectively. After how many seconds will they be together at the starting point?

2. Arrange in ascending and descending order .
   12.12, 28.7%, 121 hundredths, (21 + 0.21 + 1.012), 21% of 60

3. What least number must be added to 132.98 to make it divisible by 8?

4. Simplify: $6\frac{2}{9} + 2\frac{7}{9} - 4\frac{3}{11} + 1\frac{3}{11}$

5. 25% of 80 =

6. Simplify : $78 - [5 + 3 \text{ of } (25 - 2 \times 10)]$

7. Simplify :$78-[24-16-\{5-(4-1)\}]$

8. $\sqrt{a} = 9$; *Find the value of* $\frac{a+1}{a-1} - \frac{a-1}{a+1}$

9. $\frac{21}{39} \times \frac{78}{63} \times \frac{39}{49} \times \frac{63}{13} \times \frac{121}{270} =$

10. Mohan reached his office by 15 minutes late. It was 11:28 A.M. What was his office time?

11. While calculating perimeter of her garden Ratna calculated the length and breadth of the garden. It was 1500 m long and 600 m wide. ____ times the sum total of length and ________ will be the perimeter of the garden. Find the perimeter in km.

12. For a punch bowl, Carin needs a block of ice with a volume of at least 125 cubic inches. She has a cube of ice that is five inches on each side. Write the volume of the cube using a base and exponents. Then write it in standard form. Is the block of ice big enough? Remember that volume is calculated by multiplying length times width times height.

13. Tickets to the school play cost Rs 300 for adults and Rs 200 for students. If 235 adults and 322 students attended the play, write an expression that shows the total amount of money made on ticket sales. Then simplify the expression.

14. During vacation you spent Rs 127 out of Rs 250. There was another 500 rupees note with you. Find the money left with you.

15. The Akshi Kaikyo suspension bridge in Japan has a span of 6,570 feet. The Humber suspension bridge in England has a span of 4,626 feet. How much longer is the Humber suspension bridge than the Akshi Kaikyo suspension bridge?

16. Julio increases the laps he runs by three laps each day. If he begins on Monday running 4 laps, how many laps will he run on Wednesday at his current rate?

17. Adam is starting a business to take people on hot-air balloon rides. He knows that to carry 2 people, the balloon must have a volume of about 60,000 cubic feet. For his business, he wants a balloon that will carry 4 people. He calculates that the balloon must have a volume of 120,000 cubic feet. Is his answer reasonable? Explain.

18. _________ is the only natural number having only one factor.

19. A ___________ has no end point, a ______ has only one end point and a ______ ___________ has two endpoints.

20. A circular wire is reshaped to form a square of 20 cm side. What was the circumference of that circle?

21. Find the difference of areas of two squares having sides 30 cm and 40 cm respectively.

22. A swimming pool measures 50 m by 20 m. The manager plans to construct a cemented road around the pool, which should measure 4 m wide. What is the area of the cemented road?

23. A triangle having more than one ________ angle or more than one ______ angle is not possible.

24. A regular heptagon has ____ lines of symmetry.

25. A hexagon having only one lines of _______ is possible.

26. $5 \times 39 = 5 \times ($ _________ $+$ ______ $)$

Worksheet 12

1: Find the digit present in the thousands place in the product

a. $(11011 \div 11) \times 0.7 \qquad = P;$
b. $(29029 \div 1001) \times 0.11 \quad = Q;$
c. $(1010101 \div 101) \times 0.005 = R;$
d. $(3090 \div 103) \times 0.08 \qquad = S;$

$P = 700.7 \qquad Q = 3.29 \qquad R = 50.005 \quad S = 2.4$

Statements:

I.   They have values up to thousandths place in their like decimal from.
II. If arranged in ascending order, then Q comes at last.
III. All the results of P, Q, R and S are in decimal form.
IV. Sum total of the greatest and the smallest value is equal to a number which is 3.1 more than the seventh multiple of three digit smallest number.

Which of the above statements are not correct?

Options: A: Only I, III and IV   B: Only II, III and IV

C: Only II   D: Only IV

2: 20% of 30% of 1,00,100 + 30% of 50% of 2,00,200 = …………..

3. Half of a quarter of 8,008 + one third of one fifth of 15,015 = ………

4. Sum of five consecutive natural numbers is equal to 5,00,015. Find out the smallest number.

5. A pair of water tanks of capacity 300 l and 500 l respectively are filled up by a cistern in half of an hour. Three such cisterns are used to fill up three pairs of such water tanks. Calculate total time taken up jointly by cisterns.

6. After adding 0.125 to a decimal number the sum total becomes a decimal number having a position in the middle of 14 and 17. Find the place of that original number on the number line.

Statements:
  I.   There are more than two options possible for solving the same problem.
  II. Sum total of both the numbers to be subtracted respectively from thousands place and thousandths place will be always same.
  III. We must go for adding all the digits of the number before verifying it by using divisibility rule.
  IV. This problem can be solved without doing the actual division.

Which of the following statements are true?

A: Only II and IV   B: Only I and III

C: Only III   D: All

7: What must be subtracted from the thousands place and tens place of the following number to make it a multiple of 9?

168,213

Options: ____ from thousandths place and ___ from tenths place.

8. Richimon can finish a work in 7 days while working 8 hours a day. He preferred working seven hours a day to finish the same work in …. Days.

9. Sum of seven consecutive natural numbers is equal to 7,028. Find out the smallest number.

10. Half of a quarter of a natural number is equal to 10,001. Find out the number.

Worksheet 13

1. Points located on same line are called ______________ points.
2. A line has no ________________ but a line segment has ___ such ______ ____________.
3. A ________ can be extended endlessly in any one direction.
4. A ______ can be extended endlessly in both the directions.
5. 32 hundreds + 32 hundredths = ____________.
6. Instead of writing 321 thousands Rita has written 3 lakhs 12 thousands. Find the difference between the original and the derived answer.
7. Which natural number is having only one factor?
8. 21 tenths = ______________ hundredths.
9. Half of a gross = ________ dozens.
10. Total cost of 5 pens and 6 pencils is Rs. 145. Total cost of 6 pens and 5 pencils is Rs. 251. Find individual cost of a pen and a pencil. Also find the total cost of 5 pens and 3 pencils.
11. List all the factors of 16. Find the sum total of all these factors.
12. 5 km 5 m = ______________ m
13. Sam has a collection of 963 comic books. What are the five different ways Sam could divide his comic books into equal groups?
14. Sum total of all the factors of 6 = ________. This sum total is ____ times greater than the number itself.
15. A study table is 2 m long and 1.5 m wide. Another large table is thrice as long and twice as wide as the study table. What is the area of both the table?
16. Cost of fencing a square shaped garden at the rate of Rs. 120.00 per m was Rs. 48,000.00. Find the length of a side of that garden.
17. At the end of the party, the kids broke open the gift packs. When they assembled all the candy, Bill got 9 pieces. Sara got 3 times as many pieces as Bill. Nitin got one third of the number of candies gathered by Bill. Which of the statements depicted below are true?

I.   They have collected total number of candies which is also equal to third multiple of 3.

II.   Sara got 4 times more than Nitin.

III.   Share of Nitin and Bill was 15 less than that of Sara.

IV.   Sara got 9 times more candy than that of Nitin.

18. A wall mount clock takes 2 seconds to toll 2 bells at 2 a.m. Find the time by that clock to toll 11 bells at 11 a.m.

19. What least number must be subtracted from 129.013 to make it a multiple of 129?

20. Which value can repeat itself even after multiplying it by itself?

21. Romanika counted a bundle of sheets, excluding that of top 15 ones, as 132. She has placed 21 sheets in to the printer. How many sheets were there in all?

22. Monika calculated 15th multiple of 5 added to 5th multiple of 15. Find the digit that she might have in the one's place of the product.

23. Compare areas of two circles of 21 cm and 28 cm respectively.

24. Two concentric circles of radius 28 cm and 35 cm will enclose a ring like area of _______ sq. cm.

25. _________ non overlapping triangles can be fitted inside a hexagon.

26. How is 106.076 written in word form?

____

27. Write 16 tenths and 16 thousandths in standard form?

____

28. Pallavi prepared a sweet - dish by using 29 g sugar. She used 5 kg 800 g sugar for preparing similar types of sweet dishes for a kitty party. Find out number of sweet dishes she prepared for the party.

29. (p + 2 p + ….. 1,200 p) – 600 X 123,432 = 1,200 X 300 X 246,864.

30. Rikin covered 14 km 14 m in two hours while jogging around a circular track. Find out total time taken by him to cross the playground by following diameter of the playground.

31. 21st multiple of 100,200,300 = ………..... + 21 X 10^{8}.

Worksheet 14

1. What least number must be subtracted from a three digit greatest number to make it a common multiple of 2, 4 and 8?

2. Find the arithmetic mean of 21, 32 , -74 and 1029.

3. Find the arithmetic mean of first 100 natural numbers.

4. Arithmetic mean of three consecutive odd numbers is 27. Find all the three odd numbers.

5. Submit your answer

6. The average of 199 numbers is 1050. From these numbers average of first 99 members   is 900. Find the average of the remaining numbers.

7. A 132 m long train takes 20 seconds to cross a light post. Find its average speed in km/h. If the same train moves continuously for 45 minutes then the distance covered by it will be ………… Km.

8. 8. Fractions like ½, 1/3, ¼, 1/8, 1/12,   are also called _______________ fractions.

9. 9. Difference between 0.005 and 0.05 = _____

10. Expand: 1232.4054 =

11. Expand: 1043,546 =

12. $\dfrac{21}{100} + \dfrac{132}{1000} + \dfrac{4321}{10000} =$ _______________

13. $\dfrac{11}{144} \times \dfrac{12}{121} \times \dfrac{11}{139} \times \dfrac{13}{125} \times \dfrac{12}{25} =$

14. 10,000 + 32 hundreds + 29 tens = _____________.

15. An ice cream truck began its daily route with 95 gallons of ice cream. The truck driver sold 78% of the ice cream. How many gallons of ice cream were sold?

16. In a survey of 22,000 people, 14,300 responded that salary was the most important consideration in their ideal career. What

percent of the people felt that salary was not the most important consideration?

17. Forty-nine percent of all people who buy running shoes don't run at all. Assuming 340,000 people buy running shoes, how many will use them to run in?

18. In a month Mark makes a 22% down payment on a home in Mumbai . What was the purchase price of the home if her down payment is Rs. 35,200?

19. A family wants to keep the expenditure on sugar intact in the condition of a 20% increase in the cost of sugar. The family will curtail the consumption of sugar by _____ % for doing the same.

20. What percent of hour is equal to 76 seconds?

21. Niharika wanted to give half of a quarter of Choco bar to her friend and half of the remaining Choco bar to her younger sister. Her younger sister will receive _____% of the entire Choco bar.

22. Angles having a common arm and a common vertex are called adjacent angles.

23. Every 2nd, 5th and 10th visitor of a shopping complex receives gifts. How often do three visitors at a time will receive gifts?

24. Before last Saturday there was a rain. Weather station speculated advent of another rain after a couple of fortnight. Which of the forthcoming day would be a rainy day?

25. A circular ring was reshaped to design a square of side 39 cm. what was the circumference of the ring?

26. Sum total of five consecutive natural numbers is equal to 250,750,515. Find out the smallest number.

27. Half of a quarter of a natural number is equal to 100,200,302. Find out the number.

28. Maximum and minimum temperature of a city duly recorded in a day were 21^0 C and 39^0 C. Find out the corresponding increase of temperature in ^{0} F.

Worksheet 15

1. In an assignment 45 mathematical problems were given to all the students. Bandana can solve 30 mathematical problems in an hour. Her brother Rachit can solve $4/5^{th}$ of all problems in 40 minutes. Rohini can solve $8/9^{th}$ of these assignments in 50 minutes. Arrange these students in accord to their speed of calculations.

2. Bhavini covered $8/15^{th}$ of the entire track of a race in 80 minutes. She has another 1.5 km to go. Find the additional time that she need to finish her race without changing her speed. Also find her speed.

3. Marina added 20% of 120 and 40 % of 140 to obtain a number. If 30% of 30 is added to it, it will become a prime number having only two factors, 1 and the number itself. Find out that prime number.

4. Rohini prepared a cup of 200 ml, which can hold water equal to $1/11^{th}$ of a bowl, $1/25^{th}$ of a can and $1/100^{th}$ of a bucket. Calculate the total capacity of all the containers.

5. The difference of the length of the geometry box and scale of Andrea is 6.2 cm. sum total of both the length is 30 cm. find the length of both the object.

6. Mohan and Ravi prepared a Robotic toy which can cover a distance of 173 cm in 20 stepping. Calculate the distance covered by that robot in 180 stepping.

7. The predecessor of a five digit smallest number is the _________ digit greatest number.

8. Four electric lights are turned on at the same time. First one blinks every 4 seconds, second one blinks every 6 seconds, third one blinks every 8 seconds and the fourth one blinks every 12 seconds. In 60 seconds, how many times will they blink at the same time?

9. Seventh multiple of a number exceeds 14,009 by 40. Find out the number.

Worksheet 16

1. $(a + 2a + 3a + \ldots\ldots 900a) = 901 \times 450 \times 21{,}098{,}123$. Find out the value of a.

2. A chimp is taking a multiple-choice test. Of course the chimp can't read and is guessing for every question. If there are 4 choices for each question, and there are 84 questions on the test, how many questions can we expect the chimp to answer correctly?

   (hint: There is a 25% chance that the chimp will guess correctly.)

3. First tap can fill a water tank in 30 minutes and second tap can empty the half filled tank in 1.5 hours. By what time the empty tank will be filled up if both the tap kept open?

4. After increasing the selling price of an item by 10% the profit percent on that item is increased from 12% to 15%. Find the ratio of Cost Price and Selling Price of that item.

5. A merchant paid $500 for a table. He then marked it $820. If he then allowed the buyer a 25% discount, how much was the selling price?

6. A sofa cost a merchant $500. He priced the sofa so that he could allow a customer a 25% reduction from the marked price and still make a 23% profit.

7. Certain bank offers a deposit scheme at a simple rate of interest under which any principal doubles itself in ten years of time. Find the rate of interest.

8. If $\dfrac{1}{x} = \dfrac{1}{y} = \dfrac{1}{z} = \sqrt[3]{81}$, $p = \dfrac{xy+yz+zx}{xyz}$, then $p^3 - 1 = \underline{}$.

9. Sum of four consecutive natural number exceeds fourth multiple of six digit smallest number by 22.

10. 30% of 40% 0f 50% of 100,200,300 = ………………

Worksheet 17

1. Kavita had a piece of rope of length 9.5 m. She needed some small pieces of rope of length 1.9 m each. How many pieces of the required length will she get out of this rope?

2. In a survey of 22,000 people, 14,300 responded that watching T.V. was the most important consideration in their daily life. What percent of the people felt that watching T.V. was not the most important consideration?

3. Three boys earned a total of Rs 64.54 less than Rs. 300. What was the average amount earned per boy?

4. 45% of a number is 10 less than a hundred. Find the number.

5. Ravi earned $ 90 in a week. Calculate his annual income.

6. Interior angles of a triangle are in the ratio of 1:2:3. Find all the angles.

7. What least number must be added to the 7 digit greatest number to make it divisible by 11?

8. A shopkeeper issued three consecutive discounts of 10% on certain purchase. Find the single equivalent discount.

9. This number is the reciprocal of itself. It is also the only factor of itself. Find the number.

10. Find a natural number which is also a multiplicative inverse of 0.125.

11. 7 tenths is _______________ more than 17 hundredths.

12. One third of a number exceeds the three digit greatest number by 18. Find one fourth of that number.

13. Selling Price of 6 apples is equal to Cost Price of 8 apples. Find the gain percentage.

14. What least number must be added to the sex digit greatest number to make it divisible by 8?

15. Cost of a pen and a pencil is $ 6. Cost of 3 pens and 5 pencils is $ 22. Find the cost of 5 pens and 7 pencils. Also find the cost of a pencil.

16. Reshma uses ¾ m of cloth to stitch a shirt. How many shirts can she make with 12 m cloth?

17. 20% of a natural number exceeds 400,600,800 by 60. Find out the number.

18. Tamanna prepapred a model by using 45% of clay she had in stock. 39% of clay is used by her to prepare another model. Rest of 28 g clay she had with her in stock. Calculate total clay she had earlier?

19. Complete the following:

    a. A number that consists of a whole number and a fraction is called a/an ___________?

    b. An_____________________ is a number that represents a part of a whole.

    c. A fraction whose numerical (absolute) value is greater than 1 is called a/an ______________,

    d. A fraction whose numerical value is between 0 and 1 is called a/an _______________

20. Pallavi attended a birthday party at 9:35 P.M. She stayed there for 1 and half hours. By what time she will be returning back?

21. Ten metal cubes of volume 10 cu.cm each melted and casted again to form a larger cube of edge ________ cm.

22. What percentage of all the numbers from 1 to 500 are multiples of 20?

Worksheet 18

1. Julia stores 3,535 cans of juice on 7 shelves in a stockroom. Each shelf has the same number of cans of juice stored on it. How many cans of juice are stored on each shelf?

2. What least number should be subtracted from seven digit greatest number to obtain a multiple of 18?

3. Provide representative fraction. (13 thousandth + 103 hundredth + 1003 hundredth + 12 tens)

4. What fraction of 12.012 is equal to 3.003?

5. 20% of 30% of 2,009 + 30% of 50% of 3,012 = ………………..

6. One sixth of two seventh of 21,063 = ……………………….

7. A beaker can measure 600 ml of liquid. Another beaker can measure 200 ml of liquid. Both the beakers were used for twenty times each to fill up 90% of a container. Find total capacity of that container.

8. $(5,009 + 5,009 + \ldots 3,000 \text{ times}) \times \left(5 + \frac{9}{1,000}\right) X \left(1 - \frac{9}{5,009}\right) X \left(1 - - \frac{9}{5,009}\right)$ = ……………

. Length and breadth of a rectangle is 40 cm and 20 cm respectively. 16 such rectangles are arranged in such a way that longer sides remained side by side to form a row of all the 16 shapes. Find outer boundary of that shape.

10. Is there any pair of number having a common multiple 1,009 and a common factor 79?

11. 20% of 20,000 + 30% of 30,000 + 40% of 40,000 = …………….. X 1,000;

12. Half of a quarter of 80,016,072 = ………………..

13. Two third of a number exceeds 20,0016 by 308. Find out the number.

14. $\frac{11}{25} + \frac{7}{125} + \frac{81}{50} + 11.001 + \frac{121}{625}$ = ………… [in decimal form]

Worksheet 19

1: What fraction of the following are shaded?

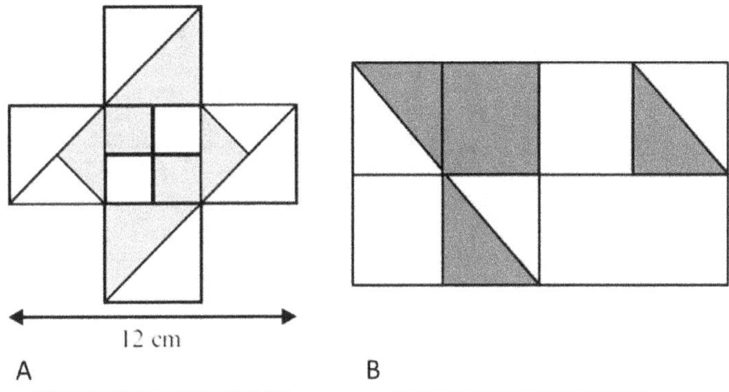

2. Find out area and outer boundary.

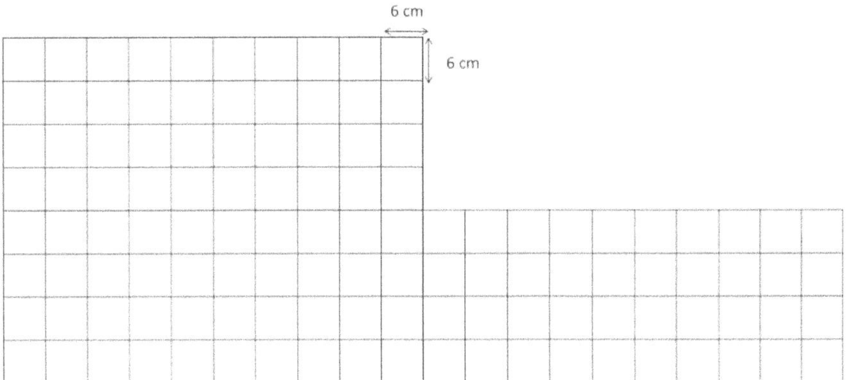

3. Represent shaded parts in decimals and fractions.

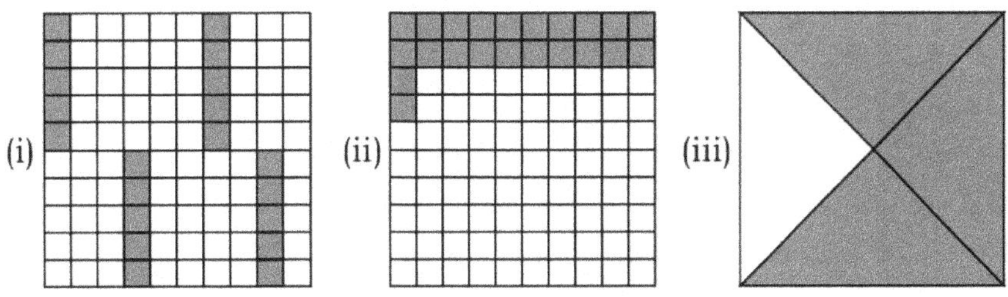

4. A train spends 45 seconds to cross a milestone while moving with an average speed of 36 km/h. find out length of the train.

5. Find out values of x.

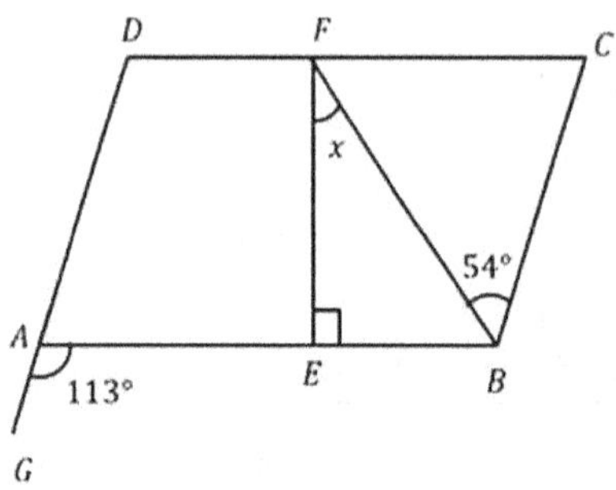 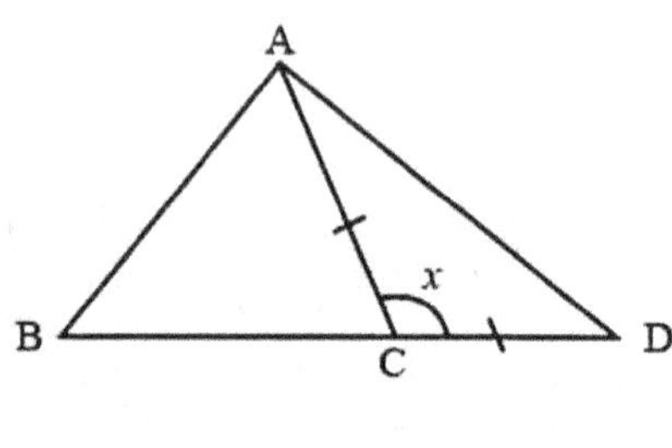

_______________________   _______________________

6. What fraction of the following are shaded?

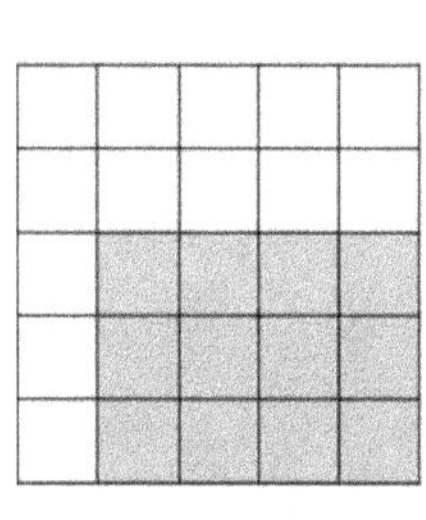 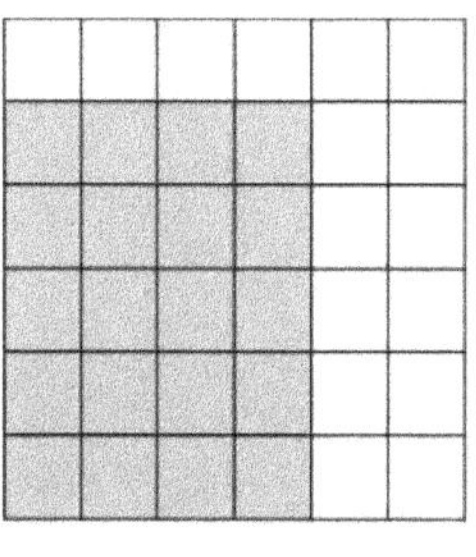 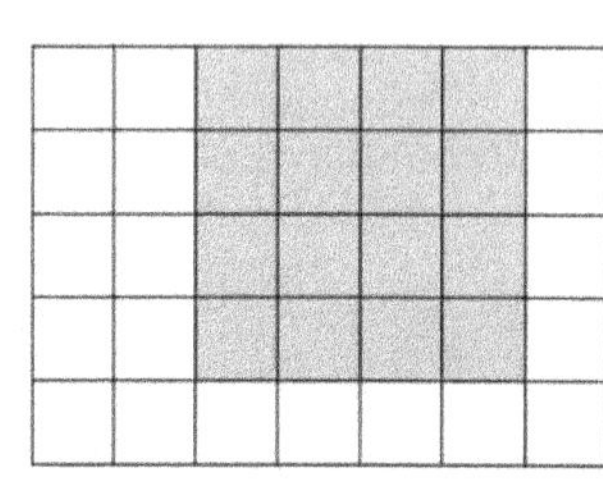

Shape P   Shape Q   Shape R

7. Area of individual unit squares is 36 sq.cm. Find outer boundary of the following grid.

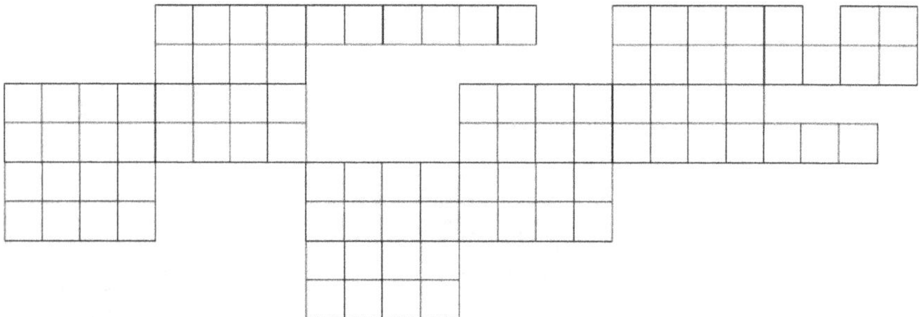

8. Ratio of three interior angles of a triangle is 2: 3: 5. Find out magnitude of the greatest angle.

9. Sum of five comsecutive natural number is equal to 15,00,050. Find out the smallest number.

Worksheet 20

1: What fraction of the following is shaded?

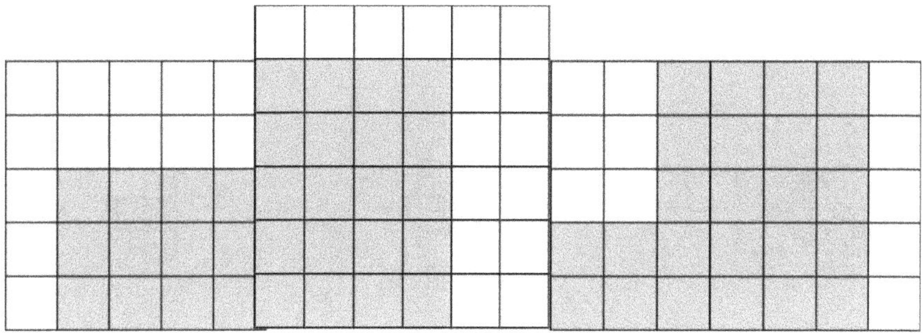

2. Arrange the following shapes on the basis of increasing area.

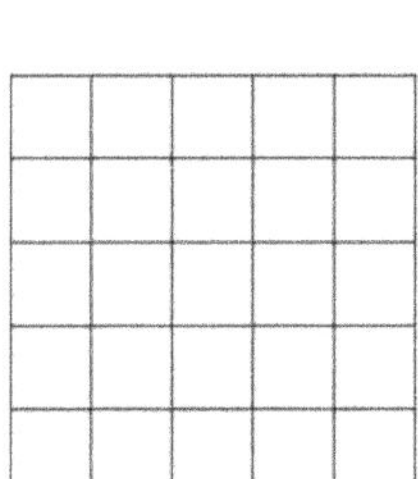

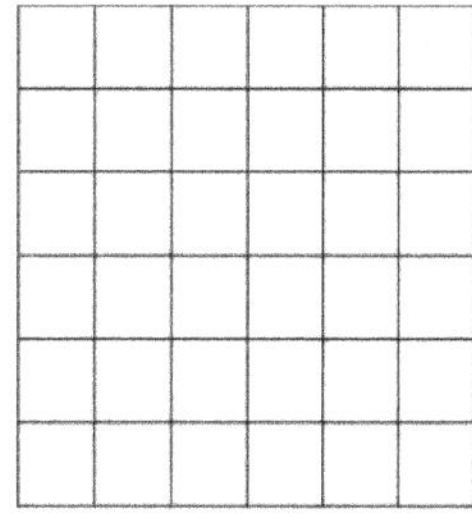

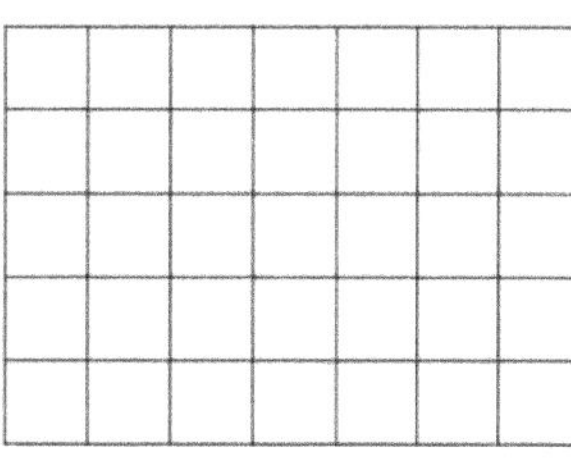

Shape P   Shape Q   Shape R

3. Complete the following:

$\bigstar$ + $\triangle$ = 2789,   6 $\bigstar$ = 36.054 and $\bigstar$ + $\triangle$ = 7,013

5 $\bigstar$ + 2 $\triangle$ = ...

4: Half of a water tank is filled up by cistern A in half on an hour and Quarter of the same tank is filled up by cistern B in 40 minutes. Both the cisterns kept open to fill up three such water tanks. Calculate total time taken by both the cisterns jointly.

5: $(x-1)(x^2-1)\ldots\ldots (x^{100}-1) = 0$; value of $(x^{99} + 10x^{101} - 199\ x^{23}) = ..$

6: Complete the following.

a. 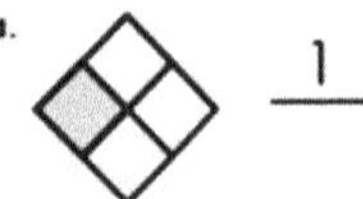 $\dfrac{1}{}$

b. 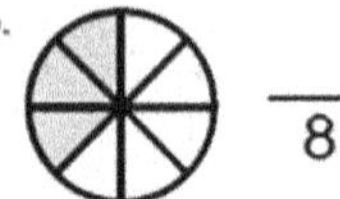 $\dfrac{}{8}$

c.  $\dfrac{1}{}$

d.  $\dfrac{6}{}$

e. 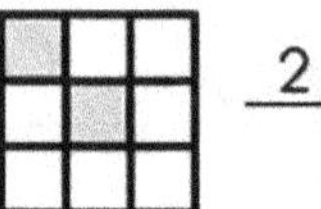 $\dfrac{2}{}$

f. 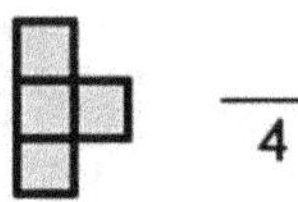 $\dfrac{}{4}$

g.  $\dfrac{}{5}$

h. 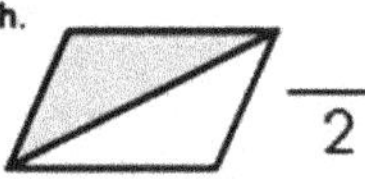 $\dfrac{}{2}$

i. 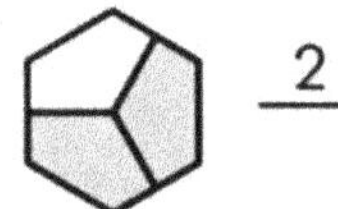 $\dfrac{2}{}$

j. 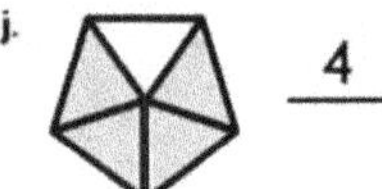 $\dfrac{4}{}$

k. 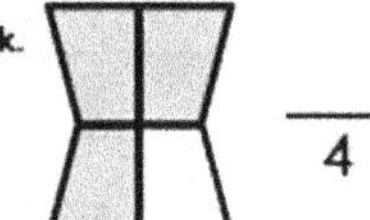 $\dfrac{}{4}$

l. 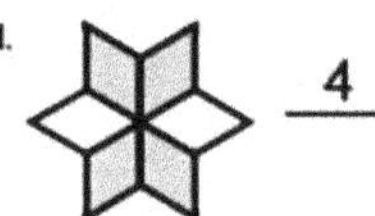 $\dfrac{4}{}$

m. 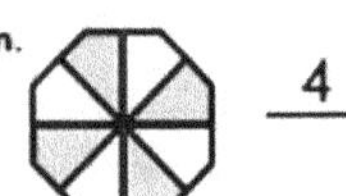 $\dfrac{4}{}$

n. 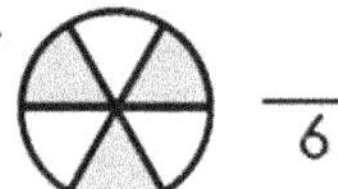 $\dfrac{}{6}$

o. 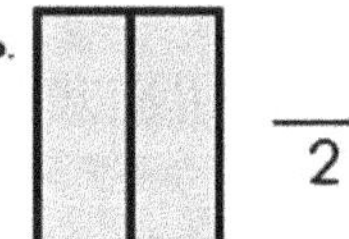 $\dfrac{}{2}$

7: Calculate value of n.

A.
$$\frac{33}{60} = \frac{n}{40}$$
$$n \approx 30$$

B.
$$\frac{32}{160} = \frac{1}{n}$$
$$n \approx 5$$

C.
$$\frac{100}{250} = \frac{n}{5}$$
$$n \approx 7.5$$

D.
$$\frac{35}{n} = \frac{0.2}{0.4}$$
$$n \approx 7\frac{1}{2}$$

***

2. Basic Geometry

Mathematics is the Science of Time and Space. .

1: Find out area of the following.

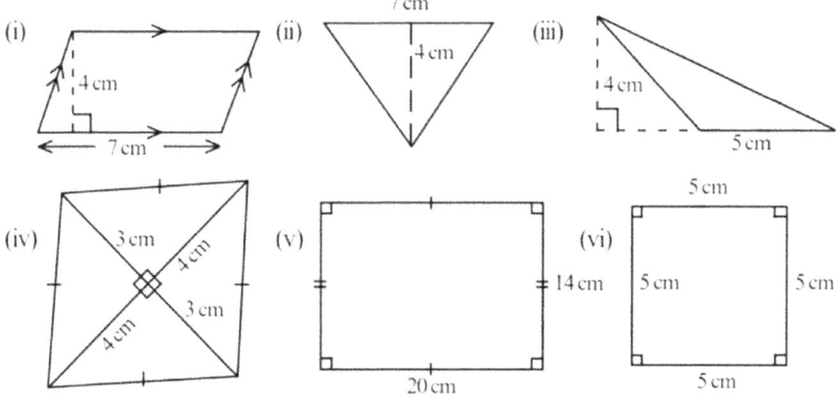

2: Find out area of the shaded portion.

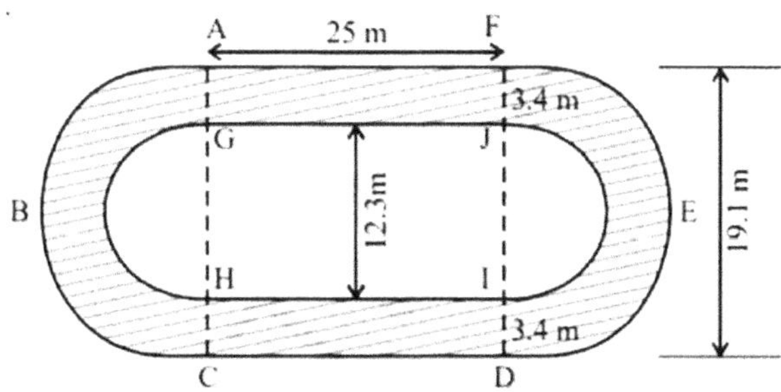

3: Interior angles of a quadrilateral are in the ratio of 2: 3: 4: 6. Find out magnitude of the greatest angle.

4: Hoow many reflex angles can be used to construct a quadrilateral?

5. A triangle can have ……… right angle(s), not more than that.

6. Compare area and outer boundary of the following.

1. 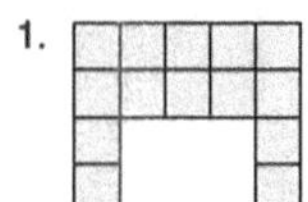   2. 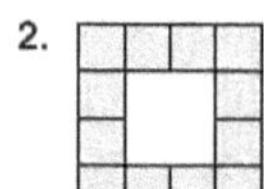   3. 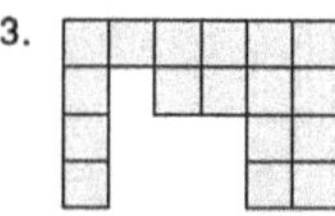

4. 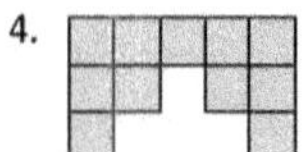   5. 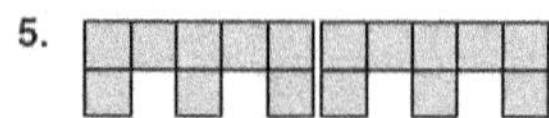   6. 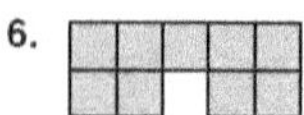

7. 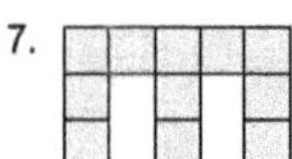   8. 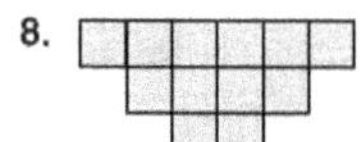   9. 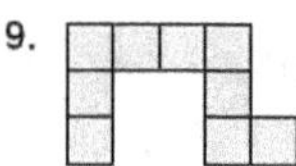

7. Which of the following represents a pair of parallel line?

1.    2. 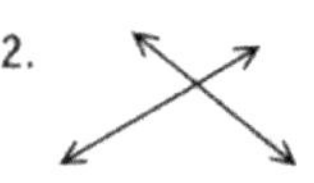   3. 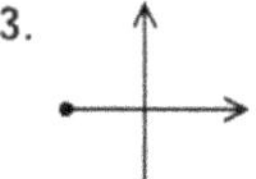   4. 

8. Area of a triangle = ½ of height X base. A parallelogram can have two identical non-overlapping triangles.

Find area of the following

1. 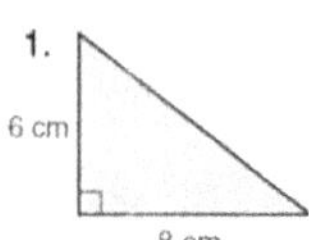   2. 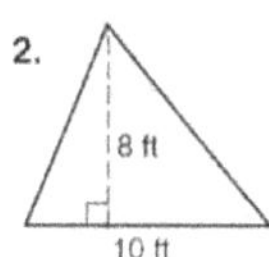   3. 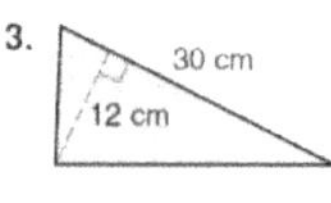   4. 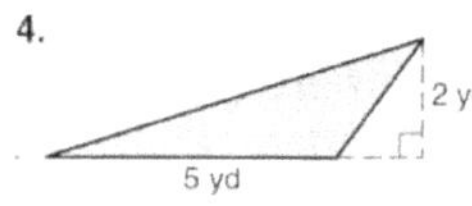

5. 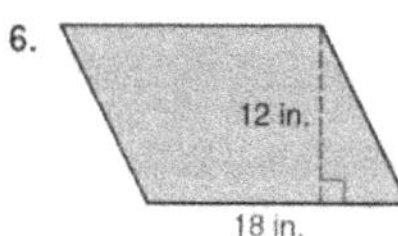   6. 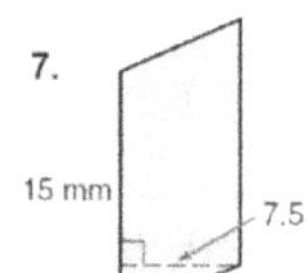   7. 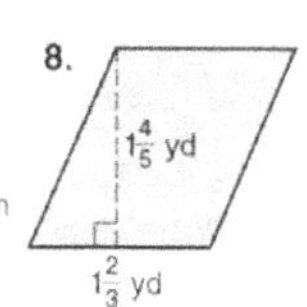   8.

9. Which of the following represents a straight angle?

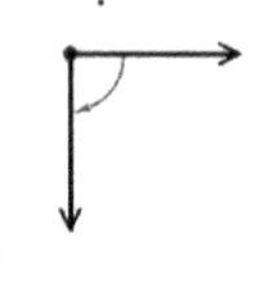      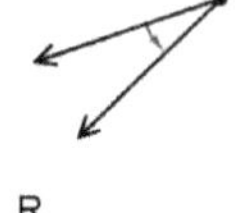   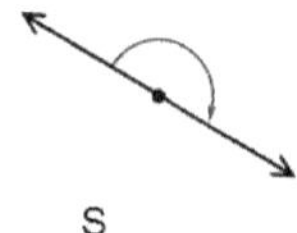

P   Q   R   S

10: Find out values of x in the following.

a.

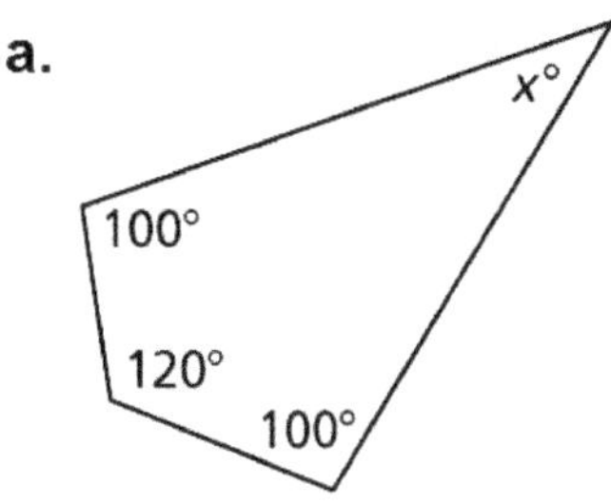

b.

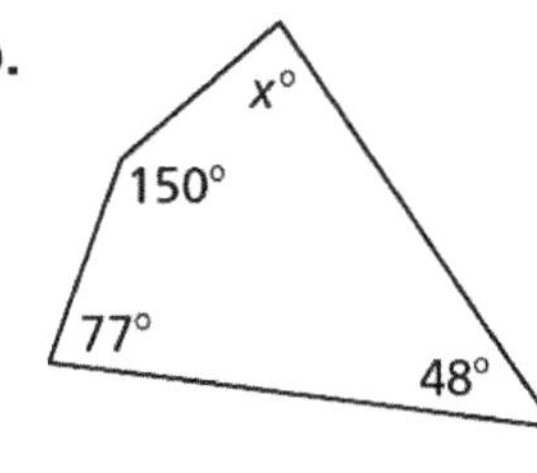

c.

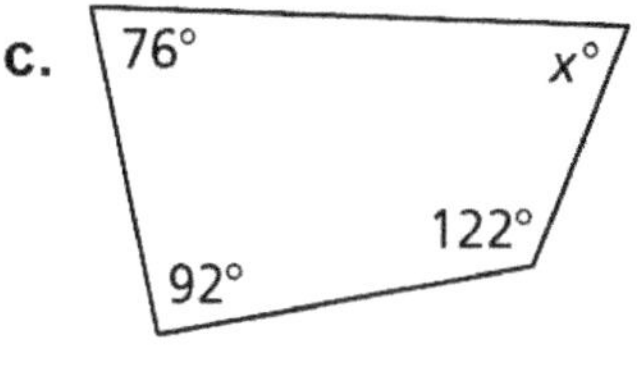

d.

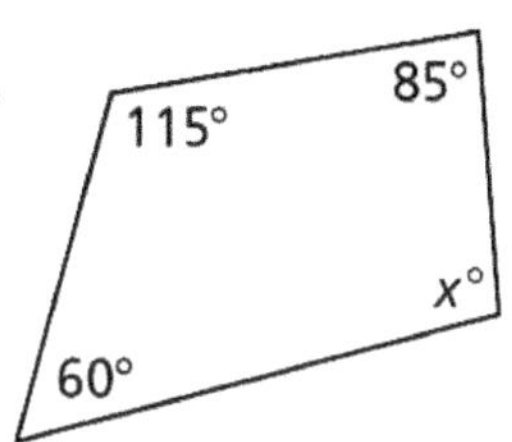

11: Side of a regular hexagon is 4 cm. Several such hexagons are used to form the following grid. Find outer boundary of the grid.

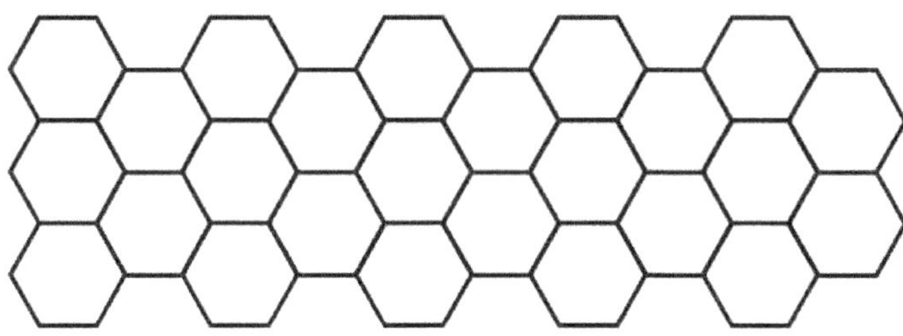

12: Find out area of each of the following.

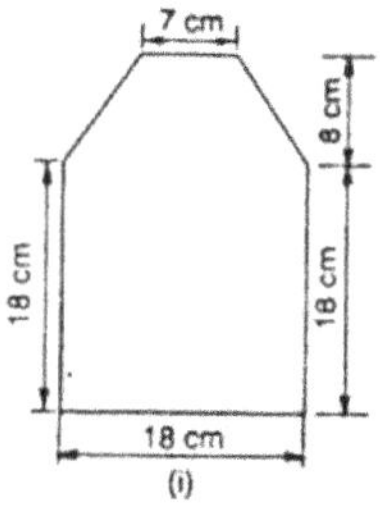

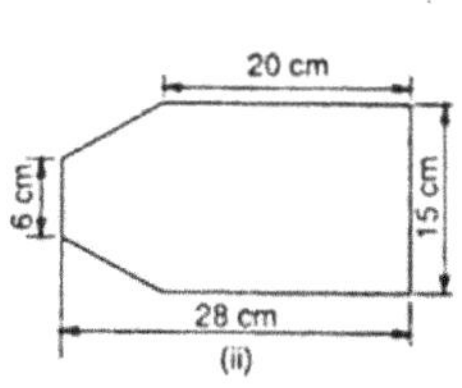

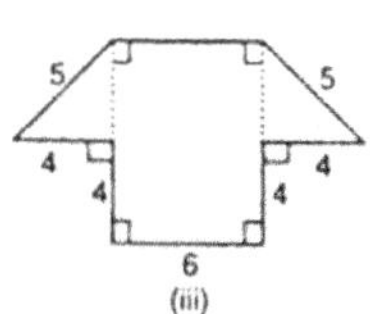

13: Calculate area of the shaded portions.

a. 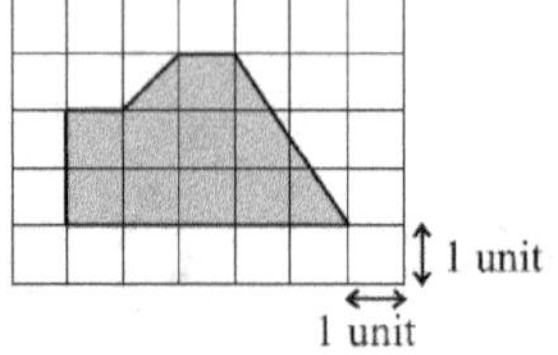

c. 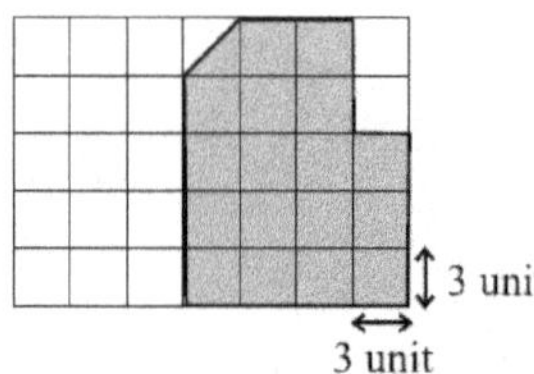

b. 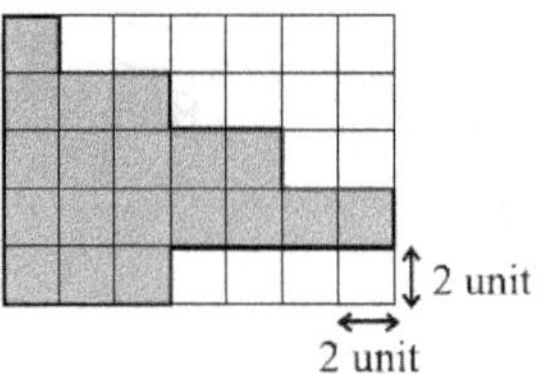

d. 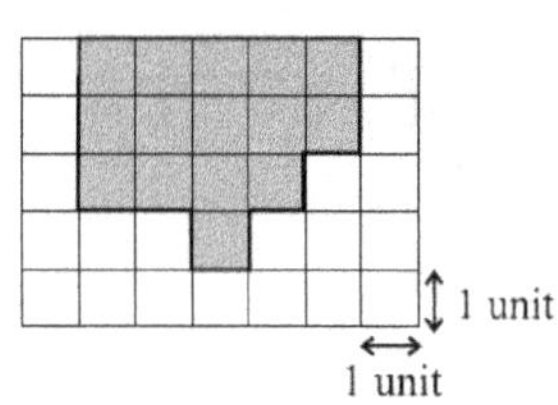

14: Find out values of x.

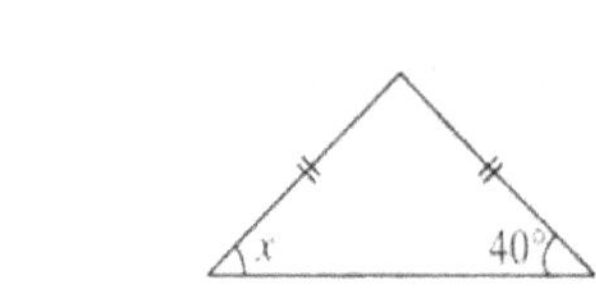

(i)

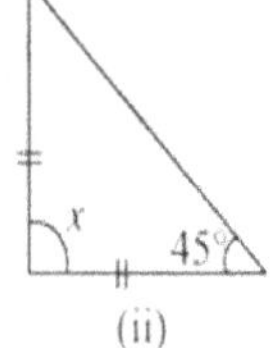

(ii)

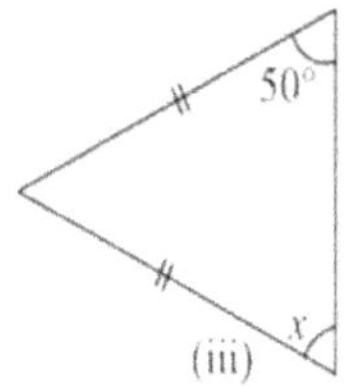

(iii)

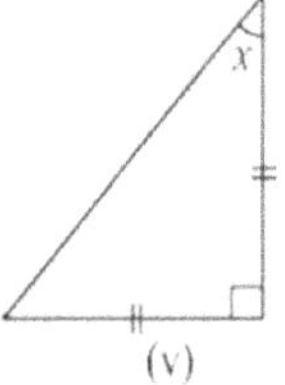

(iv)

(v)

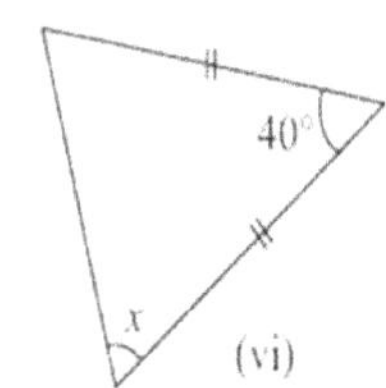

(vi)

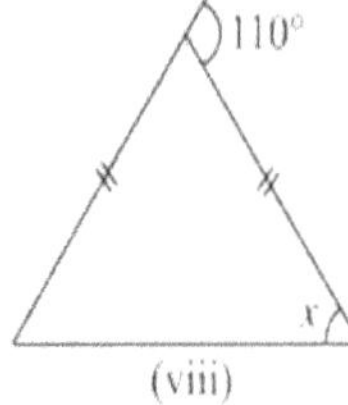

(vii)

(viii)

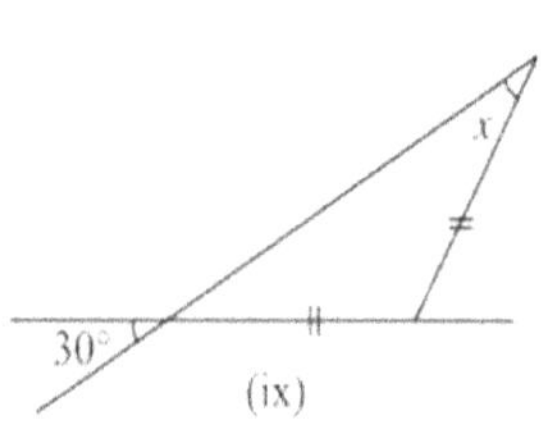

(ix)

****.**

3. H. O. T. S.

1: Find out area of the shaded portions in the following.

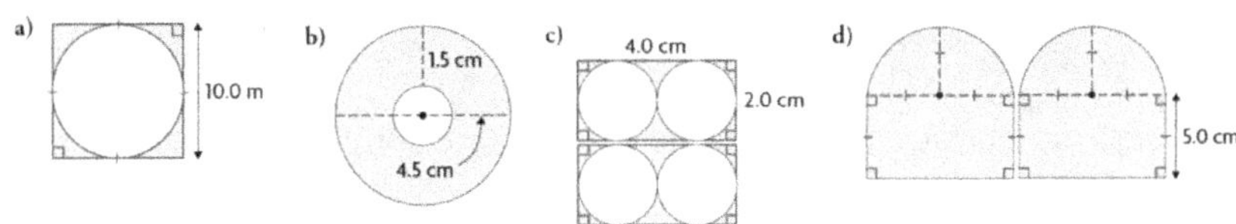

2: Calculate area of each of the following;

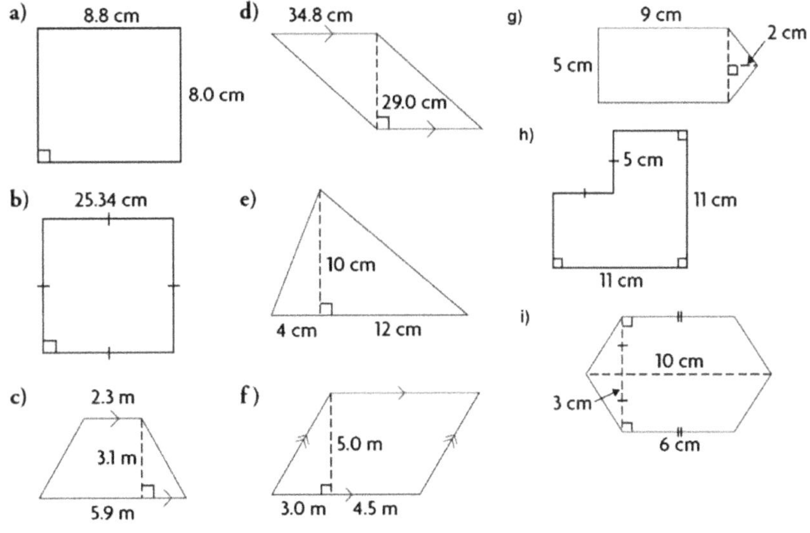

3: Find out missing angles.

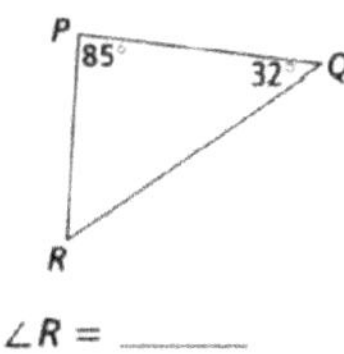

∠R = _______

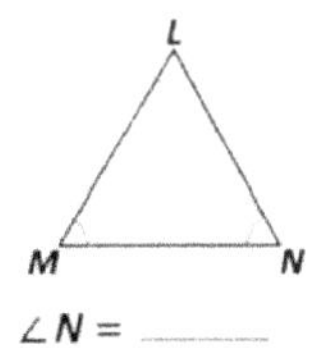

∠N = _______

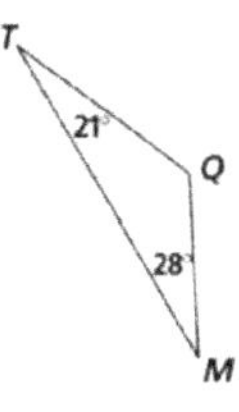

∠Q = _______

4: Find out values of x and y in the following.

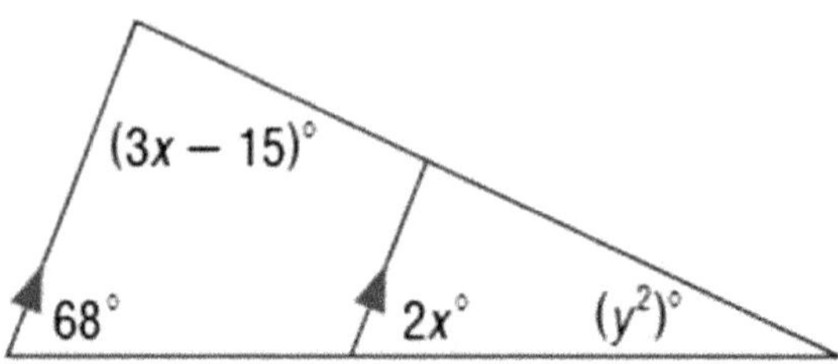

5: Find out missing angles by using angle sum property of triangle.

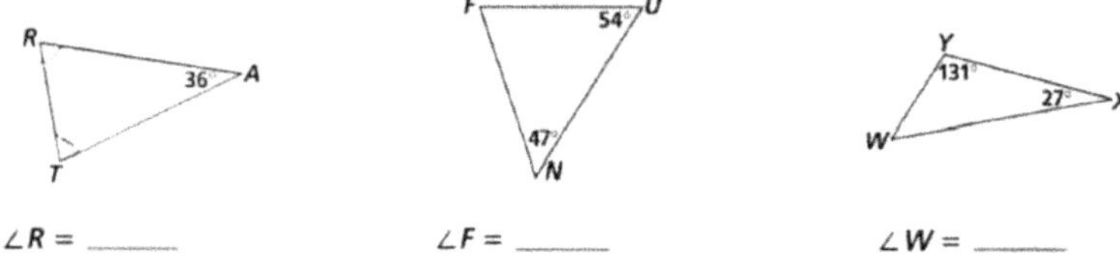

∠R = _________   ∠F = _________   ∠W = _________

6: Find out magnitude of angle 1.

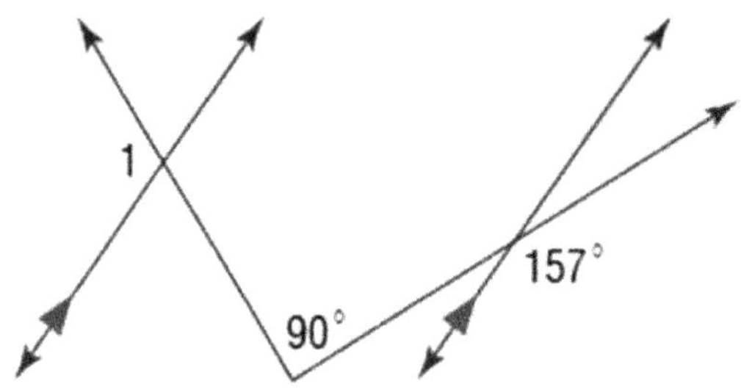

7: Find magnitude of angle 1 in the following.

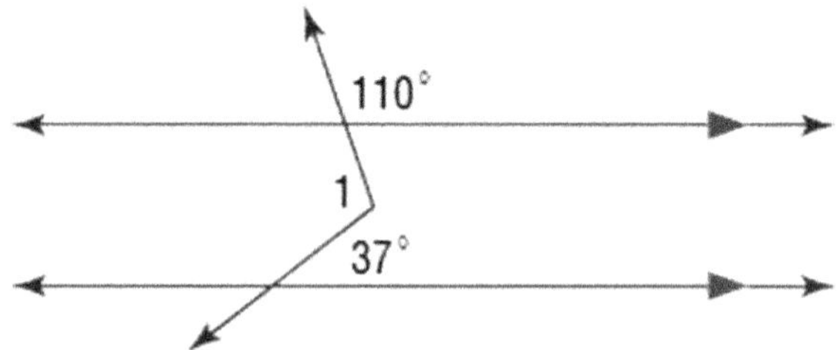

8: Find out area of shaded portions:

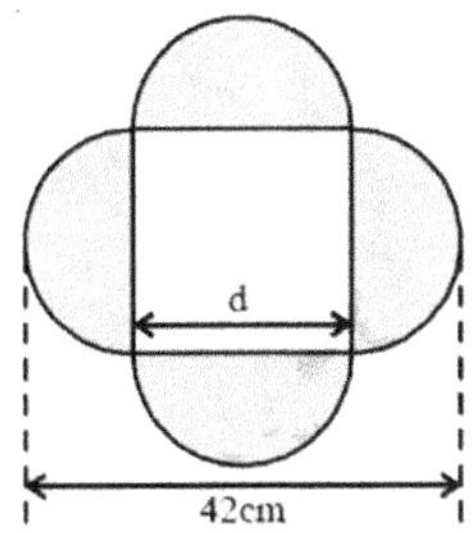

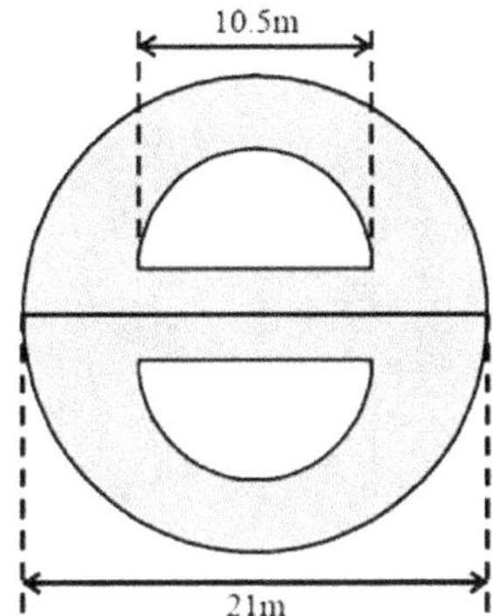

9: How many cubes are there in each of the following?

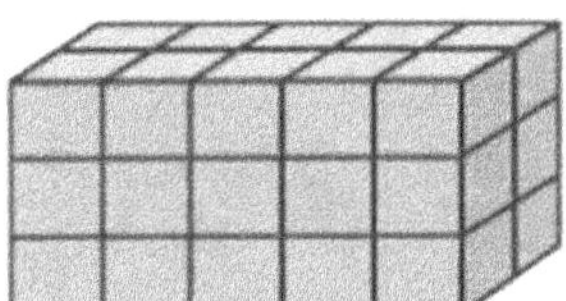

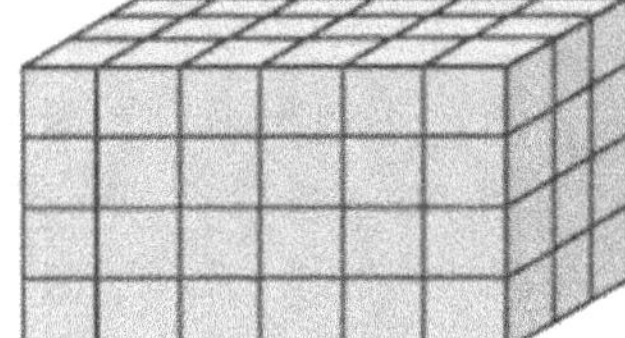

10: A large box of cakes contains same number of cakes as 12 small boxes. Each of the small boxes contains equal number of cakes. A large box contains 168 cakes. Find out total number of cakes that a large box and three small boxes contain.

11. Find out difference of digits which could be there in tens place and units place of the product of greatest six digit odd number and smallest six digit number.

12. P = (10,000 – 1); Q = (1,001 – 2); R = P X Q; The digit at ones place in standard form of R will be …………

13. Find out the missing number in the following:

683216; ………;   713216;   728216;   743216

14: 21st multiple of 100,100,203 = …………………….

167

15: Calculate area of the shaded portion.

16: Minoti had 2 m long ribbon. She used half of it and rest of the part is divided equally into 8 equal parts. Calculatre length of each of the smaller parts duly obtained.

17: There were 3/5 as many girl students as boy students in a school. There were 48 fewer boy students than girl students in the school. How many students are there in all?

18: What fraction of all the numbers from 1 to 1000 are multiples of 125?

19: Evaluate the following using suitable identites.

(i) $(99)^3$ (ii) $(102)^3$ (iii) $(1003)^3$ (iV) $(599)^3$

20: Which of the following statement is not true?

a) Only one line can pass through a given point.

b) All right angles are equal to each other.

c) Circles with same radii are equal to each other in terms of area.

d) A line segment can be extended on its both sides endlessly to get a straight line.

21: How many lines can be drawn by using ay two out of three non-collinear points?

4. Achievers

1: Angle A + B + C + D + E + F = ……

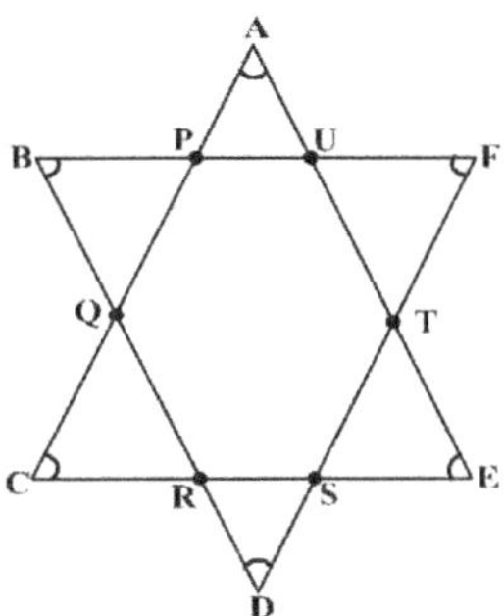

2: If the measure of an angle is 62° 32', what is the measure of its complementary angle?

3: Find value of x in the following.

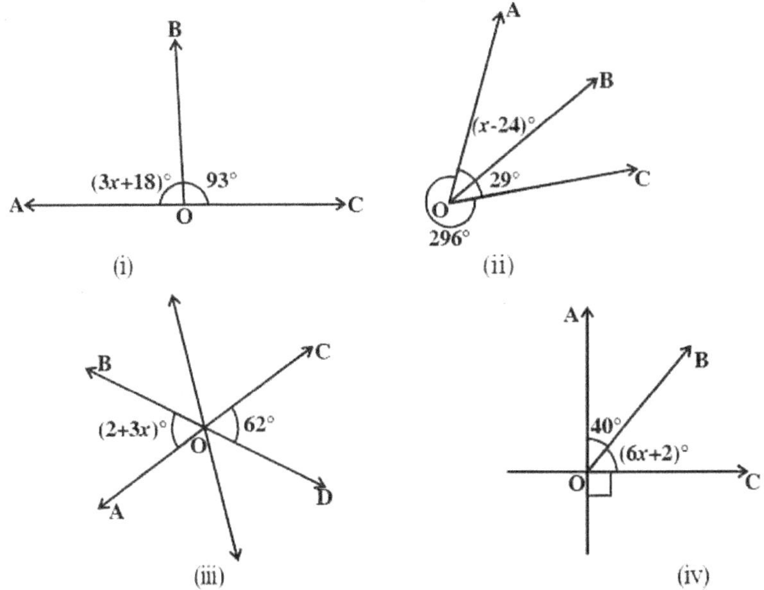

4: Two complementary angles are in the ratio 4:5. Find the angles.

5: Find angle a in each of the following.

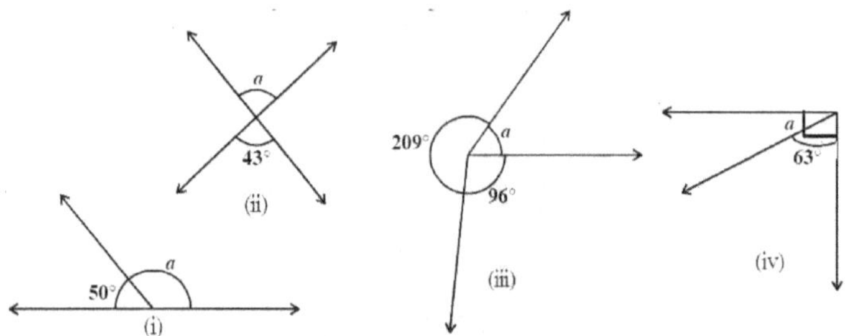

6: Find out unknown angles in the following in which $l\|m$.

a)

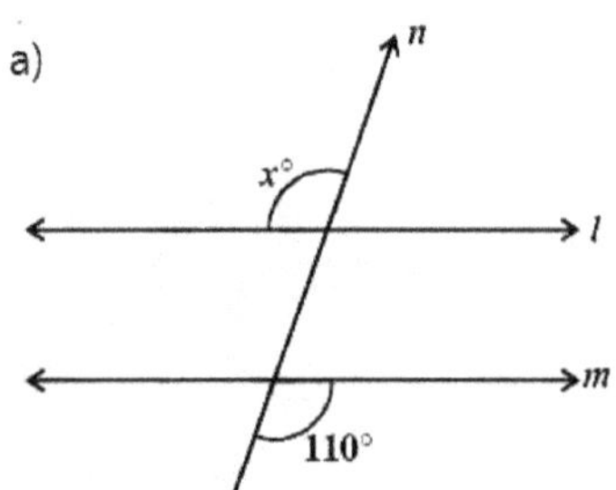

b)

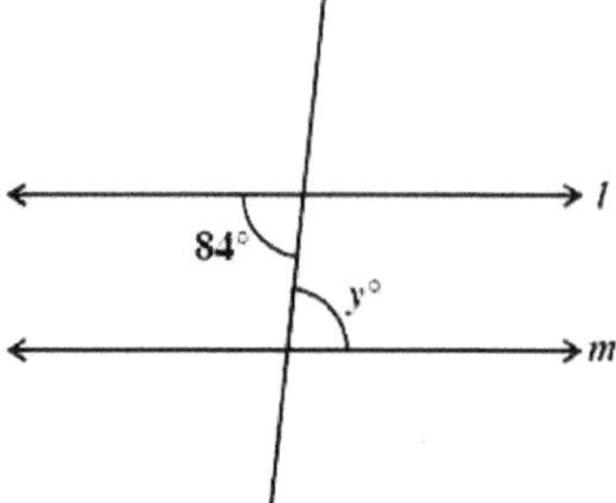

c)

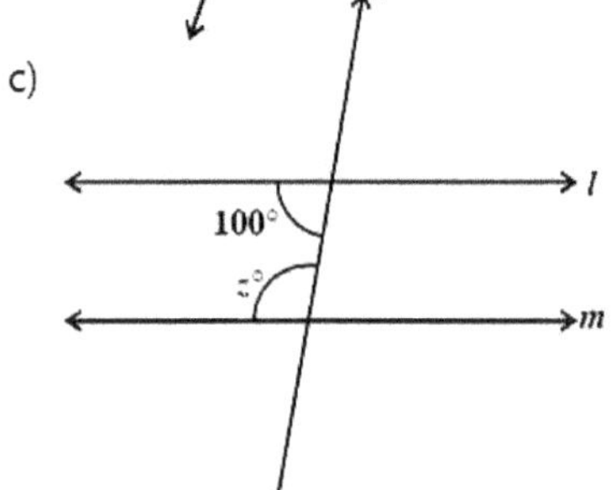

d)

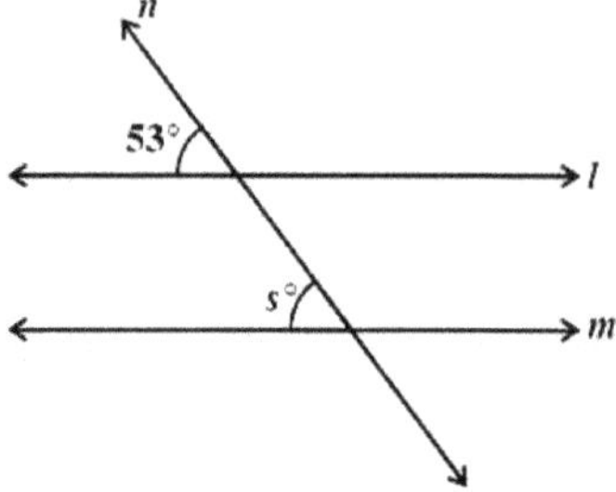

7: There are .... diagonals in a pentagon.

8: Each of the interir angles of a regular hexagon will be equal to ......

9. We can draw a triangle by taking at least .... Obtuse angle or at least ..... right angle.

10. There are .... Right angles in a rectangle.

11. In each oof the following figures AB∥CD. Find values of x.

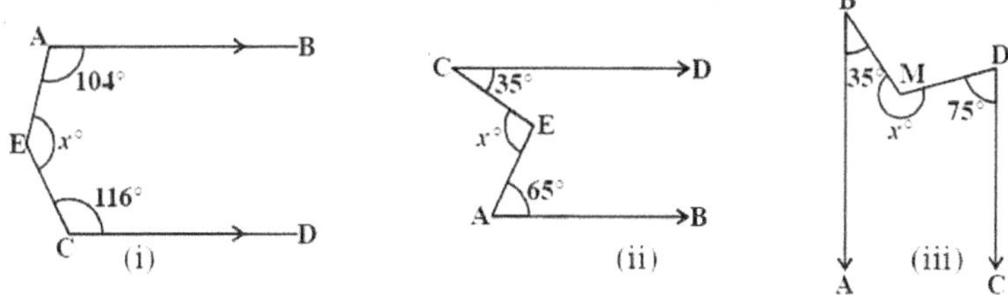

12: Find out values of x. y and z in the following.

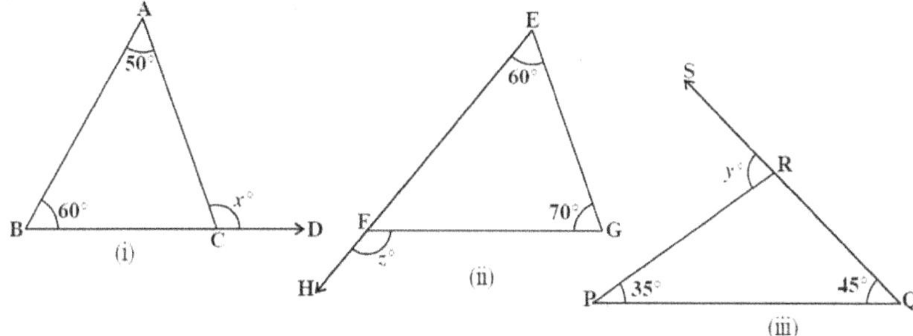

13: A metal cuboid of dimension 22 cm. × 15 cm. × 7.5 cm. was melted and cast into a cylinder of height 14 cm. What is its radius?

14: An overhead water tanker is in the shape of a cylinder has capacity of 61.6 cu.mts. The diameter of the tank is 5.6 m. Find the height of the tank.

15. A metal pipe is 77 cm. long. The inner diameter of a cross section is 4 cm., the outer diameter being 4.4 cm. Find its

(i) inner and (ii) outer curved surface area (iii) Total surface area.

16: A cylindrical piller has a diameter of 56 cm and is of 35 m high. There are 16 pillars around the building. Find the cost of painting the curved surface area of all the pillars at the rate of Rs. 5.50 per 1 m^2.

17: The diameter of a roller is 84 cm and its length is 120 cm. It takes 500 complete revolutions to roll once over the play ground to level. Find the area of the play ground in m^2.

18: The base area of a cone is 38.5 cm^2. Its volume is 77 cm^3. Find its height.

19. The volume of a cone is 462 m^3. Its base radius is 7 m. Find its height.

20. Curved surface area of a cone is 308 cm2 and its slant height is 14 cm Find. (i) radius of the base (ii) Total surface area of the cone.

21. The cost of painting the total surface area of a cone at Rs 1.25 per cm^2 is Rs. 625. Find out volume of the cone, if its slant height is 25 cm.

22. From a circle of radius 15 cm., a sector with angle 216° is cut out and its bounding radii are bent so as to form a cone. Find its volume.

23. The height of a tent is 9 m. Its base diameter is 24 m. What is its slant height? Find the cost of canvas cloth required if it costs Rs 7 per sq.m.

24. What length of tarpaulin 3 m wide will be required to make a conical tent of height 8m and base radius 6m ? Assume that extra length of material that will be required for stitching margins and wastage in cutting is approximately 20 cm (use $\pi = 3.14$)

25. Water is pouring into a conical vessel of diameter 5.2m and slant height 6.8m (as shown in the adjoining figure), at the rate of Rs 3.6 cu. m. per minute. How long will it take to fill the vessel?

26. Consider the following for a sphere:

Surface area of a hemisphere = 2 πr^2; total surface area of hemisphere = $3\pi r^2$; volume of a shere = Volume of a sphere = 4/3 πr^3;

A hemispherical bowl is made up of stone whose thickness is 5 cm. If the inner radius is 45 cm, find the total surface area of the bowl.

27. The hemispherical dome of a building needs to be painted. If the circumference of the base of dome is 17.6 m, find the cost of painting it, given the cost of painting is Rs.10 per 100 cm^2.

A Test Paper

1. Temperature of a city increased by $5\,^0$ C last week. If a corresponding increase of temperature in ^{0} F is 1.8 times more than that of the value in ^{0} C , then find the value of such increase of temperature in ^{0} F

   A: 18^0 F   B: 9^0 F   C: 8.9^0 F   D: $6\,^0$ F

2. A racing car covers 100 km in 2 hours and another 400 km 4 hours. The speed of the car during second time is ____ times more than that of the first time.

   A: 1   B: 2   C: 3   D: 4

3. The product of the place values of 5 in the following number is

   $$\overline{}$$
   $$32,435$$

   A: 9,000   B: 90,000   C: 9,00,000   D: 900

4. What must be added to 10932 to make it exactly divisible by 9?

5. $$\frac{3}{6}, \frac{7}{6}, \frac{1}{6}, \frac{5}{6}, \frac{11}{6}$$

   If we arrange these fractions in ascending order, then denominator of the product of 2nd and 3rd fraction in simplest form will be __________

   A: 12   B: 24   C: 36   D: 48

6. Half of one sixth of 72 is the ________ multiple of three.

7. A wire of a square sized shape of side 32 cm is reshaped to form a circle. Find the circumference of that circle. [Circumference of a circle is the outer boundary of a circle].

8. A solid cylinder has ____ flat faces and ____ curved faces.

9. The product of all the factors of 121 is ________ less than its greatest factor.

   A: 1   B: 11   C: 1,452   D: 1331

10. Two bells toll at an interval of 6 seconds and 8 seconds respectively. They toll together at 11:55 a.m. When do they toll together again for the second time?

   A: 12:19 pm   B: 12:19 am   C: 12: 24 pm

11. Ruchika observed that a 300 m long goods train is taking 45 seconds to cross a light-post. Find the average speed of that train.

Also find the time taken by that train to cross a 1500 m long railway platform.

12. Compare the place value of 5 in 235,934 and 54,435. Find difference of both the place values.

13. A milk-dairy produces 25,545 liters of milk every day. It supplies 15,625 liters of milk to a milk-depot and the rest to the market. How much milk is supplied to the market?

14. The sum of two numbers is 94506. One of the numbers is 49605. Find the other number.

15. The sum of two numbers is 45650. One of the numbers is 22587. Find the other number. Which part of the sum is the given number?

16. There are 35,278 students in Class III, 32,184 students in Class IV and 25,375 students in Class V in the schools of a city. Find the total number of students reading in Classes III, IV and V. Among these students 60,324 are girls. Find the number of students who are boys.

17. A person had $ 197,865. He gave $ 50,753 to his wife and $ 75,928 to his son. The rest of the money he gave to his daughter. How much did the daughter get?

18. What should be added to the sum of 3,46,068 and 3,24,263 to get the sum of 8,05,400?

19. There are 4021 students in a school. Each section can accommodate a maximum number of 25 students. There are equal number of students in each section, find their number in each section. Is there any section having less than 25 students? How many such sections are there?

20. Write in standard form:

    32 tens + 54 hundreds + 121 ones + 1001 ten thousandths = __________.

21. Points located on same line are called ______________ points.

22. A line has no __________________ but a line segment has ____ such ______ ____________.

23. A ______ can be extended endlessly in both the directions.

24. 32 hundreds + 302 hundredths + 1008 thousandths = ________.

25. Instead of writing 321 thousands Rita has written 3 lakhs 12 thousands. Find the difference between the original and the derived answer.

26. Total cost of 5 pens and 6 pencils is Rs. 145. Total cost of 6 pens and 5 pencils is Rs. 251. Find individual cost of a pen and a pencil. Also find the total cost of 5 pens and 3 pencils.

27. 5 km 5 m + 102 km 102 m + 32 km 32 m = _______________ m

28. Sam has a collection of 963 comic books. What are the five different ways Sam could divide his comic books into equal groups?

29. A study table is 3 m long and 1.5 m wide. Another large table is thrice as long and twice as wide as the study table. What is the area of both the table?

30. Cost of fencing a square shaped garden at the rate of Rs. 120.00 per m was Rs. 48,000.00. Find the length of a side of that garden.

31. At the end of the party, the kids broke open the gift packs. When they assembled all the candy, Bill got 9 pieces. Sara got 3 times as many pieces as Bill. Nitin got one third of the number of candies gathered by Bill. Which of the statements depicted below are true?

I. They have collected total number of candies which is also   equal to third multiple of 3.

II: Sara got 4 times more than Nitin.

III: Share of Nitin and Bill was 15 less than that of Sara.

IV: Sara got 9 times more candy than that of Nitin.

32. A wall mount clock takes 2 seconds to toll 2 bells at 2 a.m. Find the time by that clock to toll 11 bells at 11 a.m.

33. Simplify:

$$\left(1+\frac{1}{9}\right)\left(1+\frac{1}{10}\right)\left(1+\frac{1}{11}\right)....\left(1+\frac{1}{1,007}\right)\left(1+\frac{1}{1,008}\right) =$$

34. How many five digit numbers are there in all?

35. What least number should be subtracted from five digit greatest number to obtain a common multiple of 2, 4, 6 and 8?

36. Product of 9099, 1089, 203899 and 10879 is represented in standard form. The digit at ones lace in that product will be ....

37. Mohan wants to distribute 129 sweets and 321 almonds amongst his 63 friends equally. Calculate the number of sweets and almonds that remain to Mohan after the distribution.

38. The product of two numbers is 41310. If one of them is 270, find the other.

39. In certain division algorithm the quotient is 57, the divisor is 45 and the remainder is 29, find the dividend.

40. The annual income of Sam is Rs. 98,364. What is his monthly income if he earns an equal amount every month?

41. A number was divided by 97; the quotient was 3806 and the remainder 76. Find the number.

42. When 650 is multiplied by a number, the product is 5590. Find the number.

43. 49,000 fruits were distributed among 1,000 clubs equally. How many fruits did each club get?

44. There are 2,983 boys and 2,175 girls in a school. Find the total enrolment of the school. Find also the number of more boys than girls on the rolls of the school.

45. What least number must be added to make the six digit smallest number a multiple of 11?

46. What should be added to 79,415 to make it the greatest five-digit number?

47. By how much is 89283 is greater than 79382?

48. What should be subtracted from 98989 to get 88888?

49. There are _____ vertices, _____ faces and _____ edges in a cuboid.

50. Two cubical block of edge 30 cm each joined side by side to form a cuboidal block. Find the surface area of the top and bottom part of that cuboid.

51. Malavika prepared a 25 m long rope by joining different segments of 200 cm each. Find the number of segments she used for making that rope.

52. _______ is the predecessor of smallest four digit multiple of 9.

53. How many times do 7 appear if we write all the natural numbers from 1 to 100?   [Ans: 1]

5. Talent Search and Olympiads

1: Find out area of PQRS.

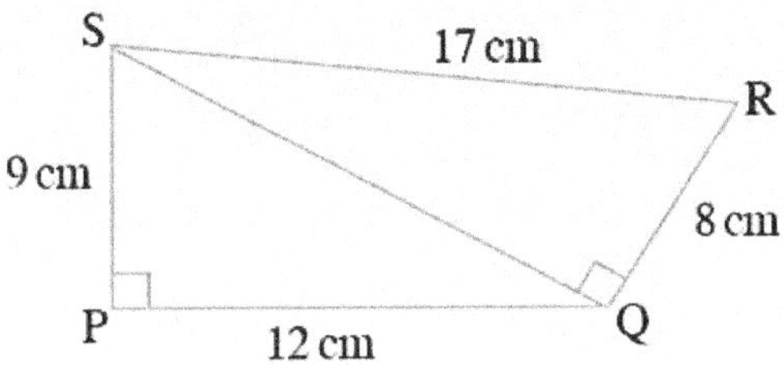

2: ABCD is a parallelogram. AE is perpendicular on DC and CF is perpendicular on AD. If AB = 10 cm, AE = 8 cm and CF = 12 cm. Find AD.

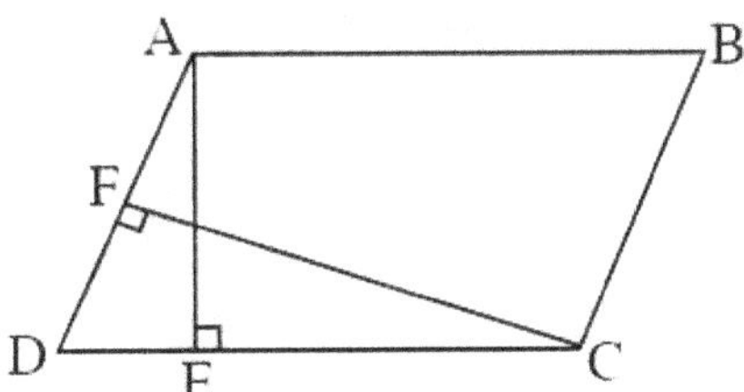

3: A farmer has a field in the form of a parallelogram PQRS as shown in the figure. He took the mid- point A on RS and joined it to points P and Q. In how many parts of field is divided? What are the shapes of these parts? The farmer wants to sow groundnuts which are equal to the sum of pulses and paddy. How should he sow? State reasons?

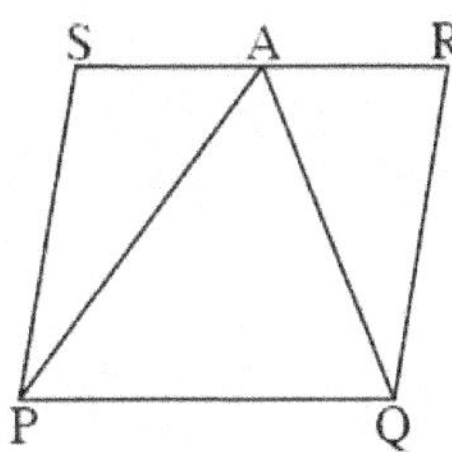

4: State true or false.

i. A circle divides the plane on which it lies into three parts.

ii. The region enclosed by a chord and the minor arc is minor segment.

iii. The region enclosed by a chord and the major arc is major segment.

iv. A diameter divides the circle into two unequal parts.

v. A sector is the area enclosed by two radii and a chord

vi. The longest of all chords of a circle is called a diameter.

vii. The mid point of any diameter of a circle is the centre.

viii. A triangle can have two obtuse angles as interior angles.

ix. A quadrilateral can have two reflex angles as interior angles.

x. Sum of all the interior angles of a quadrilateral is equal to 360^0.

5: In the given figure, point O is the centre of the circle. Find the length of CD, if AB = 5 cm.

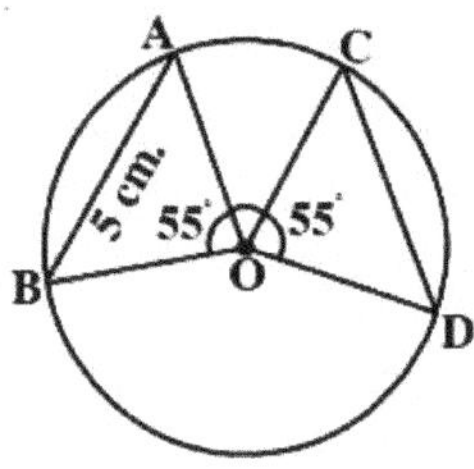

6: Calculate vlume of the following shape.

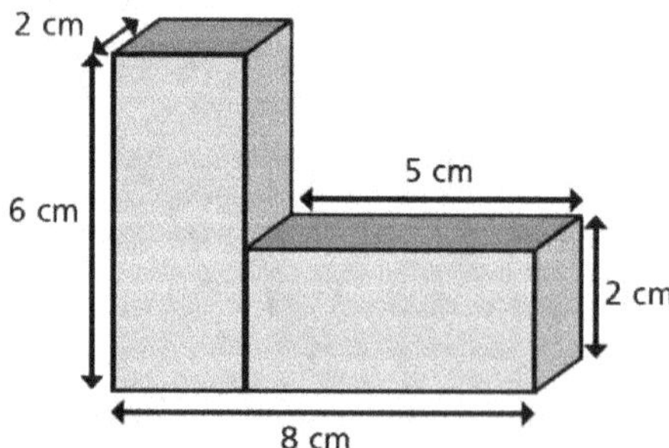

Question Bank

1: Find out missing anges.

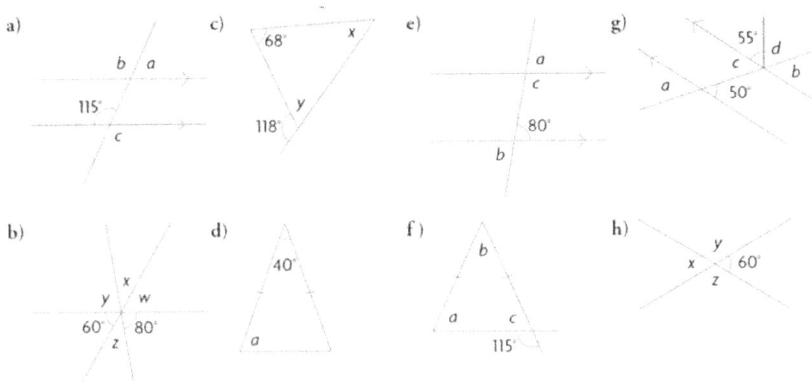

a)
b)
c)
d)
e)
f)
g)
h)

2. Find out unknown angles.

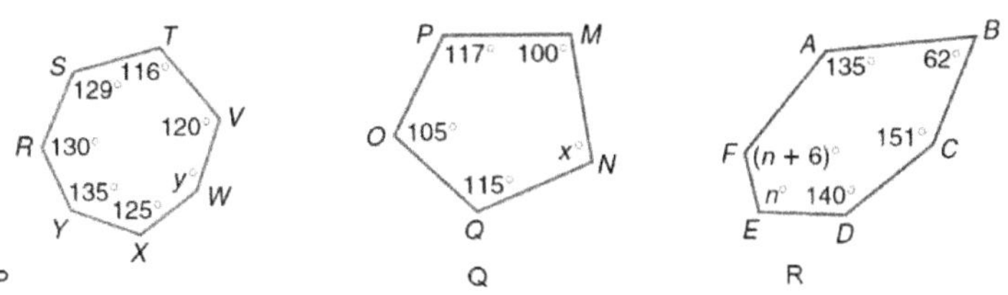

3. Mr. Jordon prepares to put fencing around his rectangular kitchen garden of width 95 m and the length 105 m. How long fencing wires does he need?

    A: 190 m   B: 200 m   C: 210 m   D: 400 m

4. A half filled oil container is used to store residue oil of capacity 125 litters. After filling the residue three eighth of the container remained empty. Find the capacity of the container.

5. One tenth of a container is equal to 16 cans of capacity 8 litters each. The entire container can hold ___________ litters of oil.

6: What least number must be subtracted from 219.376 to make the result exactly divisible by 219?   [Ans: 0.157]

7: A train, moving at the speed of 15 m per second, is taking 20 seconds to cross a telephone post. This train can take _________ seconds to cross a 1.5 km long platform.   [Ans : 2 minutes]

8. Veena rides her bike to the park for 18 minutes at an average speed of 9 m per second to meet a friend. Veena arrives at the park at 11:00 a.m. and stays there for 58 minutes. Her friend will arrive there at 12:15 p.m. they had a meeting for 32 minutes.

Try to answer the following questions.

A. What is the distance between the park and Veena's house?

B. How long could Veena have to wait for her friend?

C. How long does Veena stay at the park?

D. When will Veena leave to go home?

9. Write a number greater than 1, 50,000 by using digits 5, 4 and 2.

10. 324 thousands = _________________ tens.

11. 32 crore = __________ thousands.

12. __________ crore is 400 greater than 99,99,600.

13. Write a number smaller than 39 lakhs by using digits 4, 3 and 8. Digits can be repeated.

14. Write the predecessor of 7 digit greatest even number.

15. Calculate the sum total of place values of 3 in the following numbers

34,55,67,505,   30,56,05,506 and 35,05,04,050

16. Difference of the place value and face value of 8 in 65,76,80,653, 78,806 and 48,65,678 = ______________.

17. Numbers divisible by 2 are also called __________ numbers.

18. All prime numbers have only ______ factors. _____ and the number itself.

19. Sum total of 2 eve numbers is always an _______ number.

20. A prime number between 95 and 100 = __________.

21. All the multiples of 8 are also multiples of 2 and ______.

22. All the multiples of _____ and 4 may or may not be a multiple of 8.

23. All the multiples of ___ and _____ are not necessarily multiples of 10.

24. All multiples of 10 are also multiples of _____ and _____.

25. There are _______ flat faces and ___ curved faces in a cuboid.

26. What least number should be subtracted from the six digit greatest number to make the value divisible by 3, 6, 9 and 18 independently leaving remainder 2 in each case?

27. 59 square shaped tiles each of 20 sq. cm. are used for flooring a room. Find the area of that room.

28. Renuka prepared a bar graph that shows the number of kg of food eaten each day by each animal. What information goes on the horizontal axis? What information can be placed on the vertical axis?

29. Tim lives in New Delhi. He prepares a line graph that shows the amount of LPG used in his home kitchen for a year. Will the line graph show any change throughout the year?

30. Martin wants to represent the data related to pets owned by his classmates. He makes a bar graph that shows the number of dogs owned by members of his class. If the smallest number is 1 and the largest number is 4, what interval should Jon use for representing the data scale in the graph?

31. Find the value: $\dfrac{11}{144} \times \dfrac{12}{121} \times \dfrac{12}{49} \times \dfrac{11}{169} \times \dfrac{7}{10} \times \dfrac{7}{100} =$

32. The town newspaper is published every alternate day. One copy has 12 pages. Every alternate day 21,980 copies are printed. How many total pages are printed for all copies every month? [Consider one month equal to 30 days]

33. Simplify:

$x^2 + 5y^2 + 3xy + 6x - 7y + 8 - [\, 12x^2 - \{\, 14x^2 - 9y^2 + 4xy + 3x + 9 \,\} \,]$

34. The quotient of x by y added to product of x and y. Write the expression which is obtained.

35. What least number should be subtracted from six digit greatest common multiple of 3, 6, 9 and 18 to make the value a common multiple of 5 and 10?

36. Sum total of reciprocal of a number and half of the given number is equal to 5.1. Find sum total of 10th and 15th multiple of that number.

37. Calculate outer boundary and area of the following.

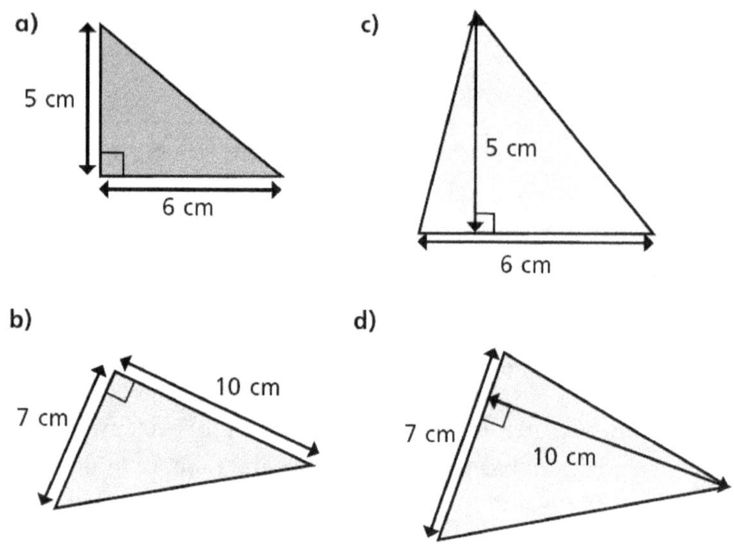

38: Calculate area and outer boundary of the following.

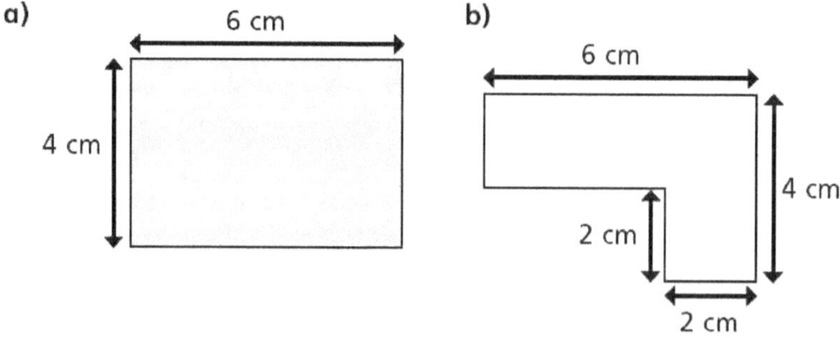

38: How many non-overlapping triangles can be accommodated inside a pentagon?

39: Find out area of the following.

a)

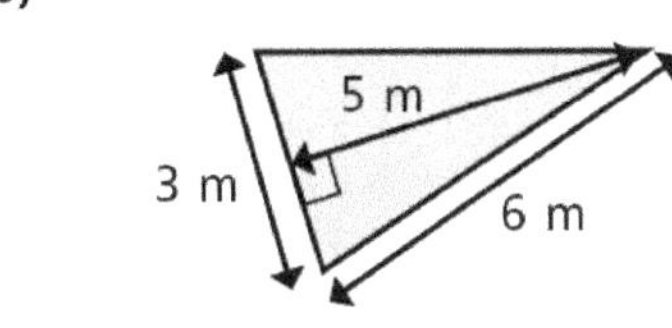

d)

b)

e)

c)

f)

40: Calculate area of the following.

a)

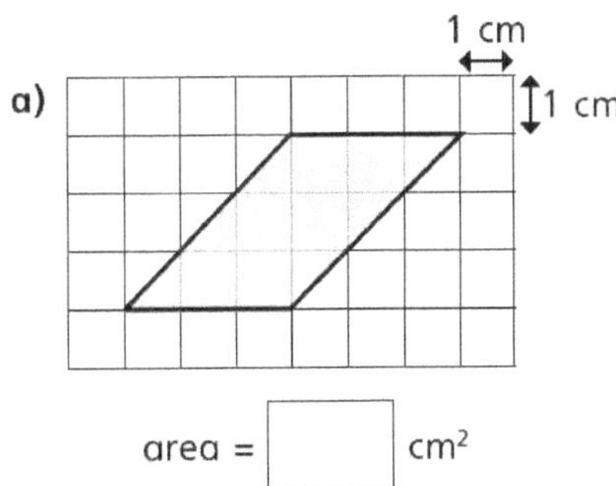

area = ___ cm²

b)

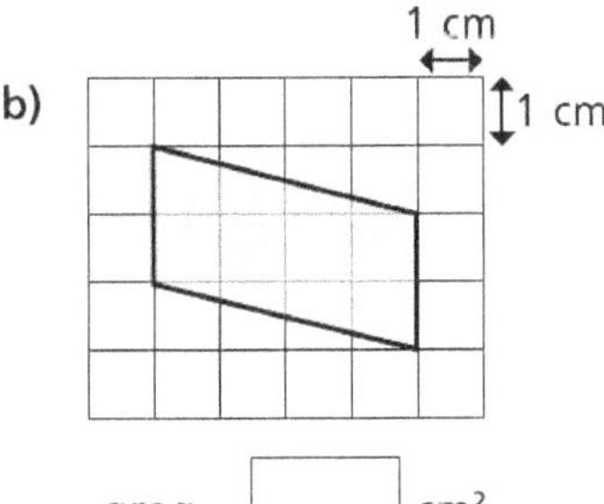

area = ___ cm²

41: Calculate area and outer boundary of the following grid.

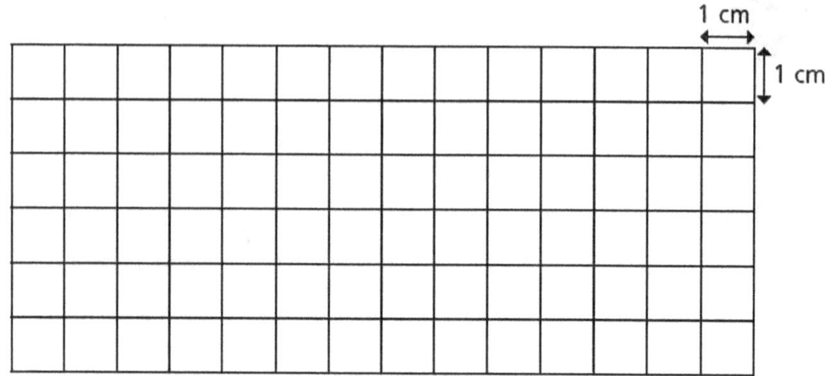

42: The area of each triangle is 12 cm^2. Find the missing lengths.

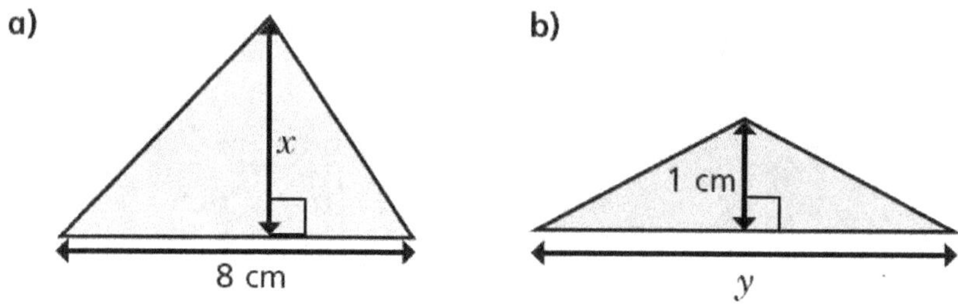

43: Which of the following is labelled incorrectly?

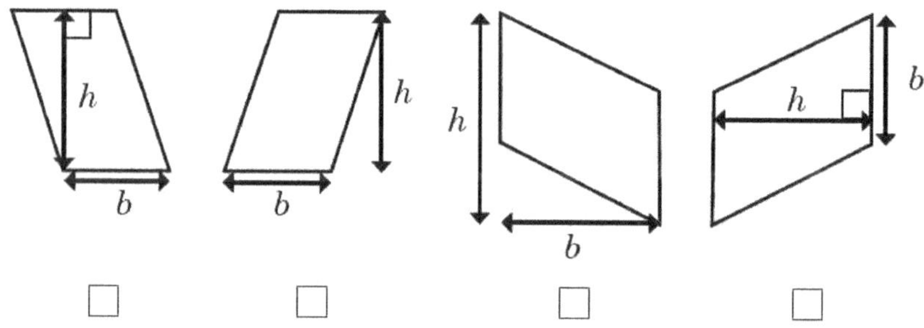

44. What least number should be subtracted from 34,56,090 to obtain a common multiple of 3, 6 and 9?

Evaluation A

1. 776 is the ______________ multiple of 97.
   A: 4th   B: 8th   C: 5th   D: 9th

2. Romanika counted a bundle of sheets, excluding that of top 15 ones, as 132. She has placed 21 sheets in to the printer. How many sheets were there in all?

3. Monika calculated 15th multiple of 5 added to 5th multiple of 15. Find the digit that she might have in the one's place of the product.

4. There are ______ flat faces and ___ curved faces in a cuboid.

5. Find the difference of place values of 5 in 22,543 and 54,432.

6. What least number must be added to make 12,543 divisible by 9?

7. What least number must be added to the hundreds place of 12,424 to make it divisible by 3?

8. A 3 m 60 cm thread is used for bordering a square shaped poster throughout edges. Find the length of each side of that poster.

9. 59 square shaped tiles each of 20 sq. cm. are used for flooring a room. Find the area of that room.

10. Renuka prepared a bar graph that shows the number of kg of food eaten each day by each animal. What information goes on the horizontal axis? What information can be placed on the vertical axis?

11. Tim lives in New Delhi. He prepares a line graph that shows the amount of LPG used in his home kitchen for a year. Will the line graph show any change throughout the year?

12. Martin wants to represent the data related to pets owned by his classmates. He makes a bar graph that shows the number of dogs owned by members of his class. If the smallest number is 1 and the largest number is 4, what interval should Jon use for representing the data scale in the graph?

13. Kim gathered information about the population of individual states of her country. If she prepares a bar graph of this data, what information will be displayed on the vertical axis? What information will be displayed on the horizontal axis?

14. 15th multiple of 5 is also a _________ multiple of 25.

15. _____________ is the smallest three digit even number.

16. 32 hundreds + 21 tens = _____________ .

17. What least number should be subtracted from five digit greatest number to make the value a common multiple of 4, 6, 8 and 12?

18. Find out a smallest five digit number which can be divided by 7, 8 and 9 leaving remainder 5 in each case.

19. Simplify:

$1/11^{th}$ of $11,011 + 1/12^{th}$ of $12,012 + 1/13^{th}$ of $13,013 + 1/15^{th}$ of $15,015 = \ldots\ldots\ldots$

20. Two bells toll at an interval of 4 seconds and 7 seconds respectively. How many times do these bells toll together in the time interval of 9 minutes 20 seconds?

21. What least number should be subtracted from the greatest number of five digits to obtain a common multiple of 3, 4, 8 and 16?

22. Find a smallest five digit number which can be divided by 2, 3, 5, 7 and 9 leaving remainder 1 in each case.

23. Find out missing angles.

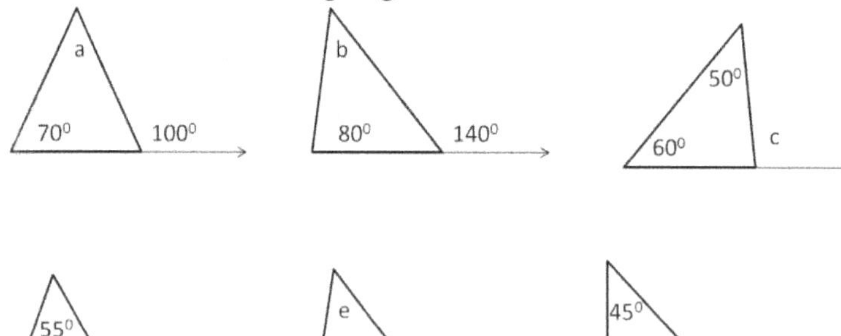

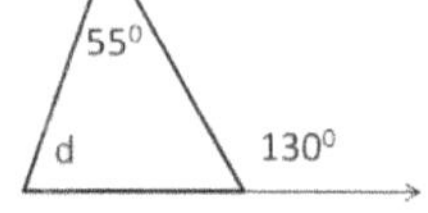

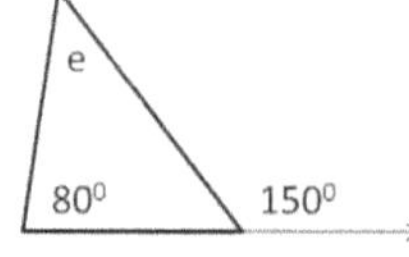

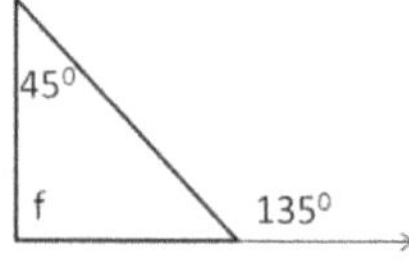

Evaluation B

1: Complete the following.

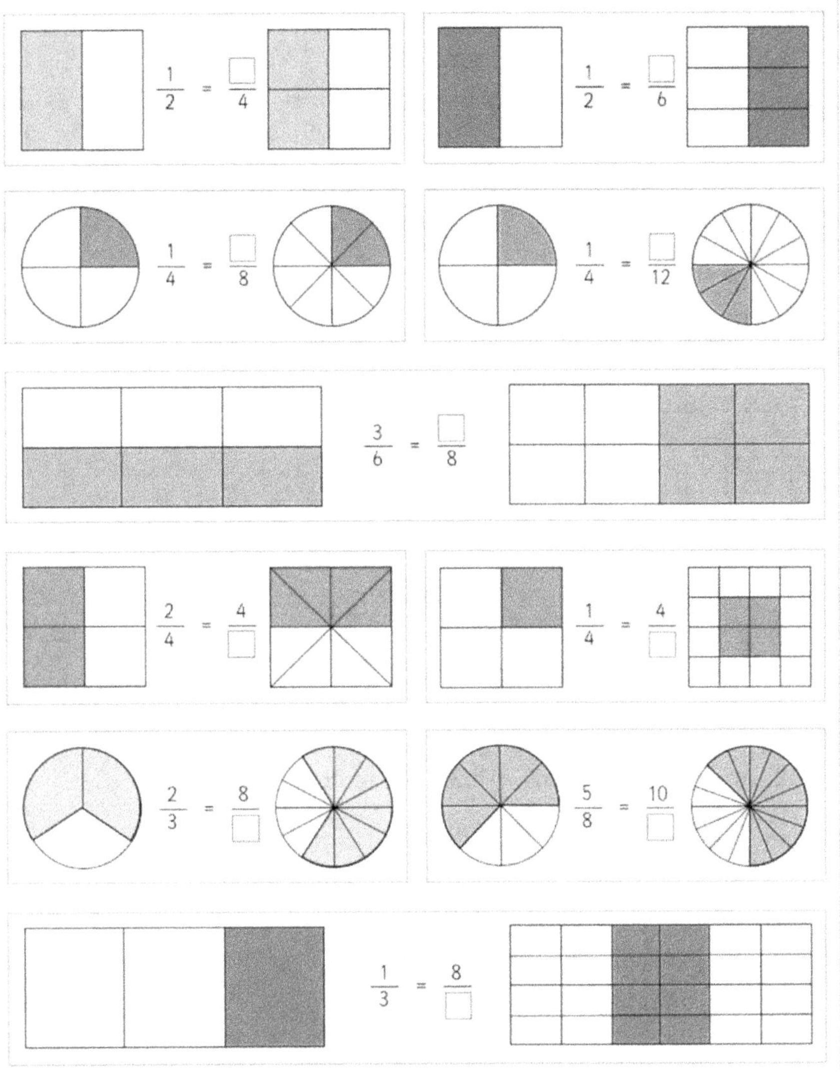

2: How many non-overlapping triangles can be accommodated inside a hexagon?

3: Each of the interior angle of a regular pentagon will be equal to ……

4: Complete the expanded form:

a: 21 thousands + 201 hundreds + 2001 tens + 20,001 = ……………

b: 21 million X 1,000 + 20 million X 11 + 1,201 = ……………………

c: $\left[\frac{1}{1,003} + \frac{1}{1,003} + \cdots\ldots\ 1,000\ times\right]$ X $\left(1 + \frac{3}{1000}\right)$ X $101,101 - \frac{101}{1000} = \ldots$

d. 605 thousands + 1,004 X 1,000 + 204 X 100 + 2,004 X 10 + 121 = …

e. (1 + 2 + 3 + ….. + 1,000) X 0.001 − 1.0001 = ……………..

f: (1.006 + 1.006 …+ 2,000 times) X $\left(1 + \frac{6}{1,000}\right)$ X 300,300 = …

g: $\frac{11}{12}$ X $\frac{12}{13}$ X … … …. $\left(1 + \frac{1}{10,000}\right)$ X $121,121$ X $\frac{5}{121}$ = …………

h: (1.001 + 11.01 + 121.003 + 1001.203) X 0.001 = ……………..

i. (121.0121 ÷ 11) + (242.0242 ÷ 22) = ………………….

5: What percentage of all the even numbers from 1 to 400 are multiples of 40?

6: (1,004 + 1,004 + ….. 3,000 times) ÷ 30,000 = ……………………

7: Is there any pair of number having a common multiple 1210 and a common factor 97?

8: (203 tens + 203 hundreds + 203 thousandths) ÷ 1,000 = ………….

9: Namrata can finish her project work in 20 days while working 8 hours a day. Pinki can finish similar type of project work in 30 days while working 6 hours a day. They jointly wanted three such projects while working 5 hours a day. In how many days do they finish three such kinds of project works?

10: How many digits will be there in the product of 100, 200, 300, 2000 and 99?

11: Is there any pair of natural number having HCF 121 and LCM 1690?

12. 4/7th of 14,56,084 + 5/9th of 81,72,054 = ………………

Evaluation C

1: Calculate outer boundary of the following grid if area of each of the unit square is equal to 1.21 sq. cm.

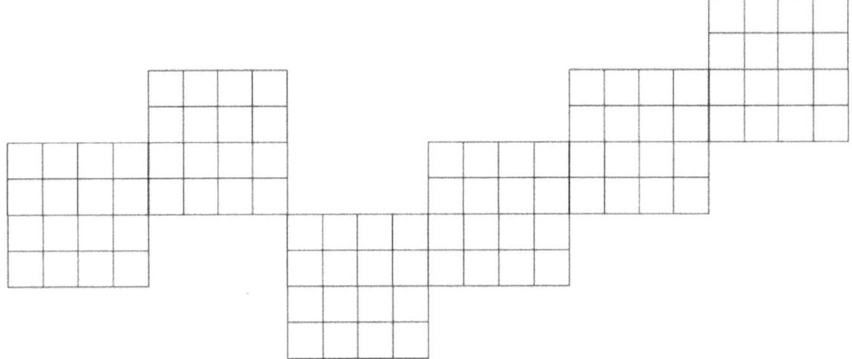

2: Calculate area of the rhombus which is embedded inside the rectangle.

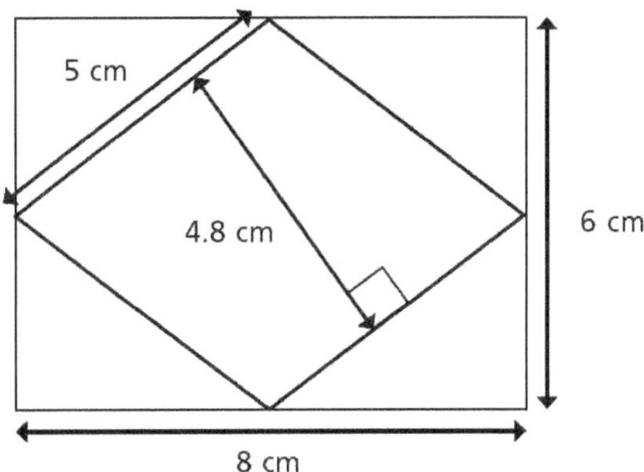

3: Claculate decrease of sale from April to May.

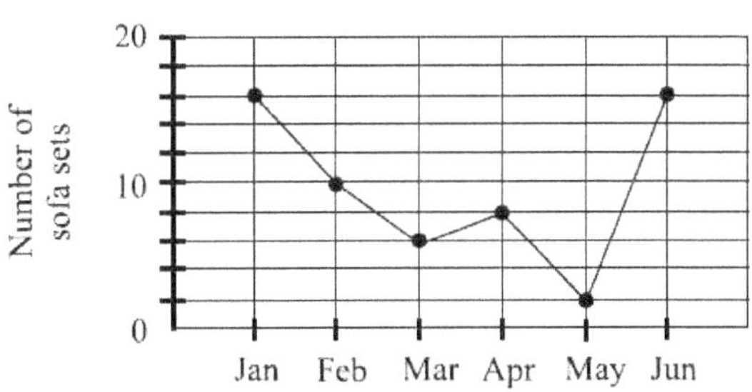

4: In 189485 place value of 8 in ten thousands place in ……. more than the place value of 8 in tens place.

5. Find out statement which is not true.

a) Number 4 have exactly three factors.

b) If a number is divisible by 21 then it must be divisible by 3 and 7 as well.

c) 78776 is divisible by 6

d) There are only 2 pairs of twin prime numbers between 10 and 20.

e) If a number is divisible only by 13 and 169 then that number is divisible by the only prime factor 13.

6. Which of the following is a convex polygon?

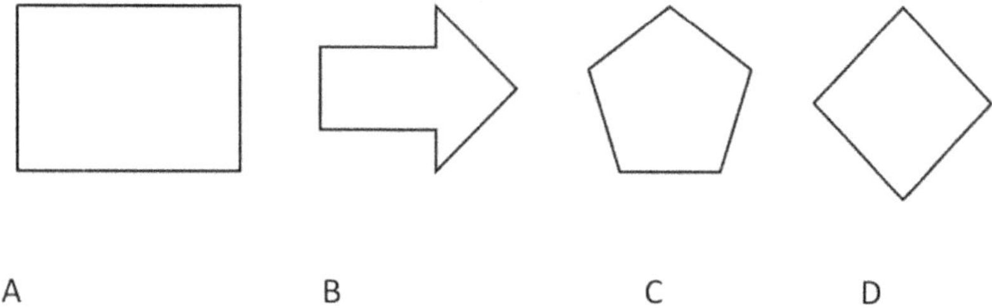

A   B   C   D

7. The area of a rectangular field is 35 times the sum of its length and breadth. If the breadth of that field is 40 metres, then what is the length of that field?

8. Snehal's uncle is 5 times as old as her age. After 15 years, her uncle will be 2 times as old as her age. Snehal is _____ years old and her uncle is __ years old.

9. The measures of the angles of a triangle are in the ratio 4 : 5 : 9. Identify the type of triangle.

***

www.ingramcontent.com/pod-product-compliance
Lightning Source LLC
Chambersburg PA
CBHW072221150726
48002CB00005B/1913